Foundations of
Dialectical Psychology

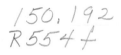
Foundations of
Dialectical Psychology

Klaus F. Riegel

DEPARTMENT OF PSYCHOLOGY
UNIVERSITY OF MICHIGAN
ANN ARBOR, MICHIGAN

AP

ACADEMIC PRESS   New York   San Francisco   London   1979

A Subsidiary of Harcourt Brace Jovanovich, Publishers

Klett–Cotta Verlag, Stuttgart, Germany will publish a German translation of
Klaus F. Riegel, <u>Foundations of Dialectical Psychology</u>.

ACADEMIC PRESS, INC.
111 Fifth Avenue, New York, New York 10003

United Kingdom Edition published by
ACADEMIC PRESS, INC. (LONDON) LTD.
24/28 Oval Road, London NW1 7DX

Library of Congress Cataloging in Publication Data

Riegel, Klaus F
    Foundations of dialectical psychology.

    1. Psychology––Philosophy. 2. Dialectic.
I. Title.
BF38.R53   150'.19'2   79–6943
ISBN 0–12–588080–4

PRINTED IN THE UNITED STATES OF AMERICA

79 80 81 82   9 8 7 6 5 4 3 2 1

Contents

Preface   *ix*

1
The Dialectics of Human Development   1

Critique of Traditional Psychology   2
Prerequisites of a Dialectical Psychology   5
Toward a Dialectical Interpretation of Development and Aging   12
A Manifesto for Dialectical Psychology   14

2
Historical Introduction   17

Paradigmatic Developmental Orientations   18
Open and Closed Developmental Systems   22
Dialectics in Soviet Psychology   27
Conclusions   32

Contents

3

Dialectical Operations: The First and Final Period of Cognitive Development — 35

Dialectical Operations — 38
Conclusions — 53

4

The Relational Basis of Language — 57

Comparison between Monetary and Linguistic Systems — 60
The Relational Basis of Language — 70
Conclusions — 82

5

The Temporal Organization of Dialogues — 85

Subject–Object Relation — 86
Situational Dialogues — 90
Developmental Dialogues — 98
Conclusions — 109

6

The Recollection of the Individual and Collective Past — 111

Developmental Recollections — 112
Historical Recollections — 120
Historical Interpretations — 124
Developmental Science as Action — 126

7

Adult Life Crises — 129

Contradictions and Development — 130
Crises and Development — 131
Preview — 132

Contradictions and Crises in Adult Life   133
Breaking of Paradigmatic Crises by Exceptional Individuals   142
Structural Stratifications in History   148
Extrascientific Bases of the Concept of "Crises"   152
Conclusions   154

8

The Dialectics of Time   157

The Concept of Change   159
Inner-Biological Changes   162
Individual-Psychological Changes   168
Cultural-Sociological Changes   172
Music, Time, and Dialectical Logic   174
Conclusions   179

References   181
Author Index   193
Subject Index   197

Preface

In recent years, an increasing number of questions and challenges have arisen within traditional psychology, and especially within developmental psychology. How can psychological theories and methodologies be modified to reflect the impact of changing social and cultural conditions upon the course of individual development? Have theories of psychology provided sufficient consideration to crucial changes and activities in human behavior, in contrast to the prevailing emphasis upon the stability of traits and abilities? To what extent do traditional research methodologies, now being pursued to their limits, come to be a barrier between the researcher and the themes and perceptions of the lives that are observed? What alternative methodologies might be more appropriate to the study by man of his own behavior? How can theories of psychology account for the continuing historical development of psychology as a discipline?

From 1971 onward, Klaus F. Riegel addressed these and similar questions in his writings. Although others have been attracted by these issues and have written on isolated facets, Riegel's work does not merely raise questions about and criticisms of traditional psychology. Rather, he constructively advances a new, integrated, and comprehensive psychological theory and methodology, based upon dialectics. A principal forum for the elaboration of dialectical psychology was the Life-Span

Developmental Psychology Conferences (Goulet & Baltes, 1970; Nessel-roade & Reese, 1973; Datan & Ginsberg, 1975; Datan & Reese, 1977), at which Riegel was both a contributor and an active participant. The early development of dialectical psychology is also reflected in a 1972 conference on structure and transformation initiated by Riegel (Riegel & Rosenwald, 1975) and in the theme chosen by Riegel for the 1973 meeting of the International Society for the Study of Behavioral Development—"The Developing Individual in a Changing World" (Riegel & Meacham, 1976). The major development of dialectical psychology, however, took place at a series of annual conferences on dialectics, initiated and guided by Riegel. The first of these was held at Rochester in 1974 (Riegel, 1975b), and conferences have been held in the following years at Toronto, Cape Cod, Shimer College, and again in 1978 in Toronto. As an outcome of these conferences, and at Riegel's initiative, the Network for Dialectical Psychologists was formed. This group supports the *Dialectical Psychology Newsletter*.

This volume brings together Riegel's extensive writings during this period. Although several of the chapters have been published previously, all were revised, edited, and integrated by Riegel early in 1977. In addition, this volume includes several previously unpublished sections that help to round out Riegel's theory of dialectical psychology. Together, the chapters provide a comprehensive survey of the major topics and issues of psychology, conducted within an integrated framework and perspective—dialectics. Thus, this volume ought to be of interest to advanced students and professionals not only in psychology, but in history, sociology, and related disciplines as well.

The first two chapters provide both a review and critique of traditional psychology, and an overview of the major themes of the dialectical perspective. Traditional psychology retains a strong commitment to the belief that traits and abilities remain stable, and to the concepts of balance and equilibrium, as in dissonance theory and Piaget's cognitive–developmental theory. In contrast to dialectical psychology, traditional psychology neglects the problem of how it is that imbalances, disequilibria, questions, doubts, challenges, and developmental changes arise. From a dialectical perspective, change and development are a result of contradictions between events occurring in different progressions, such as the biological, psychological, or cultural–sociological progressions. The resolutions of these contradictions, or crises, provide the basis for further developments—both positive and negative—of the individual and in the history of society. Riegel emphasizes that the problem of the coordination and synchronization of two time sequences or progressions is the most central issue in developmental psychology, and he provides a framework—the study of dialogues—for further investigations. He returns to the analysis of dialogues in chapter 5, and to the issue of time in developmental psychology in the final chapter.

In Chapter 2, two contrasting orientations in psychology are reviewed: the mechanistic Anglo-American paradigm, emphasizing competition and achievement, and the mentalistic Continental European paradigm, emphasizing activity and organization. Dialectical psychology provides a synthesis of these by emphasizing the interactions between individual and historical development. In addition, dialectical psychology is unique as a perspective in recognizing that dialectics can be and ought to be applied to itself, thus yielding a series of interpretations of behavioral development (rather than an accumulation of behavioral facts), each of which is appropriate to a particular social and historical context. Following a discussion of open and closed systems in the social sciences, Riegel illustrates the synthesis of the contrasting mechanistic and mentalistic paradigms by reference to Soviet psychology and, in particular, to the double interaction theory of Rubinstein. Psychological activity is related to the material world through the interactions of inner (material) dialectics and outer (historical) dialectics. Dialectical psychology makes clear the need to overcome the polarized barriers to understanding within traditional psychology—between mind and body, between individual and society, between quantity and quality, between concrete content and abstract form, between psychologists and the objects of their research, between diagnosis and therapy, between biology and the social environment, and between subject and object.

Beginning with Chapter 3, Riegel focuses on specific features and applications of dialectical psychology. The advancement of scientific knowledge—and, indeed, the basis for all thought—depends on a deemphasis of the principle of identity and an acceptance of the existence of contradiction. Piaget and others, however, maintain that cognitive development consists of removing contradictions in thought and striving for noncontradictory modes of thinking. Dialectical psychology emphasizes that in order to think in a mature manner, the child must recapture the dialectical basis of thought in a first and final developmental stage. In this stage, thinking is a process of transforming contradictory experiences into momentarily stable structures. This mature, dialectical stage does not necessarily follow the fourth stage in Piagetian theory, but instead may follow after any of the major stages. Thus, although Piaget's theory has a dialectical basis, dialectical psychology provides a modification and an extension by considering the problem of individual differences in mature thought and by emphasizing the interactions between psychological development and cultural–sociological change.

Early cognitive development and the acquisition of language and meaning are contrasted in Chapter 4, in terms of the spatial and temporal organizations of the environment. These outer organizations are reconstructed by children in the course of development, through their own activities, and based upon their own inner organizations. This developmental process is also promoted through the activities of other members of the society, based upon the products (tools, language) of activities of earlier generations. Concurrently, the activities of the children bring about changes in the immediate social environment—family, neighbors, etc. Riegel explores the processes of language acquisition by analogy with the development of monetary systems. The barter system, the coinage system, and the debenture system are compared with three levels in the origin, development, and study of language, and with the three major stages of Piaget's theory. Perceiving and producing speech are viewed as labor; this labor produces words, sentences, etc. which are capital to be reinvested in new speech productions. Chapter 4 concludes with a relational analysis, emphasizing transactions rather than fixed elements, of the inner dialectics of biological and psychological events in the course of language acquisition. In contrast to traditional psychology, for which the problem of language acquisition has been the formation of associations between already existing words, in dialectical psychology, extralingual and intralingual relations carry meaning and are prior to words or elements and to the formation of classes both logically and developmentally.

Whereas Chapter 4 is concerned with inner dialectics, Chapter 5—on the temporal organization of dialogues—emphasizes the outer dialectics between the individual and the social and cultural conditions. These interactions are explored within the framework of the dialogue, and are contrasted with the "objective" methodology of traditional psychology. Riegel argues that such methodology, adopted uncritically from the natural sciences, has neglected the participatory roles of the individual in the course of development, and of the scientist in the course of investigation. Thus, Piaget's theory, in neglecting how it is that children and researchers raise questions and problems, has remained a monologue of cognitive development rather than a dialogue of human development. In a dialogue, both persons—parent and child, researcher and subject—are subject and object at the same time. Chapter 5 is devoted to a presentation of basic properties and forms of dialogues, which may be analyzed in terms of dialogical units, each of which includes a thesis, antithesis, and synthesis. Dialogues are illustrated in parent–child relations, language acquisition, therapy, and the concepts of assimilation and accommodation in Piaget's theory. The dialogue framework provides a concrete methodology for the application and extension of dialectical psychology.

The contrast between traditional and dialectical methodologies is sharpened in Chapter 6, which focuses upon the classical problem of remembering and forgetting. This problem is conceptualized not as an abstract performance having no relevance to the personal and subjective lives of individuals, but rather as a reflection of changes in the social and historical environments in which individuals are immersed. By analogy with the activities of historians, Riegel argues that psychologists cannot attain the objective facts of development as it "really" occurs, but must strive instead for an understanding of development as it is perceived by individuals. Such interpretations include not only these individuals' critical awareness and evaluation of past events, but also their hopes for the future.

Development through the adult years is considered in Chapter 7, with particular emphasis on the careers of scientists, especially Piaget and Wundt. As individual scientists pass through various developmental stages, these stages must be coordinated with changes in the history of the scientific discipline. The discussion of these coordinations presupposes a dialectical perspective upon crises and contradictions. Crises may be described as a lack of coordination or synchrony between any of several event sequences or progressions: the inner–biological, individual–psychological, cultural–sociological, and outer–physical. In contrast to the view of traditional psychology, crises and contradictions are seen as the basis for innovation, creativity, and development. Crises are resolved by individual scientists who produce a new interpretation or paradigm and thus bring about social change; these individuals, in turn, are changed by the new social conditions.

The concluding chapter on the dialectics of time is the most crucial. In traditional psychology, time and change have been of only secondary importance, inferred from the comparison of two or more timeless cross sections. In the dialogues of dialectical psychology, however, time and change are basic properties. Temporal organization emerges from the interaction of two speakers (who also listen), and from the interaction of two or more event-sequences or progressions. Riegel contrasts various notions of time, including absolute time (which requires an idealized observer), and relational time (which depends on interactions and personalized perspectives). Both these notions are present in the concept of dialectical time. Chapter 8 concludes with a comparison of formal and dialectical logic. Traditional psychology and sciences are based on the former, and reflect primarily spatial metaphors. Dialectical logic builds upon formal logic, but also, more importantly, is capable of comprehending itself and so of generating developmental and historical progressions.

Klaus Riegel was born in Berlin on November 6, 1925, and spent his childhood there. After World War II, he worked as a mechanic and tool machine operator before studying physics and mathematics. Riegel earned his M.A. at the University of Minnesota in 1955, and received his Ph.D. in psychology at the University of Hamburg in 1958, working with Curt Bondy. Riegel then spent a year as a visiting scientist at the National Institute of Mental Health in Bethesda, where he worked with James Birren. During this time, he developed a strong interest in aging, and, together with his wife, Ruth M. Riegel, assisted in the German standardization of the Wechsler intelligence test. He then used this test, as well as various personality and social variables, in a longitudinal study of cognitive changes in old age. In 1959 Riegel joined the Department of Psychology of the University of Michigan. There, he was a participant in the Psycholinguistics Program, the Institute of Gerontology, and the Center for Human Growth and Development. A member of many professional organizations, he was elected as a fellow in both the Gerontological Society and the American Psychological Association. He also served on the Executive Committee of the International Society for the Study of Behavioral Development, and as president of the Psychological and Social Sciences Section of the Gerontological Society. In 1976, the Gerontological Society recognized Riegel's contributions by presenting to him the Robert W. Kleemeier Award. Riegel also contributed greatly to the growth and increased eminence of the international journal *Human Development,* as its editor from 1970 onward. Riegel's interests were diverse, including the development and assessment of intellectual functions of the aged, psycholinguistics, and the history and philosophy of the social sciences. He was the author or editor of several books, and a regular contributor to the journal literature. (A complete listing of his published works appears in *Human Development, 1977, 20,* 317–325.) The premature death of Klaus Riegel on July 3, 1977, was a great loss to his many students and colleagues.

My role in the production of this volume has been minor. Most of the work had been completed by early 1977. My tasks have included gathering the tables, figures, and references from a variety of sources, and preparing the indexes. In addition, I have made minor changes in the text, mainly of an editorial nature, and none that would change the meaning. I have no doubt that Klaus would have managed these tasks far better, had there been sufficient time.

Klaus was characteristically quite generous in his acknowledgments, and his published papers generally include footnotes expressing gratitude to students and colleagues. Certainly there are many whom he would have mentioned at this point. What can be done now is to acknowledge all those who over the years entered into dialogue with Klaus, regardless of whether their interpretations were consistent with or in opposition to his. Within the framework of dialectical psychology, it is dialogue and debate which is the basis for forward movement. The responsibility for maintaining the dialogue, and for the construction of new and more encompassing interpretations in the social sciences, rests with those who read this volume.

Grateful acknowledgment is given for the permissions granted by the following publishers to print either partially, or in their entirety, articles written by Klaus Riegel: Academic Press, S. Karger AG, and University of Nebraska Press. Chapter 1 was published previously as "The Dialectics of Human Development," *American Psychologist,* 1976, *31,* 689–700. Copyright 1976 by the American Psychological Association. Reprinted by permission. Portions of Chapter 2 were published previously as "The Influence of Economic and Political Ideologies upon the Development of Developmental Psychology," *Psychological Bulletin,* 1972, *78,* 129–141. Copyright 1972 by the American Psychological Association. Reprinted by permission. Portions of Chapter 6 were published previously as "The Recall of Historical Events." Reprinted from *Behavioral Science,* Volume 18, No. 5, 1973, by permission of James G. Miller, M.D., Ph.D., Editor. Additional portions of Chapter 6 were published previously in K. F. Riegel, *Psychology of development and history,* 1976, by Plenum Publishing Corporation. Chapter 4 was published previously as "Semantic Basis of Language: Language as Labor," in K. F. Riegel and G. C. Rosenwald (Eds.), *Structure and transformation: Developmental and historical aspects,* Copyright 1975 by John Wiley & Sons, Inc. Reprinted by permission of John Wiley & Sons, Inc. All rights reserved. All of the above articles were revised by Klaus Riegel in 1977 for the present volume.

JOHN A. MEACHAM
Department of Psychology
State University of New York at Buffalo
Buffalo, New York

Foundations of
Dialectical Psychology

1

The Dialectics of Human Development

The following presentation consists of four parts. The first two are critical, the last two attempt to be constructive. In the first part, I reject the preference for stable traits, abilities, and competencies deeply rooted in Western psychological thinking. Instead of searching for such abstract and supposedly universal entities, primary attention should be given to concrete events in their temporal order. In the second part, I reject an equally strong conceptual bias, the preference for equilibrium, balance, and stability. Instead of directing our attention toward the question of how such tranquility of mind or the social situation is achieved (for example, how problems are solved and answers are given), equal emphasis should be devoted to the issue of how problems are created and questions are raised.

The minimal condition for an analysis that searches not only for answers but also for the questions includes two individuals (for example, a mother and her child), both operating interactively over time and thus growing and developing together. The third part of my presentation briefly describes interactions that are most clearly revealed in language dialogues. An analysis of dialogues depicts short-term temporal patterns of situational interactions. The analysis needs to be extended into interpretations of long-term changes both in the individual and in society. The resulting dialectical interpretation is concerned with changes along several dimensions of progression. Specifically, development is brought about by crises in these progressions which create discordance and conflicts. Through the actions of individuals in society, synchronization is reestablished and thereby progress achieved. But as such a coordination is attained, new discrepancies emerge producing a continuous flux of contradictions and changes. My fourth and main focus in this presentation will be on this last aspect which leads us most distinctly toward a dialectical theory of development and aging (Riegel, 1975c).

Critique of Traditional Psychology

The Abstractness of Abilities

In the discussion of stable entities, either general substances or analytical elements were emphasized. Nowadays this distinction, rooted in the early Greek philosophy both of the Eleatic school and of Democritos, is expressed in the psychology of individual differences and personality, on one hand, and in experimental psychology, on the other.

The inquiry into stable entities is founded upon *Vermögenspsychologie* or faculty psychology of the eighteenth century. On the basis of common observations and introspections, a number of entities were proposed, such as passion, prudishness, courage, intelligence, etc., and the occurrence of specific behaviors was explained by the preponderance of these capacities or—in modern terms—competencies for such behavior. Although disreputed many times, the seemingly more advanced forms of inquiry in psychometric and diagnostic testing and theorizing do not differ decisively from these original concepts. Nowadays however, we speak of genotypes and phenotypes, of deep structure and surface structure; it is the same story. To give a concrete example, we still say that a mother does not feed her baby appropriately because she does not have the intelligence to do so.

The experimental psychology of the later nineteenth century, because of its methodological rigor and the firm adaptation of natural science conceptions, appeared to be superior to the attempts by students of individual differences and personality. But just as for those the search was directed toward the "detection" of universal, stable entities, now conceived as the smallest indivisable mental elements (sensations, images, and simple feelings in the formulation of Wundt), rather than as global potentialities of the organism and competencies of the mind.

The progressive refinement of both approaches led to the complex systems of modern experimental psychology (as, for example, expressed in the theories of memory [Tulving & Donaldson, 1972]), and to the implementation of modern research designs in the study of individual and cultural changes. But not even all the King's horses and all the King's men could put Humpty-Dumpty together again, and, thus, experimentalists were bound to fail in their attempts of putting meaning back into their psychology from which they had eliminated it so radically. Meaning is not something that can be added later to the system analysed; rather, it is the most fundamental topic. Strictly speaking, it is the only topic for any inquiry by human beings of human beings.

Likewise in the study of individual differences and personality, much important progress has been made, most notably, through the development of developmental research designs by Schaie (1965) and Baltes (1968). As a consequence, the argument has come to be accepted that the individual must be seen as a changing individual in a changing world (Riegel & Meacham, 1976). While this recognition expresses clearly the main theme of dialectical psychology, it remains insufficiently implemented as long as we continue to depict the individual in terms of underlying traits and competencies. What we need to do is to direct our efforts toward the concrete actions of the individual in a concrete social world. In order to show the implications of this issue let me extend my previous example.

At a symposium of the American Psychological Association convention, attention was given to the usefulness of intelligence testing for social actions. It was argued that information on the distribution of intelligence scores within a ghetto population would produce valuable information. For example, there might be a correlation between intelligence scores and mothers who are providing insufficient nutrition to their children. Disregarding the enormous efforts required to obtain such information, the underlying idea is abstract. Why should one gather information about the intelligence of the mothers if one could ask them directly about their feeding procedures? By engaging them in a supportive dialogue one would, at the very same time, begin to change their orientation and actions. This, of course, is inconceivable for the "scientific" approach to psychology in which we try so hard to segregate the diagnostic from the therapeutic part of the exploration. The conversation with the mother would assign a status to her which is almost equal to that of the interviewer, that is, the status of a dialogue partner rather than the status of a "subject." These two issues, the separation of the diagnostic from the therapeutic part and the segregation of the observer

3

from the subject of the study, reveal most clearly the abstract, alien, if not absurd, character of traditional psychology which a dialectical approach is bound and determined to overcome.

The Tranquility of Balance

The preference for an equilibrium model in the behavioral sciences has been as firmly established as the preference for abstract traits or competencies. Without any debate it has been taken for granted that a state of balance, stability, and rest is more desirable than a state of upheaval, uncertainty, and change. Thus what we aim for is a psychology of satisfaction but not of excitement. This preference has found expression in balance theory, equilibrium theory, steady-state theory, and indirectly in the theory of cognitive dissonance. With the possible exception of the latter, these interpretations fail to explore that every change has to be explained by the process of imbalance which forms the basis for any movement. In recognizing this prerequisite, stability appears as a transitory condition in the stream of ceaseless changes. Although the condition of stability might be easier to depict than the flux of discrepancies and changes—in the same sense that it is easier to describe a single frame rather than the continuous actions of a movie—the latter constitute the conditions from which everything new emerges, on which any development is based. An instructive example for the overemphasis of stability at the expense of change, of the state of equilibrium rather than the process of transformation, is Piaget's theory of cognitive development (1950).

Without any notable exception, Piaget's work is concerned with the question of how children solve problems, such as in tasks of conservation, grouping, or seriation. He investigates how children resolve conflicting situations, contradictory evidence, or inconsistent impressions, but rarely how children come to question their earlier judgements. Undoubtedly Piaget's concern with the process of resolving discrepancies in experience and thought is of great importance, but he disregards at least one half, the other half, of the topic of operative and cognitive activity.

Piaget's preference for studying how problems are solved rather than generated, how questions are answered rather than raised is concretely revealed by the experimental conditions chosen for his studies. The experimenter always poses the problem and expects the child to solve it. Further questioning by the experimenter aims at eliciting from the child answers that would allow the experimenter to draw inferences about the structure of the child's operations and thoughts. Without any

4

noteworthy exception, all questions are asked by the experimenter and all answers are given by the child.

Piaget's preference reflects his commitment to an equilibrium model that describes the child's development as a succession of plateaus at which the operational structures are at balance. Whenever new questions and doubts arise in the child, triggered by new experiences but not explained by the theory, the balance is disturbed and new operativity is generated in the child. Eventually a new equilibrium will be attained, and thus the child has moved into the next higher level of cognitive balance. While the sequence of progression described by Piaget is convincing and a great step forward in comparison to the earlier mechanistic interpretations of a continuous accumulation of bits and pieces of information during development, little attention is given to the question of how transitions are initiated and come about.

Raising the same argument from a different perspective, Piaget considers only the child's interactive operations with objects, but he does not consider that some of these objects may be other subjects who, like the child, operate actively upon objects and, in particular, upon other subjects. Piaget has paid little attention to the outer or social dialectics of interacting individuals. By restricting his analysis to the interactions of the subject with objects, he succeeded in describing the logic of stages in rational thinking but failed to elaborate the basis of cognitive operations, the social basis of human being.

Prerequisites of a Dialectical Psychology

Dialogic Interactions

By turning away from the abstract concept of abilities, traits, and competencies and by turning away from the blind preference for stability, balance, and equilibrium, I call attention to the concrete interactive changes in common activities and everyday situations. In emphasizing the social basis of human beings, the interaction between two persons in the form of dialogue provides the prototypical example for such explorations.

1. A dialogue has temporal structure or structured order. The speakers alternate in their presentations, and each successive statement has to reflect at least the one immediately preceding it. Incorporating only the preceding statements represents, of course, a minimum re-

quirement for a dialogue. A maximum is attained if each utterance reflects all of the earlier statements. It has to be consistent with the proponent's own views and has to represent equally consistent or systematically modified reactions to all statements made by the opponent. Moreover each statement should reflect basic issues of the topic or theme that are presupposed but not necessarily openly expressed in the dialogue. Figure 1.1 shows a case which is comparable to a truss of a bridge and will be called a *simple dialogue* (Riegel, 1975c).

If such a reflective coordination did not take place, the dialogue would degenerate into alternating monologues in which speakers would merely follow-up on their own earlier statements without reacting to their opponent's elaborations. The other speaker's statements would appear as distractive interruptions, and the only remaining dialogical feature would consist of the alternations between the participants. If these alternations cease, the dialogue becomes what Piaget (1926) has described as *collective monologues.* Here two or more speakers continue their productions uninterruptedly and parallel to one another.

2. Like the distinction between "primitive" and "scientific" dialectics (Lawler, 1975), development of language relies at the beginning on intuitive "understanding" between speaker and listener, in particular between mother and child (Harris, 1975). With increasing experience in linguistic–cognitive operations, the dialogue becomes explicit. Eventually a person might be clearly aware of its conditions and might consciously select certain topics, registers, or expressions.

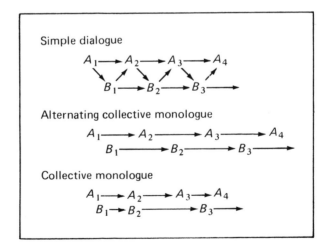

Figure 1.1. Examples of dialogic interactions.

Dialogues require temporal coordination or synchronization that, at first, depends heavily on shared extralingual knowledge, demands, and affects between mother and child. But increasingly with age, the synchronization relies on the mother's and the child's language experience and selective cognitive operations. Already a few weeks after birth, their actions have become finely tuned to one another. The child begins to look at the mother's face; when the mother moves, the child follows her with its eyes. When she speaks, the child looks at her mouth; when she stops, the child vocalizes and switches its attention from her mouth to her eyes. Interactive social situations have been investigated by Rheingold (1961), Moss (1967), and Sameroff (1975) and those of language development by Lewis and Freedle (1973). The interactions between mother and child represent the basis for sociolinguistic dialogues at the adult level.

During the early parts of life, dialogues are asymmetric. The mother has available a large repertoire of signs, rules, topics, and registers; the child has only a few of these acquired forms and operations at its command. Consequently the mother has to be highly restricted in her communication with the child; she retreats to the mode of "primitive" dialogues. But independent of her efforts, she will talk and sing along, and the child, eventually, will follow her activities and participate in them.

The sign system shared by mother and child is at first private to both of them. As development advances the signs become congruent with those of the linguistic system of the society. In this process of change, the mother functions as an intermediary between the child and society. Thus the developmental dialogue is not only an exchange between two individuals, but, through the activities of the mother, the knowledge and values of society are introduced into the dialogical interactions. The conditions are similar in a short-term situational dialogue. The two speakers might represent quite different social groups with very different orientations, preferences, and goals. Communication between them is possible only because the groups which the speakers represent are part of the same society and thus share many properties of a more fundamental communication system.

3. Recently Marxist structuralists have raised similar arguments in regard to the remote interactions between authors and readers (see Fieguth, 1973; Mao Tse-Tung, 1968; Riegel, 1975c; Schmid, 1973). The activities of authors are not merely determined by their personal knowledge but also by the thoughts, intentions, and feelings of the readers in the contemporary society, developed from their past history and reflected in their society's philosophy and ideology. The authors try to

7

translate and to transmit the knowledge and direction developed in a society to their readers. The authors' task consists of their participatory efforts to transform the cultural–historical conditions for the benefit of their readers. Thus the authors, like the mothers, like the priests, and like the commissars, function as intermediaries between the knowledge- and direction-seeking individuals and the ideas and values of the society.

For both the authors and the mothers the coordination and synchronization of their efforts with those of their readers and children, respectively, are most important. The load for the reader as well as for the child should neither be too heavy nor too light. Information has to be given at the right moment, in the right amount, and of the right kind. This is achieved through dialectical interactions with the knowledge seeker. If the authors fail, they may have become too abstract, they may have progressed too fast, or they may lag behind. The mother, in a more concrete sense, has to speak, direct, and prevent, but she has also to listen and change her own activities according to the demands of her child. The synchronization of these two time sequences, that is, the changes and the development of the child and the changes and the development of the mother, is of central importance in their dialogue. The topic of coordination and synchronization of two time sequences is also the most central issue in dialectical theory.

Dialectical Changes

A dialectical interpretation of development and aging focuses upon the simultaneous movements along at least the following four dimensions: (a) inner-biological, (b) individual-psychological, (c) cultural-sociological, and (d) outer-physical. Different progressions within one particular and between two different dimensions are not always coordinated and synchronized. Whenever two sequences are out of step, it is said that a crisis takes place. However crises should never be exclusively considered in a negative manner. As to be discussed in Chapter 7, most crises represent constructive confrontations leading to new developments. In the following, I describe a few of such confrontations out of the possible total of 16 types shown in Table 1.1. Sometimes, that is, when major reorganizations are required, these new developments may be said to represent a new stage or period in development.

1. Crises originating along the inner-biological dimension, such as illness, incapacitations, or death, are rarely synchronized with individual-psychological events, and therefore create critical problems

TABLE 1.1

Crises with Negative (Upper Lines) and Positive Outcomes (Lower Lines) Generated By Asynchronies Along Four Planes of Developmental Progressions

	Inner biological	Individual psychological	Cultural sociological	Outer physical
Inner biological	Infection fertilization	Illness maturation	Epidemic cultivation	Deterioration vitalization
Individual psychological	Disorder control	Discordance concordance	Dissidence organization	Destruction creation
Cultural sociological	Distortion adaptation	Exploitation acculturation	Conflict cooperation	Devastation conservation
Outer physical	Annihilation nutrition	Catastrophy welfare	Disaster enrichment	Chaos harmony

for the persons affected. Nevertheless successful synchronization constitutes the goal in these and simpler situations, and whenever a crisis is resolved, a synchronizing reinterpretation has taken place. Crises could be prevented if synchronization could be prospectively achieved. In this case incapacitations and even death could become meaningful phases in one's life.

Inner-biological progressions lead individuals away from home, to work, marriage, and parenthood. Most of these events will be well-synchronized with progressions along other dimensions. For example, individuals marry when they are mature enough, when they have the appropriate psychological stature and intention, and when the social conditions are conducive and appropriate. In many other instances, such a synchronization is not achieved. Individuals marry without having reached a sufficient level of maturity; others may have attained the proper level but fail to find the right partner. Thus the inner-biological and individual-psychological progressions are not always synchronized with the cultural-sociological or outer-physical conditions (for example, the traditions and laws about marriage or the reduced availability of marriage partners). Under successful conditions, however, coordinated interdependence between the progressions along all of the different dimensions will be achieved by the individual and by society.

2. The relations between children and their parents, brothers and sisters, husbands and wives constitute basic forms of interactions during the life span in which a synchronization of two interdependent progressions along the individual-psychological dimension is attempted.

9

Numerous other forms of coordination exist between relatives, friends, neighbors, classmates, teachers and students, employers and employees, creditors and debtors, vendors and sellers, etc. The progressions within the family are intimately dependent upon one another; the progressions outside of the family exhibit a higher degree of independence and flexibility. Both types of interactive developments are crisis producing. For example, a child may not be wanted; this creates difficulties for the child, the parents, and their relation to one another. Children may be born with defects; frequently this results in the breakdown of their parents' marriage. An employee may be fired. Students may not live up to their teachers' expectations.

Although individual-psychological interactions are always mutual in their progression, the degree of mutuality or symmetry may vary. This I have shown already for the dialogues between the mother and her child. The synchronization of the career developments of marriage partners, to use another example, has been traditionally achieved by subordinating the wife's progression to that of her husband. Thus, a coordination was achieved at the expense of the wife's individual-psychological development. Liberation movements are trying to change this form of solution. But enabling the woman to create her own career development does not necessarily lead to a better coordination of the progressions of the two partners. During its antithetical phase, liberation might indeed prevent the development of synchronized progressions. A dialectical synthesis (Hefner, Rebecca, & Oleshansky, 1975) will be achieved only at a level beyond that of present day thinking and stereotypes.

3. In order to achieve these differentiations and coordinations, major changes are necessary in the developmental interactions between the individual and the social group. Although the development and status of social groups is generated by individual efforts, these groups exert a formative influence upon the individual's development as they begin to establish their means of existence (housing, communities, resources), of communication (language, trade, customs), and of organization (institutions, laws, traditions). But development lies neither in the individual alone nor in the social group but in the dialectical interactions of both. If progressions within individuals, within social groups, and/or between both fail to be synchronized, a crisis will result.

The career development of scientists who participate in one paradigmatic orientation and who are led into a crisis as this orientation fades into the background of scientific consideration represents an instructive example for the coordination of individual and social progressions. A programmed change in their academic roles (for example, by assigning administrative and ceremonial duties to them during the later parts of their careers) would enable these scientists to resolve more effectively the crises which they experience.

A few outstanding scientists are not only instrumental in generating a single paradigmatic orientation, but as this orientation is implemented through research and publications, they may already propose other conceptualizations. Despite the gratified lives that these individuals apparently live, they may experience crises since the community of "normal" scientists (Kuhn, 1962) is not always ready to accept their new ideas. The scientific community may either neglect or reject those contributions, which they regarded as the most advanced achievements of their careers. Wundt's proposal of transformational grammar, for example, was disregarded until recently (Blumenthal, 1970) and has remained neglected by modern proponents of such interpretations.

4. The forms of interactions and the range of organizational units at the cultural-sociological dimension are even more extensive than those at the individual-psychological level. The family is perhaps the most basic group. Different families within the kin compete for leadership. But they also cooperate in order to achieve welfare and security for all of their members. Families, kins, and tribes play a decisive role in the maintenance of nonindustrialized societies. These functions are in part taken over by interest groups, political parties, manufacturing companies, and business organizations in industrial societies. But this stratification is not unidimensional. It crosscuts society in various ways, such as linguistic, political, religious, economic, occupational, and scientific groups, and—most important—cohorts or generations.

In historical progressions and through their competition and cooperation, the various groups make their contributions until they are replaced by others and fade into the background. Not all of the changes generated provide improvements for all groups and, ultimately, for all individuals. Lack of coordination and synchronization creates crises which reveal themselves negatively in conquests, wars, depressions, inflations, bankruptcies, strikes, and unemployment. More important, however, such crises will also lead to creative artistic styles, provocative scientific interpretations, improved processing technologies, constructive economic upheavals, and fairer social orders.

In the traditional family, the development of women has been subordinated to that of her husband; in the traditional society the development of minority groups has been subordinated to that of the majority. Liberation movements have justifiably claimed the right for separate developments of the minority group—the right to express their own culture, language, and institutions. Such attempts are the prerequisites for any coordinated development in the larger society. Such a synthesis can take place only when the two developmental progressions have achieved a sufficient degree of autonomy that is reflected in mutual appreciation and respect. But the need for coordination has been traditionally overemphasized, and the need for separate developments has been disregarded by the majority. Furthermore, the need for subsequent developmental synchronization has been recognized neither by the majority nor by the minority. However, such synchronization is the only mode by which progress can be achieved.

5. Societies composed of well-coordinated subgroups have achieved the conquests of nature and the intellectual heights that make up the history of civilizations. Most of these efforts have been directed toward increasing the security and welfare of the whole society and, as a consequence, of all its individual members. However, these attempts have frequently led to conflicts with other groups creating crisis for the individual and for society. In some extreme cases, social groups have engaged in reckless strife for power without any justifiable and deeper reasons. In many other instances outer-physical conditions have determined far-reaching cultural changes and have exerted their impact upon whole civilizations. As outer-physical events, such as earthquakes, climatic changes, draughts, floods, etc., influence societies, the task of a society consists of protecting itself and its individual members from the catastrophies encountered. In the extreme case, however, outer-physical catastrophies have a direct impact upon single organisms—they may annihilate their biological existence.

Developmental disruptions created by inner-biological or outer-physical changes are relatively rare however. Most crisis are generated by asynchronies in individual-psychological and cultural-sociological progressions. Since these events can be avoided through improved planning and coordination, they deserve the label of a "crisis" with lesser justification. The constructive rearrangements that they demand lead to new cognitive–social achievements and individual and cultural progress.

Toward a Dialectical Interpretation of Development and Aging

A dialectical interpretation of development and aging always considers at least two concurrent temporal sequences, representing progressions that are either inner-biological, individual-psychological, cultural-sociological, or outer-physical. Taken separately these sequences are mere abstractions. Development results from the coordination and synchronization of any two and, indirectly, of all of these progressions. Developmental leaps are brought about by lack of coordination and synchrony. Rather than regarding these critical episodes in a negative manner or from a fatalistic point of view, they provide the fundamental basis for the development of the individual and for the history of the society. Only the inner-biological and the outer-physical sequences occasionally produce events that justifiably appear as crises to the individual and society. But even here refined structural transformations at the individual-psychological or cultural-sociological level will succeed in assimilating these disruptive conditions by coordinating them in a manner that gives meaning to every event in the development of the individual and in the history of society.

In contrast to theories of traits and competencies, stable entities or elements have no part in a dialectical interpretation of development and aging. As such concepts as intelligence and need for achievement have convincingly shown, traits and competencies represent abstractions; their investigations lead to fictitious results. The concept of intelligence, although originally conceived in a rather pragmatic and socially relevant manner, soon attained a metaphysical character through reification and substantification. These mystifications made it increasingly more difficult for us to understand the human being as a changing individual in a changing world (Riegel, 1975c).

A dialectical interpretation of development and aging, in contrast to Piaget's theory of cognitive development, does not emphasize the plateaus at which equilibrium or balance is achieved. Development rather consists in continuing changes along several dimensions of progressions at the same time. Critical changes occur whenever two sequences are out of step, that is when coordination fails and synchronization breaks down. These contradictions are the basis for developmental progressions. Stable plateaus of balance, stability, and equilibrium occur when a developmental or historical task is completed. But developmental and historical tasks are never completed. At the very moment when completion seems to be achieved, new questions and doubts arise in the individual and in society. The organism, the individual, society, and even outer nature are never at rest, and in their restlessness they are rarely perfectly synchronized. Nevertheless, synchronization is the major goal. It can only be achieved through human efforts. There is no preestablished harmony.

Development requires a delicate synchronization between the progressions along the different dimensions. Synchronization is comparable to balance, but it is a balance structured in time. Such a temporal balance can be understood only if the state of imbalance is simultaneously taken into consideration. Balance and imbalance are dialectically determined, and their relationship changes continuously. In this sense, a dialectical interpretation of development and aging is comparable to orchestral compositions. If there were only two instruments in an orchestra and if both were always playing in unison, they would merely increase the sound volume of the melody. Orchestral arrangements from classical music to modern jazz create deviations. Classical music allows the different voices to vary the theme but retains synchrony through its harmony. Modern music produces deviations through disharmonies but retains synchrony through rhythm and beat. Only random alignments create sounds that have neither temporal patterns nor synchronies. They represent music as inappropriately as a series of uncoordinated progressions would represent development and aging.

A dialectical interpretation of development and aging remains a goal to be fulfilled. Undoubtedly much more work has to be done in theory, methodology, and, last but not least, in the application of dialectical thinking research, education, and social praxis. In attempting to summarize once more the critical features of a dialectical interpretation of development and aging, I have prepared the following statements.

A Manifesto for Dialectical Psychology

A specter is haunting Western psychology; the specter of scientific dialectics. The scaffold of the academic world is shaking; the time for its transformation is near. By segregating the subject from the object, we escaped into abstract formalism; by preferring static traits and balanced equilibria, we substituted for the human being a mechanistic monster or a mentalistic mirage; by disregarding our commitment to the human being and to human culture, we increased our self-constriction instead of our self-awareness; by focusing upon synchronic universality, we forgot that the human being is a changing being in a changing world.

1. Dialectical psychology is committed to the study of actions and changes. Therefore both Hegel and Marx have sought their roots in Heraclitus' notion of "ceaseless flux" rather than in the static abstractions of Eleatic being. But even our cherished modern theories of development, most notably that of Piaget, are emphasizing the stable over the unstable, the rest over the unrest, and the static over the changing. After all, Piaget describes development in stages of equilibria at each of which

the mind finds itself at rest. Dialectical psychology, in contrast, is primarily concerned with how individuals and groups succeed in overcoming their tranquility and balance. Consequently dialectical psychology reinterprets crises and contradictions in positive terms. For dialectical psychology it is more important to find out how challenges are recognized and how questions are asked, rather than how problems are solved and how answers are given.

2. Dialectical psychology is concerned with short term situational changes, as well as with long-term individual and cultural developments. The short-term conception of dialectics is historically the earlier form and has been elaborated in Socrates' and Plato's philosophy. It is presently retained in studies of dialogues by Freedle (1975, 1978), in explorations of the social basis of language acquisition as emphasized by Harris (1975), in experimental work as discussed by Kvale (1975), Meacham (1972, 1975b, 1977a, 1977b), and Mitroff and Betz (1972), and in personality theories as promoted by Rychlak (1973, 1976a, 1976b), Chandler (1975), Meacham (1975a), and van den Daele (1975). In contrast to this orientation, the long-term conception of dialectics is concerned with developmental changes in the individual and historical changes in society. In particular, such an orientation points at the necessary interdependence of both. In psychology these viewpoints were first expressed by Krüger (1915), Wundt's last student and successor at Leipzig, in sociology by Mannheim (1952), and more recently by developmental psychologists and sociologists at the University of Chicago (Mead, Burgess, Havighurst, Neugarten, & Ryder) and at the University of West Virginia (Baltes, Datan, Nesselroade, Reese, and Schaie). With the coordinated emphasis upon individual development and social changes, the emerging interpretation has lead us away from the traditional child-centered approach toward an adult or rather life-span emphasis in development.

3. Dialectical psychology is concerned with primitive and scientific dialectics. Most developmental psychologists consent to the notion of primitive dialectics in the child and in the child–mother interactions (Freud, Werner, Piaget). There is a fine tuning, almost from birth, in the interaction between a child and a mother which often makes it impossible to determine who initiated an action and who followed it (Lewis & Freedle, 1973; Sameroff, 1975). As cogently discussed by Lawler (1975), Buck-Morss (1975), and Wozniak (1975a, 1975b), primitive dialectics provide the basis of individual and social activities. Through these activities, new levels of consciousness are created until finally the individual becomes aware of dialectics itself; scientific dialectics has emerged. Scientific dialectics finds expression in dialogues and debates, both in the

thoughts and operations of a single individual and between many individuals. In particular, scientific dialectics leads to developmental and historical awareness that is expressed, for example, in the understanding of the struggle between different scientific theories.

4. Dialectical psychology is concerned with inner and outer dialectics but, most notably, with both at the same time. Inner dialectics is well expressed by Piaget's concepts of assimilation and accommodation leading to adaptation and reorganization of the individual's cognitive structure. Although assimilation takes something from and accommodation gives something to the outside world, both are processes within the organism. Without notable exception linguistic and cognitive theories of development have not recognized that there are other individuals intimately related to those under concern who, like them, are continuously engaged in assimilations and accommodations. The interactions between different active individuals, the outer dialectics, represent an aspect of development equally important to that of the inner dialectics. However a comprehensive and appropriate interpretation of development has to consider both. As convincingly expressed by Rubinstein (1958, 1963; see Payne, 1968) the individual finds himself at the intersection of interactions, his activities represent relations of relations.

5. Perhaps in their attempt to escape the difficult concept of the relations of relations, Marxist dialecticians have preferred to anchor the dialectics upon an inner-biological and outer-physical material base. But their attempts, in the end, seem to give away the notion of activity, labor, and effort in preference for commodity, product, and result. But dialectical theory neither needs to be materialistic nor idealistic; it can encompass a manifold of different conceptions. The theme of the dialectics always needs to be translated however into new forms appropriate for a society (including its sciences) at a particular historical time, that is, dialectics needs to be applied to dialectics itself. I am committed to help in the new translation. Let there be a hundred new flowers blooming.

Dialectic psychologists unite! You have nothing to lose but the respect of vulgar mechanists and pretentious mentalists; you will win a world, a changing world created by ever-changing human beings.

2

Historical Introduction

Traditionally, treatises on the history of sciences have been restricted to intellectual changes in Europe and North America. The extensive developments in other civilizations, based on distinctively different philosophical, political and economic conditions, have been disregarded (see, however, Murphy & Murphy, 1968). Moreover, within the European and North American tradition, history of science has been described as a universal progression which, through increased empirical work and abstractions, would move us closer and closer to true scientific knowledge and help us in the detection of the "laws of nature." Rarely has it been emphasized that several divergent, and often contradictory, conceptions of these "laws" and nature exist even within a single cultural orientation and rarely has it been recognized that scientific progress itself becomes possible only through confrontations between these contradictory conceptions.

As in past presentations, the following discussion will be restricted to the history in Europe and North America, but within this geographical and intellectual arena, three distinct paradigmatic orientations will be compared that are based upon different social, political, and economic conditions. For simplicity, they will be called mechanistic or Anglo-American, mentalistic or continental European, and the dialectical orientations (Riegel, 1972c).

Paradigmatic Developmental Orientations

Mechanistic Orientation

An early indication of this mode of scientific and social philosophy is provided by Hobbes' (1558–1679) discussion of the origin of social order. According to his interpretation, at the beginning there is a "fight of everyone against everyone" (*bellum omnium contra omnes*); the human being is compared to a selfish and untamed beast; social order has to be imposed upon the original chaotic conditions by a rational contract. Several centuries later, similar ideas dominate Darwin's (1809–1882) naturalistic interpretations of the "struggle for survival" and the "survival of the fittest." Where else could such viewpoints originate and succeed than in a society in which free trade, competition, and achievement were valued so highly, in Great Britain and in the United States!

Mental organizations were neglected in epistemology just as social structures were ignored as principles of society. The mind was compared by Locke (1682–1704) to a *tabula rasa* or a black box upon which external contingencies were to impinge. Neither the outside nor the individuals themselves participated actively in the selection and organization of knowledge. Subsequently the main, if not the sole, criterion for intellectual excellence was the amount of information accumulated in the black box, as much as the criterion for social respectability was the amount of cash deposited in the bank account and of property registered in the registrar's office.

Not surprisingly either, when considering development, the young white adult male, engaged in manufacturing or trade, was bound to appear as the most successful competitor of all and became the single standard for comparisons. None of the other individuals and groups, the very young and the old, the delinquent and deprived, the female and the colonial subject, were evaluated in their own terms but rather against this single yardstick. They were described in negative terms only, as retarded, deficient, deteriorated, or simply as deviant.

Most distinctly, this philosophy of man and society entered into psychology through the spectacular efforts of Sir Francis Galton (1822–1911), who is considered to be the founder of the psychology of individual and developmental differences, including those of adulthood and aging. When merged with the pragmatic goals of stock farming, this orientation led to Eugenics which Galton justified as follows:

> It may seem monstrous that the weak should be crowded out by the strong, but it is still more monstrous that the races best fitted to play their part on the

stage of life, should be crowded out by the incompetent, the ailing, and the desponding [1869, p. 343].

Mentalistic Orientation

Although implied in Leibniz' philosophy (1646-1716) with its emphasis upon active organizing forces of the mind, the scientific and social philosophy of the alternative orientation was most clearly expressed by Rousseau (1712-1778). In contrast to the ceaseless strife for achievement, he proposed a social philosophy in which the young were considered and evaluated by independent standards rather than by those of the successful young adult. In this way, Rousseau provided an option for multiage, multigenerational, and also, multicultural standards.

In his romantic zeal, Rousseau refused to consider development as the taming of ineffective and uncontrolled drives. The child as well as primitive man (*bon savage*) were regarded as reflecting the inherent harmony of the human being more perfectly than the acculturated adult. Civilization was seen as a restrictive cloak covering the natural beauty and knowledge of children and as generating social differences and injustice. Education, therefore, should treat children as children. It should keep them in their innocent state as long as possible and should not aim at making them assimilate the adult world quickly and completely.

Through the efforts of Pestalozzi (1746-1827), Fröbel (1782-1852), Montessori (1870-1952), and many others, Rousseau's social philosophy began to influence profoundly the educational institutions on the European continent. At the same time, upheavals from within various age groups led to refined age stratification and the assignment of specific roles to different groups within society.

Already during the Napoleonic wars, clandestine student organizations charted out distinct roles for this privileged group of young adults. Toward the end of the nineteenth century the far-spread "youth movement" (see Hardesty, 1976) tried to liberate the adolescent, an attempt which received scholarly sanction in Spranger's (1924) influential book on adolescence (see Thomae, 1976). Most recently, the continental European movement has found expression in Piaget's work (see Flavell, 1963; Furth, 1969). His psychology is characterized by the notion of a stepwise progression in development. Each stage has to be evaluated in the framework of its own standards and, strictly speaking, is incompatible with other levels of behavior.

The continental European paradigm emerged in societies with strong social stratification governed by landed aristocracies. Competition within but not between classes was permitted. The political and economic decisions were directed from the top down, and as the privileges decreased in this order, the duties increased. Nevertheless, such a seemingly archaic social organization led to a sensitive educational philosophy which was appreciative of differences between ages and social groups and assigned appropriate roles to them.

But in spite of its innovations, the continental European paradigm continued to focus emphatically upon the individual alone in his conquest of the outer world. Development was seen as emerging from within. Although the interaction of the individual with the social world was recognized, the latter merely functioned as a testing ground and, in the case of Rousseau, as coercive power against which the individual would have to rise. But society not only emerges from within organisms. It emerges outside the individual, through the combined efforts of many other individuals. Since this issue was not recognized with sufficient determination, we must depart from the second paradigm and, most notably, from the cognitive developmental psychology of Piaget.

Dialectical Orientation

The third paradigm focuses upon the developmental interdependence of organism and environment. Thereby, it tries to overcome the separation of subject and object. The split between the observing subject and the observed object has characterized psychology's desire to mimic the conception and success of the natural sciences. But even if the separation of the subject from scientific discourse has led to the success of the natural sciences up through the nineteenth century (Wundt, 1949; see Chapter 3, this volume), the creation of these "objective" conditions has never been of exceptional benefit for the behavioral and social sciences (Giorgi, 1969; Riegel, 1973a). Rather than generating knowledge through the process of such a separation as in the continental European orientation or by searching for it out there in the "objective world" through the elimination of the participating subject, as in the Anglo-American orientation, the epistemological foundation for behavioral and social sciences lies in the interactions between individuals or groups of individuals. These interactions, being dependent on both inner-individual and outer-cultural development, are dialectical in character.

The topic of a dialectic psychology can be most clearly elaborated by contrasting it with traditional approaches representing three levels of abstraction or alienation in psychological research.

1. The first and still rather common approach in psychology represents the path used by general-experimental psychologists. This approach is the most abstract and alienated form of a scientific inquiry. Both individual-developmental and cultural-historical changes are eliminated, and thus, the human being represents a fictitious point in a developmental–historical vacuum.

2. The situation is not much better for the second approach used by individual-developmental psychologists. Although they study developmental differences (and sometimes changes), they eliminated, with few exceptions, any consideration of history. For example, young and old persons tested at one particular historical time differ widely in regard to the social–historical conditions under which they grew up. Although the impact of historical changes during an extended period, for example, in education, health care, nutrition, communication, etc., is often much more dramatic than any differences in performance between young and old persons, this factor is generally disregarded in developmental studies.

3. Thus, the only valid approach to the study of the individual has to take account of both individual-developmental and cultural–historical changes. This approach synthesizes the two other orientations mentioned in the earlier parts of the presentation. It absorbs the mechanistic or Anglo-American paradigm of a passive organism in an unstructured world, directed by a relentless drive toward a uniform standard of achievement. It absorbs the mentalistic or continental European paradigm of an organism actively constructing a world which, nevertheless, remains passive and does not induce its direction upon the organisms but merely provides multigenerational and multicultural options to them.

The dialectic paradigm emphasizes the interaction between individual and historical development which are both traced to their inner and outer foundations. Thereby, man retains a much higher and humane role than that of an untamed beast, an empty wax plate, a playful child, or a good barbarian. Through their ceaseless efforts, men change nature; the changing nature, changes men. For example, early men, by inventing a tool, a sign, or a linguistic expression, change at the same time the social–physical conditions under which they live. In the process of history, these changed conditions change men. Thus, through dialectic interactions, the individual as well as society move forward to ever new achievements and ever new structures.

Open and Closed Developmental Systems

Overlapping, though not identical with the comparison between the first two paradigmatic developmental orientations described above, is the distinction between open and closed developmental systems. The former is akin to the mechanistic orientation which implies the concept of quantitative, continuous growth and the latter to the mentalistic orientation which implies the concept of qualitative, discrete growth. Both orientations reveal again the impact of our concept of development and of our philosophy of man upon the research activity in which we are engaged; they limit our scientific decisions and determine the type of research data which we are bound to obtain.

Four Models of Development

In the past, developmental psychology, being dominated by the notion of continuous growth processes, has shown an implicit preference for open developmental systems. According to such an interpretation, growth consists in the acquisition of bits and pieces of information, habits, or experiences which are accumulated in the individuals' repertoires, making them increasingly more effective and able. If certain tasks or problems can not be resolved at a given moment, *the individuals will have to acquire more information so that they may finally succeed.* In contrast to such a notion of unlimited expansion, a closed developmental system is characterized by the principle that *everything that grows, grows at the expense of something else.* Such a model assumes that the limits in capacity are basically fixed. Development consists in an increasingly finer organization and, perhaps, in sudden, systematic restructuring of information, habits, and experiences, but not in a ceaseless addition of new materials.

The distinction between open and closed psychological systems has been introduced by Bertalanffy (1960). A detailed and comprehensive recent discussion has been presented by Overton (1975). In analogy to physics, a closed system, such as an ideal gas in a container, changes its state only through the intervention of external forces, and, even after these have been applied, the system will eventually return to the original state of equilibrium. Modifications of the open system, on the other hand, imply an exchange of information or energy with the external world. Subsequently, changes are irreversible and the system does not return to its original condition.

In contrast to these physical models, our interpretation emphasizes the internal organization and the changes in organization of these systems (see Riegel, 1973b). Thus, in order to arrive at a complete comparison of these interpretations, we would have to introduce a double classification, one dimension denoting (in analogy to physics) systems in which information or energy is exchanged (or not), the other denoting (in the sense given to it here) systems which are undergoing internal reorganizations (or not). Thus, we have four possible cases: (*a*) Systems that neither incorporate information nor change their internal organization except for brief losses of their equilibrium; (*b*) systems that accumulate information but do not change their internal organization. Such systems are similar to the mechanistic model of continuous or quantitative growth; (*c*) systems that do not accumulate information but change their internal organization. Such systems are similar to the mentalistic model of discrete or qualitative growth; and (*d*) systems that both accumulate information and change their internal organization. Such systems represent a synthesis of the open and the closed models (as used in the present context) and describe the dialectics of developmental processes. They represent what in Marxist terminology is often called the change from quantity into quality.

The distinction between open and closed developmental systems has a wide range of applications. It can be applied, for instance, to political, economic, and administrative conditions.

Sociological Examples

Rural communities in nonindustrialized societies are frequently cited as examples of closed political, economic, and social systems. Usually, members of such communities have been engaged in the same activities for countless generations. Changes in these activities are often viewed with suspicion and, if possible, prevented. Since little or no information is acquired, such social systems would represent Case A of Table 2.1. It is inappropriate, however, to limit the description of closed systems to communities that are, essentially, unchanging. Numerous other groups, though stable in the size of their population or in the area occupied, have shown considerable growth through internal reorganization, better utilization of their resources, more efficient planning, better designed settlements, etc. Most of the former city states in central

TABLE 2.1
Comparison between Four Models of Development

	No information exchanged (closed)	Information exchanged (open)
No reorganization	Case A—no growth	Case B—quantitative
Reorganization	Case C—qualitative	Case D—dialectical

Europe as well as in ancient Greece and the eastern Mediterranean are cases in point. In modern times, the highly developed smaller European countries such as Sweden, Switzerland, and the Netherlands serve as outstanding examples. They increased the quality of their products, of their living conditions, education, and welfare to a higher degree than accomplished in the most advanced expansionistic industrialized nation, the United States. Improving the quality of life and social conditions through internal reorganizations represents Case C of Table 2.1.

In comparison to the first two examples, the concept of open and accumulative social systems has become singularly associated with the development of modern industrialized societies. Both West and East, Democrats and Republicans, subscribe wholeheartedly and completely to the political, social, and economic philosophy of imperialistic, ceaseless expansions. Although questioned in recent debates, this commitment has not been abandoned nor seriously challenged in the political praxis yet. Whenever problems arise, such as a business slump, a high rate of unemployment, a trade deficit, an instability of exchange rates, the single, overall solution proposed consists in accelerating production and/or increasing spending. Undoubtedly, there are minor variations between different camps: the Democrats willingly subscribe to Keynes and deficit spending, the Republicans are more reluctant and aim for a balanced budget; the farmers care less about the unemployment; the urbanites favor increases in governmental subsidies. But in spite of any specific and often forceful disagreements and in spite of the social decay created, the belief in such an open system is not questioned. Closed systems, on the other hand, are seen as backward, as unable to produce solutions, and as antithetical to growth.

Undoubtedly, optimal conditions for growth and development depend upon synchronized changes in quantity and quality. Such conditions are represented as Case D in Table 2.1 and can be best demonstrated by examples from cognitive developmental psychology and from the history of sciences.

Psychological Examples

According to the quantitative, open model of growth, individual development is seen as a ceaseless, continuing expansion, produced by the addition of bits and pieces of information, experiences, or habits. The more material individuals have accumulated, the brighter, the better adjusted, and the more successful these individuals are thought to be. In contrast to such a concept of growth, a good example for a closed developmental system is the interpretation of Piaget's theory (1958) by McLaughlin (1963). This author described the four major developmental periods of Piaget as qualitative changes in the child's ability to operate with classes. During the sensorimotor period, children attend to one concept at a time and do not discriminate along any dimension or attribute. During the period of pre-operational intelligence, they handle two concepts along one dimension, such as red versus non-red. During the period of concrete operational intelligence, children succeed in double classifications of four concepts along two dimensions, such as red versus non-red, plus square versus non-square, and during the period of formal operational intelligence, they perform triple classifications of eight concepts. Thus the children approach and apprehend the same material in successively more differentiated and structurally more complex ways. At the beginning they lack discriminability; at the end they make succinct differentiations and perform complex operations and judgements in full conformity with the requirements of the adult world.

While McLaughlin's interpretation seems to represent Case C, that is, development through internal reorganization, in further extension, he equates this qualitative progression with increases in immediate memory span that enable the child to deal simultaneously with an increasingly larger number of concepts and, by implication, with an increasingly larger number of dimensions or attributes. With this extension, McLaughlin demonstrates that the evaluations in terms of qualitative and quantitative growth are intimately interwoven. Increases in immediate memory span, though discrete in any instance of testing, when averaged over repeated measures or groups of individuals provide smooth, continuous growth curves as demonstrated in many textbooks. The concomitant increases in cognitive operations, however, are qualitative in nature.

McLaughlin's interpretation represents an important demonstration of a switch from quantity to quality in developmental progression; it represents Case D of the developmental system. In all fairness, the same has to be concluded about Piaget's developmental theory. For Piaget, too, the intellectual operations of a child at successive periods of de-

25

velopment are characterized by distinctly different types of logics that are only partially embedded in one another. Development does not merely consist in the discrimination along additional dimensions, but in the appearance of new types of operations at successive stages. Thus, children acquire, at each period, a unique logic which they continue to improve during these periods until, suddenly, they shift toward a more complex form of behavior and a more advanced logic. Piaget's theory, therefore, represents Case D, that is, a system that does not only accumulate information but also changes its internal organization

Kuhn's (1962) interpretation of the structure of scientific revolutions resembles Piaget's theory of cognitive development. He distinguishes between paradigmatic and normal sciences. The former are initiated by outstanding scientists who provide new perspectives and interpretations of data either already available or collected in view of the proposed new paradigm. Different scientific paradigms may coexist, such as the wave theory and the particle theory of light. New paradigms shift the attention to scientific aspects which were disregarded in the past and place them into a qualitatively different context. Other examples from the natural sciences are the Ptolemaic and the Copernican astronomy, the Newtonian mechanics, etc., and in the social sciences, for example in linguistics, the conflicts between historical philology, structural linguistics, transformational linguistics. Like Piaget's theory of cognitive development, Kuhn's interpretation proposes an accumulation of information within paradigms. He compares this process with the solving of jig-saw puzzles. Major progress in sciences is brought about, however, by shifts from paradigm to paradigm. Each paradigm will contribute knowledge to the overall growth of a discipline, that is, to the growth of normal science.

Kuhn's interpretation of the history of science, like Piaget's interpretation of cognitive development, suggests a synthesis between qualitative and quantitative developmental systems of Cases C and B; it promotes the dialectical system of Case D. In the past, interpretations in the history of sciences have been dominated by a preference for open, or more specifically, by quantitative systems. Progress has been seen as a ceaseless accumulation of data leading to more and more information, thereby, stripping nature of secret after secret. Such an interpretation is compatible with utopian views of political and cultural history as expressed both in democratic and socialistic theories. An interpretation of political and cultural history in terms of a closed, or more specifically, of a qualitative system has been proposed by Spengler (1918–1922). According to his view, a civilization starts with a basic theme which through artistic, philosophical, and scientific advances is explicated in successive steps until, toward the end, it deteriorates through over-differentiation. Even though such an interpretation is one-sided, it provides a challenging alternative to the traditional view of history in which event follows event and person follows person without any explicit origin or goal.

In contrast to such a random match, a meaningful interpretation will have to integrate open and closed developmental systems, quantitative and qualitative growth models. Such an interpretation, as represented by Case D of Table 2.1, prepares the way for a dialectical analysis. While more will be said about such an analysis in the remaining chapters of this book, it is to be shown in the following section that both viewpoints have been merged into the social philosophy dominating the behavioral and social sciences in the Soviet Union, if not in praxis then at least in theory.

Dialectics in Soviet Psychology

The two paradigmatic orientations which in the first section of this chapter I have called "mechanistic" and "mentalistic" conceive of psychological activities and development as either an accumulation of information by essentially passive organisms, or as the spontaneous generation of new modes of operations for which the environment merely provides information as necessary material so that the organisms are able to make their own selections. Overlapping, though not identical with the distinction of these two paradigmatic developmental orientations, is the comparison between open and closed developmental systems or, more specifically, between quantitative and qualitative growth models (see previous section—"Open and Closed Developmental Systems"). Dialectical psychology incorporates these divergent viewpoints by arguing that new operations and new knowledge represent the internalization of external structures, such as speech, but that these operations and new knowledge represent the externalization of internal structures, such as cognition. Dialectical psychology insists, for example, that men create language but that, at the same time, men are created by language. Dialectical psychology, thus, focuses upon and tries to overcome the separation of organism and environment, consciousness and behavior, subject and object.

In some dialectical interpretations, both the material basis within and the material basis without the individual are recognized as foundations of the interaction processes through which activity and knowledge emerge. While we do not need to agree with such an interpretation, that is, with the interpretation proposed by dialectical materialists, the best known inroads into the behavioral and social sciences have been made from this perspective, that is, by Soviet psychologists.

The Beginnings of Soviet Psychology

In the years following the Russian revolution of 1917, the dominant figure in Soviet psychology was Pavlov (1849–1936). According to his interpretations, conditioned and unconditioned reflexes realize the connection of the organism with its environment and are directed towards the maintenance of an equilibrium between the organism and external conditions. The activity involved in the formation of this connection is called "higher nervous activity." It is distinguished from "lower nervous activity" which serves to integrate the different parts of the organism. The signals from the environment indicating the conditions necessary for the organism's survival (such as food, shelter, and danger) belong to the "first signaling system." The first signaling system is common to both men and animals.

Through culture and history, the human being has also developed a "second signaling system" which does not directly signalize "reality" but rather the data of the first signaling system. The second signaling system, mainly through the development of language labels and instructions, allows for an expansion of the organism's activities and results in the cultural–historical achievements of human society. This extension of Pavlov's theory of conditioning paved the way for a consolidation of the dialectical materialism which characterizes his earlier work on the first signaling system with the historical dialecticism of Marx, Engels, and Lenin, which characterizes the intentions for his later work on the second signaling system. One of the most penetrating proponents of this development was Rubinstein (1889–1960) (1958, 1963; see also Payne, 1968).

The synthesis envisaged did not succeed without an internal struggle. During this controversy, the purge of the educational movement known as Pedology gained special significance. According to the criticism, this movement (especially connected with the work of Blonsky) undermined the responsibility of the teacher and developed a *laissez-faire* if not a negative attitude toward so-called "backward" children. The use of psychological tests had been recommended by Blonsky (1884–1941) for the categorization of these children who, then, were kept in their "backward" states by assigning them to "special" schools in which "bad habits" became even harder to correct. Individual differences were either related to inherited biological factors or to the social environment. Especially the proponents of the former view, the "biologists," came under sharp attack for preserving the compartmentalizing concepts of the bourgeois society instead of emphasizing the duty of the educators toward active modification of the child's development. Instead of accepting the child's development as predetermined, the participatory role of the teacher as a representative of the cultural–historical conditions of the society became the dominant theme not only for education, but for the behavioral and social sciences in general.

Although criticized for his support of the bifurcation of psychological activities into heredity and environmental components, Vygotsky (1896–1934) was credited with directing full attention to the constructive effects of the cultural–sociological factors. This interpretation was juxtaposed to that of the biologists and has been occasionally identified as that of the sociologists. It was consonant with the historical dialecticism of Marx, Engels, and Lenin. According to Vygotsky (1929, 1962) psychological processes (including consciousness) emerge through historical and social evolutions that, in turn, originate from human labor.

The victory of historical dialectics was greatly enhanced by Vygotsky. His arguments were carried forward by his associates and students, especially Leont'ev and Luria (1968). When united with Pavlov's interpretations of the first and second signal system, a theory could emerge in full conformity with the goals of Marxist ideology. This synthesis has been most clearly elaborated in the system of psychology proposed by Rubinstein.

Double Interaction Theory

Rubinstein's interpretations imply nothing else than a reformulation of the old mind–body problem. Traditionally the solution to this problem has been sought by, first, determining the nature of both, the mind and the body, and second, by contemplating their interdependence. For Rubinstein the solution has to proceed in the reverse order. The relationship determines how we conceive of mind and how we conceive of body.

Rubinstein's synthesis tries to overcome the mind–body dualism which has remained unbridgeable in western thought and has led to development of several different "psychologies." On the one hand, the mental introspectionists, such as Wundt (1832–1920), Titchener (1867–

1927), and the psychologists at Würzburg, focused exclusively upon consciousness. But because of its subjective character, consciousness has remained unattainable for scientific descriptions. On the other hand, the methodologically powerful opponents, the behaviorists, focused upon the overt stimulation of the organism, for example, upon food, drink, or shock, and the overt reactions, for example, eating, drinking, or withdrawal. With its exclusive emphasis on physical conditions, behaviorism represents nothing but the denial or inverse of introspectionism. According to Rubinstein, it represents "vulgar mechanism" and is not of greater worth than introspective mentalism.

Rubinstein's synthesis emphasizes the unity of consciousness and behavior. These two terms do not denote separate systems; neither is the former all internal nor the latter all external, but both interpenetrate each other. Consciousness is not a passive contemplative state but an activity; behavior is not merely a movement but is directed by internal organization. On the one hand, activity objectifies the inner subjective world; on the other hand, the objective world is reflected in and by the subject. Both processes are interdependent and produce the continuous changes of the individual and society. Rubinstein refers to Marx: "By acting on the external world and changing it, man, at the same time, changes his own nature." For example, by inventing a tool or by employing linguistic expressions, men change the world in which they live. The changed world, in turn, changes men.

Development does not merely consist in the continuous accumulation of information and goods but progresses in dialectical leaps. Modifications are brought about by structural changes created by the organism. But as these structures change, the functions change. The invention of some tools and linguistic forms changes the expression and significance of men's work and communication. Structure and function develop as a unit. At the beginning the development of an organism is mainly determined by biological evolution. With the historical growth of psychic activities, however, development becomes codetermined by cultural–sociological evolution. Men, through their activities and labor, transform their environment and create new conditions for the individuals' development.

The individuals' development consists in the acquisition of human culture through their own activities. But this process is supplemented by the activities of the society. The activities permeate in both directions; from the individuals to the society and from the society to the individuals. Knowledge is acquired through the individuals' activities, but the activities of the society are equally important. Knowedge is social in nature.

Constitutive Relationism

The dialectical interactions between the individual-psychological and cultural–sociological conditions are codetermined by a second system of interactions, the interactions between inner-biological and individual-psychological activities. Rubinstein does not elaborate this interaction system at length but refers to Pavlov's extensive work on the conditioning process. Contrary to the American behaviorists, Pavlov regarded the reflex as a basic organic action unit which only in the process of conditioning is broken up into a stimulus-response sequence. American behaviorists have taken the separation of the stimulus and response for granted and have developed their "psychology" on the basis of this separation. The unfolding of the reflex is demonstrated by Pavlov's dog who, first, salivated only when exposed to food powder but, later, to the sound of the bell that had always preceded the presentation of the unconditioned stimulus, the food powder. The ringing of the bell was not, but became, the substitute for this exposure; it was not, but it became the (conditioned) stimulus.

With the emphasis on the inner-biological basis, Rubinstein completes his synthesis. In the words of Payne (1968),

> The relation of the psychic to the material world is fundamentally two-fold: to the inner matter of the brain (this relation constitutes the psychic in the quality of higher nervous activity) and to the outer matter of the external world in which relationship the psychic takes on the quality of ideal and subjective. The first quality Rubinstein calls the *ontological* (or theory-of-being) aspect of the psychic; the second he calls *epistemological* (or theory-of-knowledge) aspect [p. 98].

In the view of most western scholars, reflexes merely represent reactions, that is external responses of an organism to external stimuli. In contrast, Rubinstein emphasizes reflexes as basic relational units which, though triggered by external stimuli, are also being modified by the responses produced. In modern philosophy, the idea of such a relational interpretation originated with Hegel's dialectical idealism (1770–1831) and reappeared in Lenin's writings.

Rubinstein emphasizes the material basis from which relations originate and through which they generate double interaction systems, namely between psychological and cultural-sociological conditions (representing the historical dialectics of Soviet psychology) and between psychological and inner-biological conditions (representing the material dialectics of Soviet psychology). Similarly, Rubinstein regarded the material world as having both an internal structure, for example, the molecular structure of a diamond, and an external structure that relates the diamond to other objects as well as to subject, for example, to the craftsman using it as a tool, the merchant using it as a commodity, and the lover using it as a treasure. The observable results of those external interactions can be defined by the diamond's physical and social qualities. For example, the diamond will appear hard and pointed to the craftsman, as a sound investment to the merchant, and as enchanting to the lover. Finally, both the internal and external interactions represent processes within individual and cultural developments. For example, diamonds, like gold and silver, have been useless though attractive stones for uncivilized men, they have been raw material for craftsmen and artisans, and they have been standard commodities by which the wealth of people and nations has been evaluated.

Psychological activity is determined by the dual relationships to outer and inner matter. But matter, too, appears in this dual relationship. For instance, a diamond is determined by its inner atomic structure as well as by its relationships to the outer material conditions. Thus, the boundaries between mind and matter are not fixed but determined in multiple ways. The inner and outer material reality provides the anchoring conditions for two interaction processes. Through these two interaction processes psychological activity emerges. Psychological activities represent the interaction of these two interaction processes or, in dialectical jargon, they represent relations of relations. Thus, like the two interlaced links of a chain, psychological activities are to be found at the center of these interactions but, at the same time, they are delegated to a secondary position. Their study has to be founded upon the inner-biological and the outer cultural–sociological processes. Psychology without these foundations would be fictitious.

Conclusions

In the past, the mechanistic interpretations, promoted by sensualism, associationism, and behaviorism have compartmentalized human activities and, consequently, have led to the development of separated sciences, such as biology, psychology, and sociology. Implied in these approaches is the tendency to segregate parts and components analytically. Little attention was given and little success was achieved in putting the pieces together again. The main task of science was seen as breaking the unity apart. If a synthesis was attempted at all, it aimed at an additive composition or conglomeration of the separate parts. Thus, we find the peculiar notions that sentences are the sum of words, words are the sum of syllables, and syllables are the sum of letters; performance time is the sum of reaction time and movement time, and, most devastating of all, a trait is the sum of hereditary and environmental features, intelligence is 20% environmental and 80% innate.

In comparison to the mechanists, mentalists have emphasized organismic units. These units were either of the inner-biological or outer-social type. Thus, Piaget, like Pavlov, sees development emerging from the unit of the reflex and proceeding through the process of the organism's accommodation to outer conditions and the organism's assimilation of outer conditions to higher and higher levels of perceptual-cognitive operations. In spite of their relationship to outer conditions, both accommodation and assimilation are processes within the organism, however, and do not involve the physical and social conditions as active forces in the developmental process.

In contrast to Piaget, others have emphasized the outer units. In his symbolic interactionism, George Herbert Mead (1862–1931) [1934], for example, regards the individual and the self as emerging through the conflict between the inner core of the "I" and the various forms of the "me's," that is, the various social attitudes and roles that the individual enacts and is induced to enact by the prevailing social conditions. Although there is consideration for the inner conditions of the "I," this connection is not elaborated and remains a mysterious part of Mead's interpretation. As much as Piaget has focused upon the inner dialectics, so has Mead focused upon the outer dialectics of the organism. Thus, nothing else seems to be our task than to put the inner and outer dialectics together again, to put Piaget and Mead together.

However, there are additional problems. Both the mechanists and the mentalists have given disproportionate emphasis to the individual. The mechanists compared the isolated subject to an empty box or a wax plate where pieces of outside information are accumulated. In emphasizing the sensory basis of knowledge, for some mechanists, the perceptionists, knowledge resides exclusively inside such a box and is subjective in nature. For others, for behaviorists, it is of no interest at all, precisely because it is subjective in nature. For the mentalist, of course, knowledge is very much a matter of concern. But here too, it resides exclusively inside the individual and is attained through the individual's creative struggle, often—as emphasized by Rousseau—against an alien or hostile world.

In comparison to these individualistic viewpoints, dialectical psychology regards knowledge as being both individual and social at one and the same time. On the basis of the inner dialectics, men are creative, but as they produce objects and generate knowledge, they are being transformed by their own creations. Thus, a dialectical interpretation emphasizes individual and human qualities of knowledge, but these qualities are recognized as the result of cultural–historical development.

3

Dialectical Operations:
The First and Final Period
of Cognitive Development

Natural sciences—not to speak of the behavioral and social sciences—have been plagued by implicit contradictions. Since Huygens, it has been recognized, for example, that phenomena such as interference and diffraction, are best explained by a wave theory of light. However, polarization (at least prior to Fresnel) is best explained by Newton's corpuscle or emission theory. Although attempts to synthesize both interpretations have succeeded, notably in Planck's quantum theory, modern scientists have come to accept and to live with coexistent, contradictory theories. Some scientists have not hesitated to admit that these inconsistencies are basic properties of nature rather than insufficiencies in the knowledge acquired.

> Wave theory of light and corpuscle theory are both reliably substantiated through experiments and both represent inescapable conclusions from experience. But both contradict each other . . . Today, we can no longer doubt that the dualism of wave and corpuscle represents a very general physical lawfulness [Jordan, 1943, pp. 84–85].

The antagonism between such different interpretations could reach its distinctiveness only because both groups of scientists succeeded in eliminating from their experiments the participatory role of the subject. "It is impossible to deny that, so far, all acquisition of knowledge in

35

physics has in principle aimed at the widest possible separation of processes in the outer nature and processes in the realm of human sensations [Planck, 1934, p. 45]." The importance of the subject was unadmittedly retained outside of the context of experimentation only, namely, in the selective preference for one theory or the other and in the selective performance of particular series of experiments.

Modern scientists have realized that the activities of the observing subjects are intimately connected with the scientific investigations. When dealing with subatomic particles, for example, it is in principle impossible to observe, with equal precision, both their location in space and their movement in time. Since each measurement exerts a causal effect upon the process to be observed, the investigator is prevented from separating these conditions from the measurements chosen. Both location and movement, or mass and velocity, have to be studied in their mutual dependence and in their dependence upon the observations. This recognition implies nothing else but to admit that the object is influenced by the subject and that the subject is influenced by the object.

The abstract status of classical natural sciences, which the theory of mechanics represents a prototypical example, was achieved through a strict adherence to the postulate of identity and the rejection of explicit or implicit contradictions. The laws of classical mechanics—as well as those of any of the other theories of classical natural sciences—

> represent idealizations which we derive by considering only those portions of our experience, in which we can achieve an order with our concepts of space, time, etc . . . (but) . . . such a conceptualization of a world proceeding in objective space and time is, again, only an idealization of nature, carried out in the desire to objectify as much as possible [Heisenberg, 1942, pp. 41, 94].

The theory of mechanics was built upon the traditional logic, the most important property of which is that any observations, definitions, or postulates would be noncontradictory, that is, A should always equal A, but not B at one time and A at another. It was inconceivable, in the very general case, that light could be a wave and a particle at the same time. Only one of these alternatives could be true.

The issue of identity and contradiction separates most distinctly Hegel's dialectical logic from the formal logic of his predecessors, especially Aristotle and Kant, to which most contemporary scientists have remained uncritically committed. Hegel delineates his own from traditional logic in the following manner:

> It is one of the basic prejudices of traditional logic and of common-sense conception that contradiction is not such an essential and immanent determi-

nation as identity; if we were to consider their rank, however, and if both determinations were to be kept separated, contradiction would have to be accepted as deeper and more essential. For identity, in contrast to it, is only the recognition of the single immediate, the dead being; but contradiction is the source of all motion and vitality; only in so far as something contains contradiction does it move, has it drive and activity [1969a, p. 545].

The adherence to the principle of identity and noncontradiction characterizes both the scientists who are founding their inquiries upon the viewpoints of philosophical realism as well as those who prefer the experiential basis of positivism. The former believe that their observations represent the objective conditions in space and time of the "real" world (most commonly within the Newtonian frame of reference). The observer can err or lack precision and sophistication but, ultimately, these shortcomings can be overcome and, thus, "true" answers can be "detected." The task for the philosophical realists is not to determine those principles which " ... we are projecting into things in order to make them comprehensible and practically accessible to us, but these which can be detected by us in the things themselves [Bavink, 1940, p. 273]."

The positivists did not subscribe to the metaphysical notion of "real" space and time in which things exist and "objective" processes take place. They, exclusively, attend to the sensory-perceptual basis of knowledge and did not consider it the task of sciences to detect "explanations for processes in nature but to describe them as simply and as completely as possible. The genuine object of sciences is only the immediate observations and experiences themselves [Jordan, 1935, p. 37]." But, like the philosophical realists, they emphasize the need for noncontradictory observations. Thus, the first group reaches the abstractness of its interpretations through a belief in an objective world and by its disregard of the subject. The second group emphasizes the subjective nature of our knowledge, but by clinging to the principle of noncontradiction, operates with the same abstract theories as the realists.

A dismissal of the principle of identity and noncontradiction synthesizes both philosophical bases. In science, according to Hegel, thought perception is as much the object, as the object (thing) is thought. Any theory derived from such a synthesis will be concrete rather than abstract. Abstract theories are disengaged from the subject observer. Concrete theories take the intimate interdependence between subject and object into account. By abandoning the principle of identity, these theories also allow for the coexistence of different interpretations. Dialectical interpenetration of subject and object and of contradictory theories is not only possible but positively necessary for science and knowledge. However, they dissolve much of what, hitherto, has been clear and firm.

In the following pages I will demonstrate that dialectical conceptualization characterizes the origin of thought in the individual and in society. More important, dialectical conceptualization represents a necessary synthesis in the development of thought toward maturity. In particular, I examine Piaget's theory that, also, depicts cognitive development as originating from a dialectical basis. But all of the remaining explications in Piaget's theory characterize development as a progression toward abstract thought, away from its implicit contradictions. Thus, development represents an alienation of the subject from the object. Since Piaget fails to emphasize that, ultimately, all thought has to return to its concrete dialectical form, I am led to propose a fifth stage of cognitive development, the period of dialectical operations.

Dialectical Operations

My introduction relied on the insightful essay by the late Max Wundt (1949), philosopher and son of Wilhelm Wundt. In particular, I emphasized the dialectical reinterpretations of coexisting theories, the subject–object relations, the realism–positivism controversy, and the distinction between concrete and abstract thought. The dialectical solutions, as proposed by Hegel, rested upon a reconsideration of the identity principle. It has not been Hegel's intention (nor is it mine) to dismiss this principle out of hand and once and for all. For the purpose of particular logical constructions, mathematical models or measurement systems, scientists will rely on its usefulness or formal explications. The blind adherence to the identity principle and, thus, to classical logic, hinders the understanding of the contradictory nature of human thought in its mature, as well as in its very early stages.

Hegel's Dialectical Theory

Contradictions, in Hegel's (1969a, b; see also Kaufman, 1966; Soll, 1969) dialectical theory, are not conditions of error and insufficiencies, but are the most basic property of nature and mind. Only *rational thinking* (Verstand) separates certain attributes and, then, by connecting them in a systematic manner, tries to depict the phenomena under concern (such as those of optics or mechanics, learning or cognition) in an unequivocal manner. The concurrent acceptance of alternative theories reduces the status of unequivocality. But contradiction is not only a principle applicable to show the complementary nature of such general abstract theories, it is a necessary condition of all thought.

Each thing is itself and, at the same time, many other things. For example, any concrete object, such as a chair, is itself but, at the same time, is of many different properties. By selecting some and disregarding others we might develop one or another abstract notion (theory) about the chair. But only when we see all of these properties in their complementary dependencies do we reach an appropriate, concrete comprehension. But what is, then, the thing itself? It is the totality of all the different, contradictory notions about it to which the thing itself stands in contradictory relation. *Dialectical thinking* (Vernunft) comprehends itself, the world, and each concrete object in its multitude of contradictory relations. As Lenin would put it many years later: "Every concrete thing, every concrete something, stands in multifarious and often contradictory relations to everything else: ergo it is itself and some other [1929, p. 124]."

Hegel's discussion of "master and slave" in his "Phenomenology of Spirit" provides another example of dialectical thinking. The master is independent and therefore enjoys for his own sake; the slave is dependent, he does not partake in enjoyment but has to carry the load of labor. But the master becomes dependent upon the labor, whereas the slave, through his labor, gains consciousness and, thus, independence. Each side can be described unambiguously and without contradiction. Such a description would be abstract, however. Only a description of both in their mutual relation provides a concrete representation of the totality without covering up one or the other. Such a description represents dialectical thought with its intrinsic contradictions.

The dialectical nature of our conceptualization, both in our everyday and in our scientific efforts, can be demonstrated through other examples. Concepts like being and becoming, cause and effect, passivity and activity, structure and transformation can not be thought of in isolation but only in their mutual dependence. For a further demonstration, let us consider the concepts of element and simple relation as well as those of class and general relations. As to be discussed in the following sections and, especially, in Chapter 4, all of these concepts are fundamental in their developmental implications.

If we conceive of elements as represented by points in a geometrical space and of simple relations as represented by lines or vectors, we realize their dialectical interdependence: Points are defined as the intersection of two or more lines; lines are defined as the (shortest) connection between two points. The same holds for classes and the general relations between them, both of which can be deduced from the former. But here again we are confronted with dialectical ambivalence. On the one hand, we might derive classes from sets of simple relations, such as the class of "actors" and the class of "actions." Conjoining them we can, subsequently, define the general relation of "activity," that is, the general relation of "acting actors." On the other hand, we might consider this general relationship as given; subsequently, we define the classes of "actors" and "actions" on the basis of this relationship. In either case, we unravelled the interpenetration of elements and relations as well as of classes and general relations. Thereby we derived abstract descriptions; concrete thought considers both of these concepts in their mutual determination.

On the following pages I will try to elaborate the implication for developmental psychology of the concept of dialectic interpenetration and of uncritical acceptance of the identity principle. In particular, I will demonstrate these implications in regard to the development of logical operations with classes and of linguistic operations with explicit relations, that is, comparative terms. In a third section, I discuss some of the difficulties encountered when one tries to apply Piaget's theory to the study of maturity and aging. In a fourth section I summarize the necessary modification and extension of Piaget's theory of cognitive development.

Development of Logical Operations with Classes

In considering Piaget's theory and observation of cognitive development, we recognize its dialectical basis. This dialecticism is most clearly revealed in the accommodation–assimilation paradigm leading to adaptation and readaptation. Accommodation denotes the changes of the subject to (in view of) the object (for example, the eating child). Assimilation denotes the change of the object to (for the benefit of) the subject, for example, the physical and chemical changes of the eaten food. In the dialectical sense, both accommodation and assimilation are complementary, they are standing in contradictory, mutual relation.

While Piaget's theory is based upon such a dialectical foundation, critics have often wondered how the accommodation–assimilation paradigm is carried forward into the interpretations of the higher and later stages of cognitive development. Undoubtedly, Piaget uses this paradigm convincingly and skillfully for depicting basic biological interactions and early cognitive differentiations, such as those of sucking, grasping, touching, as well as the coordination and sequencing of these early schemata. As soon as the child reaches the second major period in Piaget's theory, the period of preoperational intelligence, and as soon as Piaget shifts from a methodology of observational interpretations to those of experimentation, the dialectical paradigm of accommodation and assimilation is slowly abandoned or, at least, disregarded, and the interpretations are proposed in terms of traditional logic.

For a discussion of the next three major periods in Piaget's theory, I rely on a much simplified interpretation of cognitive development by McLaughlin (1963). This interpretation deals exclusively with the operation of classes and regards development as a consecutive addition of dimensions of categorical judgments. At the sensory-motor period children are not yet able to classify within a dimension; they are able to attend to only one concept at a time. In order to categorize they would need to attend to at least one other concept or to negate the former, the attended concept.

Sensory-motor children focus upon distinct singular objects that happen to come into their field of attention. Neither do they discriminate any of these objects against others nor against negative instances of the same object. For example, children are able to focus upon a block, but they do not discriminate this block from beads or nonblocks. All that they are able to do is to achieve a gross figure–ground differentiation. McLaughlin's interpretation is supportive of Piaget's observations and theory. The dialectical character of the early form of cognitive operations is attested to by the fludity with which children's attention might switch from item to item or from figure to ground and from ground to figure.

The dialectical character is also revealed at the next higher level of cognitive operations corresponding to Piaget's period of preoperational thought. At this level children attend to two concepts simultaneously. Thus they are able to sort items by their color into those that are red and those that are green or, more generally, into those which show the presence of an attribute, such as the color red, and those which show its absence, that is, nonred. The positive and negative instances of an attribute are mutually dependent. Red determines as much that which is not red, as not-red determines red. Both together define the attribute or dimension of discrimination, that is, color. Such a dimension, at different instances or at higher levels of development, might be contrasted sequentially or simultaneously with new alternatives, such as form or materiality. Moreover, the mutual determination of an instance and a noninstance of one attribute is not fixed but variable. In one case, red might be contrasted with all other colors; in another case, red might be contrasted with all other reddish colors. The determination of the kind and the range of a dimension is dependent upon extraattributional and contextual factors.

The discussion of the remaining two developmental periods, the concrete and the formal operational periods, can be relatively brief. In McLaughlin's simplified interpretation, children become able to operate simultaneously with two attributional dimensions and four concepts, or with three attributional dimensions and eight concepts. Both steps imply important expansions of the children's conceptualization. At the period of concrete intellectual operations, for example, the children succeed in double classifications and thus, can form the products A and B, A but not B, B but not A, neither A nor B. At the period of formal operational thought, still further-reaching expansions occur.

All of these operations could be interpreted in a dialectical form if the mutual determination of a class and its inverse, that is, of the classes A and nonA, were consistently emphasized. While this seems to be obvious enough from a theoretical perspective, in the reports of his research observations, Piaget searches systematically for contradictions in the child's judgements, and thereby undermines his own dialectical interpretations as well as degrades the dialecticity of the children. Of course, Piaget merely reports these contradictions, and thus, the dialectically minded readers could use this information adequately to substantiate their own interpretations, but since Piaget's theory subsequently progresses to higher and higher levels at which earlier contradictions cease to occur, his theory becomes antidialectical and the progress of the children as described by Piaget is one of increasing alienation of thought. With the following examples I will try to show the continuing dialectical character of the child's thought, and later on, I will claim that the older, alienated child, in order to reach maturity, will have to return to a dialectical basis of thinking.

Piaget's Theory of Cognitive Development as a Theory of Alienation

Various research reports (see for example, Piaget, 1962, 1963, 1965; Piaget & Inhelder, 1967) provide rich sources for demonstrating the dialectical character of the child's thought. The following example from Piaget shows shifts in the identity concept of a child at an age of 2 years and 7 months.

> J. seeing L. in a new bathing suit, with a cap, J. asked, *What's the baby's name?*
> Her mother explained that it was a bathing costume, but J. pointed to L.

herself and said, *But, what's the name of that?* (indicating L's face) and repeated the question several times. But as soon as L. had her dress on again, J. exclaimed very seriously, *It's Lucienne again,* as if her sister had changed her identity in changing her clothes [1962, p. 224].

At an early age, children are not embarrassed by their own contradictory judgments as shown in the following example on a numerical comparison of sets of items at an age of 6 years 9 months.

Are there more wooden beads or more brown ones? *More brown ones.* If we make a necklace with the wooden beads and a necklace with the brown ones. which would be longer? *The one with the wooden beads* (without hesitating). Why? *Because there are the two extra white ones* [1965, p. 176].

Regardless of whether one attributes these contradictory judgments to a change in the child's opinion, to a lack of short-term retention, or to disability to operate simultaneously with two conceptual dimensions, development is seen by Piaget (as well as by almost all developmental psychologists) as removing these inconsistencies and as reaching toward a coherent, noncontradictory mode of thinking. These examples also show, however, that thinking originates from a dialectical basis and, as I will try to demonstrate, creative and mature thinking returns to its dialectical mode or rather fails to separate itself clearly and firmly from this foundation.

Additional support for my interpretation comes from a recent study by Miller (1972) with the specific purpose of examining children's reactions to the violation of their expectancies concerning the conservation of weight. Eight and 10-year old nonconservers and conservers were studied under a condition (among others) where the outcome of the weighing of two clay balls could be overridden by the experimenter, thus creating a result contradictory to the experience of, at least, the conserving children. Contrary to the investigator's expectation, observable surprise was infrequent, and changes in judgment were readily made. Contrary to some earlier findings, active resistance to change was apparent in about half the conservers, but older conservers did not show resistance more often than young conservers.

Miller derives the interpretation of his findings from Piaget's notion of the "logical necessity" for the persistence of cognitive structures. This notion (as vague as it is) is, in turn, derived from the concept of equilibrium. If a conflict is created through new experiences or cognitive changes, the organism tends to resolve such an incongruity. If such an equilibration is not successfully achieved, children, especially younger ones, will simply state their observation without persistent attempts to consolidate it with their earlier judgments of conservation. Within Piaget's theory, such a solution represents a regression toward a preconservational level of operation. To us, it merely indicates that the thoughts of children are flexible enough to exist with ambiguities and to tolerate contradictions. Eventually, through alienating training and abstractions, they will be induced to consolidate these contractions for the sake of educationally accepted interpretations. In principle, however, these contradictions remain to coexist even within the superimposed structures of later interpretations as demonstrated in the following report by Zaporozhets and Elkonin (1971).

These authors presented a pan filled with water to children and allowed them to test whether various small objects would float or not. At about 3½ years of age, children will successively propose various discrete alternative reasons whenever their previous answer becomes incongruous with new experience. Thus, they will switch their interpretation from "It doesn't hold itself on water" (brass disk), to "It is small" (needle), to "It doesn't know how to swim" (when asked to predict whether a match will swim). At an age of 4 to 5 years, children are able to produce compounded answers, such as, "A splinter swims because it is little and it is light." Subsequently, they will be faced less often with contradictory experience. In emphasizing with Piaget the development toward abstract and general structures, Zaporozhets and Elkonin (1971) conclude

> The child is so convinced of her own judgment that it is difficult for her to refute it even in the light of contradictory facts. However, does it mean then that the child is not aware of the contradictions, that she ignores reality whenever it does not correspond to her understanding? The observations show that this is not so [p. 240].

The interpretations by the Soviet investigators, in spite of their likely commitment to dialectical materialism, agree with those by Piaget: The thoughts of young children are founded upon dialectical contradictions. But increasing with age and experience, they acquire stable structures that consolidate contradictory evidence into consistent interpretations. In regard to floating objects, children, at first, consider either the attribute small *or* the attribute light as criterial; later they begin to realize that objects have to be both small *and* light at the same time; still later they might relate their weight to their volume in the form of a ratio, and they might consider whether the objects are hollow or solid, the type of liquid they are placed on, etc.

But as children apprehend increasingly complex structures that consolidate all the contradictory evidence experienced, the different concrete observations remain to coexist, that is, a small object floating, a small object sinking, a heavy object floating, a heavy object sinking, etc. Each new situation demands an immediate transformation of these experiences into a consolidated structure. Each new situation remains contradictory as each thought remains tied to its dialectical basis. As for students puzzled by an ambiguous multiple choice item (and which item fails to be ambiguous) the "correct" answer might be clearly known by the teacher. But it does not matter for an understanding of the students' thinking whether or not they finally found the "correct" answer; what matters are the ambiguities and the contradictions that they experience and through which they succeed in moving toward a solution. Thinking, in the dialectical sense, is the process of transforming contradictory experience into momentary stable structures. These structures consolidate the contradictory evidence but do not by themselves represent thinking, they merely represent the products of thinking.

Development of Linguistic Operations with Relations

Recently several studies explored the acquisition and use of comparative terms, such as "more" and "less," "tall," "taller," and "tallest," as well as constructions such as "beautiful," "more beautiful," and "most beautiful." These investigations have been conducted and summarized either by emphasizing a linguistic (Clark, 1970) or a perceptual-cognitive basis (Huttenlocher & Higgins, 1971). Undoubtedly, the study of comparative terms is intimately related to Piaget's work. In particular, his interpretations of conservation have been criticized for failing to take account of the child's ability to operate and comprehend such terms as "more," "less," "same," etc. (Bickford & Looft, 1973; Donaldson & Balfour, 1968; Griffiths, Shantz, & Sigel, 1967).

According to the available evidence—simplified to a considerable extent—the following stages in the development of comparative terms may be distinguished. At level 1, when children are producing single-word sentences, expressions (such as "more") are sometimes used as imperative demands without comparative implications. Paraphrasing their expression, children seem to say "I want this or that." At level 2, when children operate simultaneously with two terms, they might use such words as "more" in an absolute, dichotomizing manner, contrasting it with "not more" but not implying a gradation of magnitudes. At level 3, when children operate simultaneously with three terms, true transitivity and, subsequently, comparativity is established. For instance, they might apply terms like "small, medium, tall" or "tall, taller, tallest." By dropping off either one of the extreme items of a series, they are able to extend it without limitation.

Level 3 represents an important step in an additional sense. All previous comparisons implied absolute anchor points. In one-term expressions, the conditions and desires of the speakers serve as an absolute point of reference. In two-term comparisons, the expression "more" serves as the positive instance; "not more" represents merely its negation. At level 3, the anchor point becomes variable. Applying a spatial representation, usually the left-hand term (as in "tall, taller, tallest") serves as such an anchor point but can always be modified by adding a new element, such as "less tall," or—more radically—by changing the sequence into "tall," "less tall," "least tall."

At level 4, when children operate simultaneously with four terms, they ought to be able to make comparisons between two dichotomized variables and perform class multiplications such as between "wide and narrow vs. short and tall." This performance is one of the logical prerequisites for conservation tasks. Similar performances, although they do not represent any new form of operation, imply hierarchical comparisons. For example, children might, first, classify objects into large and small items and then subdivide each class again in the same manner. This operation, when executed repeatedly, results in a series in which all items are ordered transitively. Finally, we might expect level 5 and level 6 children to compare simultaneously items along three or more dimensions.

My discussion demonstrates the use of comparatives within a conceptual framework related to Piaget's developmental model, especially to the simplified version proposed by McLaughlin (1963). In general, it relates to the traditional logic of classes and relations. But development consists neither of a continuous refinement of gradating comparisons nor of the compounding of an increasing number of dimensions into the comparison; development also involves an increasing relativisation of standards in comparative expressions. The necessity of applying alternate evaluations characterizes already the behavior of older children in role playing activities, for example, in judging some event as fortunate but from another person's view as unfortunate. It characterizes more clearly the mediating operations of adult persons and—in a general sense—the modern scientific notions of relativity of movements in space.

If an object is fast, when compared within a fixed system of coordinates, but slow, when compared with another moving object, or if we say that "a small elephant is a large animal," we recognize, once more, the dialectical principle of contradiction. This principle implies that a thing has a given quality and, at the same time, does not have it. In regard to comparatives, the statement that something is tall and at the same time small, namely, when viewed within two different frames of reference, is equally characteristic of mature judgments. Such a statement can not be captured easily within a simple logic of classes and relations.

Dialectical thinking emphasizes the interdependence of form and content. In its narrow sense, this principle deals with the interrelationship between methods and results, in its most general sense, between subject and object. As one person pronounces a judgment, he or she externalizes a standard which will direct and modify another person's judgments, which, once it too has been pronounced, will produce further modifications. Thus, these interactions set a process in motion that is in continuous flux and only temporarily at rest, namely, at those moments in which a pronouncement takes place. Such a process of evaluation and reevaluation characterizes best the thought and judgments of the mature person.

In regard to the aged it may be questioned, of course, whether their thinking also is characterized by this mode of operation. Processes of simplification and rigidification might have altered their conceptualizations. But such an evaluation holds only if the development of their thinking is considered to be preceded by all four periods described in Piaget's theory and compared against the final outcome of the last of these periods, that is, of formal operations. If dialectical thinking emerges directly from any of the earlier levels, especially from any level other than that of formal operations, a more successful cognitive aging will result. Uncritical adherence to traditional educational and academic goals has made us firmly believe that successful development would always have to proceed through all of the four periods; the further a person advances in his progression, the more successful his development has been considered to be. The option to be proposed, that dialectical or mature thinking might emerge from any one of the succeeding periods, opens new perspectives for the study and understanding of adult thinking and successful aging (Riegel & Riegel, 1972; Riegel, 1972a). Previous investigations of cognitive and linguistic development have clearly failed to provide adequate interpretations. The following review reveals these inadequacies.

Cognitive Changes during Adulthood and Aging

Thus far only a few studies of normal aged persons have been conducted with tasks taken from the rich repertoire of Piagetian investigations (see Papalia, 1972). Others have been made on senile older individuals by de Ajuriaguerra (see Hooper, 1973).

The two earliest studies (Kominski, 1968; Sanders, Laurendau, & Bergeron, 1966) investigated the conservation of surface areas by means of two green cardboards which were described as meadows on which two cows could graze. By placing various numbers of blocks in various positions upon either one or both cardboards, individuals were asked whether equal amounts of grass were available under these different conditions. According to the evidence obtained, older adults do not conserve area as we would expect them and as older children do. They rather seem to have regressed to judgments based on their immediate perceptual impressions, much like those of younger children.

These results raise the puzzling question of the disappearance of personal knowledge, for example, the knowledge of the conservation of matter. Is it conceivable that a person, once he or she has realized that an amount of liquid remains the same when poured from one beaker into another one of different shape, can ever lose this insight? Don't we always keep knowing what we know?

In one of the discussions on cognitive changes during adulthood and aging, Flavell (1970) argues for the "disappearance of knowledge" under conditions of serious neuro-physiological damage. According to available information, such changes are not necessarily affecting all aging persons to a sufficient extent. Arguments against the "disappearance of knowledge" are based upon the distinction between competence and performance as introduced into linguistics by Chomsky and as translated into cognitive developmental psychology by Flavell and Wohlwill (1969).

Competence refers to the knowledge about language; it is intuitive, immmediate, and ideal. Performance refers to the execution of linguistic tasks; it is acquired, incomplete, and concrete. This distinction reflects (as well as it fails to overcome) the mind–body dualism of Descartes; in its idealistic extension it argues for the immutability of competence or knowledge; in its mechanistic extension it proposes that competence is innate.

A second theoretical discussion on the transition in cognitive operations between adolescence and adulthood has been published by Piaget himself (1972). Here Piaget seems to weaken his earlier interpretations by giving more attention to individual and societal differences in speed of development, developmental diversification, and professional specialization.

Originally, the four major periods in the cognitive development of the child were regarded as universal progressions through which all children would move at about the same pace. Studies of crosscultural and subcultural variations have often failed to confirm such an interpretation and led Piaget to suggest that the *speed of progression* is not the same under all social conditions, leading to retardation in deprived and to accelerations in stimulating surroundings. Differences between individuals are especially marked at the later periods of development; during the early periods, the progression seems to be most uniform.

Developmental diversifications in regard to types of tasks also seem to affect least the early developmental periods. Even operations that are not successfully performed before an age of 10 or 12 years, such as conservation of matter, weight, volume, or space, seem to have universal significance; few differences have been observed across cultures or social groups. When dealing with the propositional logic of formal operations at the fourth period, however, marked differences exist. Most of Piaget's tasks use constructs from mathematics, physics, or chemistry. Probably, such topics are not only inadequately handled by children from lesser developed countries, but also well-trained students in advanced countries, having other areas of specialization, such as business, medicine, or law, often fail to do well on them.

Finally, *professional specialization* produces variations within a culture. Here, Piaget argues that carpenters, plumbers, mechanics, etc. might be able to apply, for example, formal operations within the contexts of their specific occupational activities but might fail in laboratory settings and with material unfamiliar and irrelevant to them. Thus, factors of interests and motivations, practical and social significance codetermine operations, originally thought of as being universal qualities.

Piaget's statements on the transition from adolescence to adulthood provide concessions to individuals and social groups who "fail" to progress all the way through the elaborated structures of formal thought. But his statements neither indicate the cultural–historical implications of such "failures" nor do they elaborate in positive terms the types of intellectual operations "failing" individuals will have to choose or are bound to end up with.

Piaget's concessions seem most reasonable because it has never been shown convincingly that the highest level of operation (i.e., formal operational intelligence) characterizes the thinking of mature adults. Only under the most exceptional circumstances of logical argumentations and scholastic disputes would a person engage in such a form of thinking. In daily activities, logics and operations of much lower power will be applied. Indeed, even in their scientific activities researchers will very rarely engage in the propositional logic of the fourth period in Piaget's theory and systematically calculate all possibilities in the search for a solution. Such forms of thinking merely provide the last straw in the process of a scientific inquiry that might be applied after intuitive thought is exhausted. Creative scientific activities are dominated by playful manipulations of contradictions and by conceiving issues integratively which have been torn apart through formal operational thinking. The same type of intuitive inquest characterizes even more clearly the performance at levels below those of formal operational intelligence.

For all these reasons, Piaget's theory describes thought in its alienation from its creative, dialectical basis. It represents a prototype reflecting the goals of our higher educational system that, in turn, are reflecting the nonartistic and noncreative aspects in the intellectual history of western man (Riegel, 1972b, 1973b). Although Piaget's theory is founded on a dialectical basis, it fails to make the transition from the formal intellectualism of Kant to the concrete dialecticism of Hegel. Thus, his theory is not only incapable of interpreting mature thinking but also fails to give sufficient emphasis to their dialectical character and the creative features of children's cognitions. A commitment to Hegel enables us to reinterpret Piaget's theory with due consideration of mature and creative thinking. It leads us to an extension of Piaget's developmental sequence and to a modification of his cognitive theory.

A Modified Model of Cognitive Development

In a recent publication (Riegel, 1972e), I have discussed three models of qualitative developmental changes. These models were derived from the earlier work by van den Daele (1969). In both publications, Piaget's theory of cognitive development was considered to represent the simplest of all three models, the single sequence model. In this model qualitatively different sets of operations or behavior succeed each other in temporal sequence; no provisions for difference in progression between persons or between skills were made, nor were there any statements on the transition and accumulation of behavior across stages. Undoubtedly, this representation oversimplifies the richness of Piaget's theory, but on the other hand, there are insufficient or only ambiguous reasons to assign any of the other two models, the multiple sequence or the complex sequence model, to represent Piaget's theory.

In view of such an assignment and in view of the present discussion the question arises as to what happens at later stages to the behavior or operations acquired and representative of the earlier stages? Are the schemata of the sensorimotor period lost or are they modified and transformed into those of the preoperational and the higher periods? Moreover, is it conceivable that an individual operates simultaneously at different levels of cognition, perhaps switching back and forth between them or choosing one for one area of activity and another for another area?

Recently Furth (1973) has maintained that Piaget does not "pretend that stages of thinking reached in one domain will necessarily be found in the thinking of the same person in another domain [p. 8]." But Piaget does not state explicitly and does not specify the conditions under which such switching across stages might or has to occur. Even if we consider the simplified interpretation by McLaughlin (1963), we fail to derive any definite conclusion. The progression depicted in this model represents, as we have seen, a successive increase in the number of attributional dimensions and, thus, in the number of concepts with which a child operates simultaneously. But if children at the level of preoperational thinking categorize items according to the presence or absence of one attribute, are they, then, also able to dismiss the attributional dimension altogether and to conceive items "as such" without any categorizing efforts, that is, in the manner of the sensorimotor child?

Presumably the further children have advanced in their development, the harder it will be to "regress" to the "naive" mode of early conceptualizations. For this reason, the growth of cognitive organization, as depicted in any of these models, represents an alienation from original thought. Dialectical operations represent a step forward and, at the same time, a return to early thinking that in the opinion of many writers (e.g., Stern, Werner, Freud, Zeininger, Levy-Strauss, *et al.*) is dialectical in nature.

As shown in Figure 3.1, I propose that an individual at any developmental level may directly progress to its corresponding mode of dialectical operations, reaching thereby a mature stage of thinking. This provision introduces interindividual variation at the level of maturity. Persons might reach dialectic maturity without ever having passed through the period of formal operations or even through that of concrete operations. This provision also introduces intraindividual variation. The skills and competence in one area of concern (for instance, the sciences) might be of the type of formal dialectical operations; those in a second area (for instance, everyday business transactions) might be of the type of concrete dialectical operations; those in a third area (for instance, artistic activities) might be of the type of preoperational dialectical intelligence; finally, those of intimate personal interactions might be of the sensorimotor and therefore of the original or "primitive" dialectical type (see Lawler, 1975).

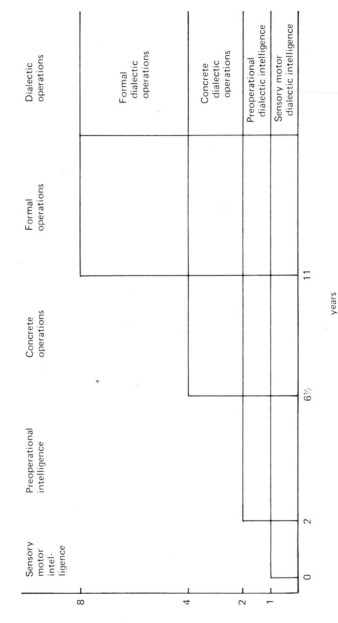

Figure 3.1. Schematic representation of five developmental periods for Piaget's extended theory of cognitive development.

In his discussion of equilibration and disequilibration, Piaget touches most explicitly upon the issue of optional, multilevel operations. At the same time, his discussion reveals clearly that his concept of development is one of consecutive alienation. According to Piaget, organisms inherently tend toward equilibrated states. Disequilibrium represents conflict and contradiction that organisms try to overcome through their activities. The state of disequilibrium characterizes, in particular, the moments prior to the transitions into each of the next higher levels of operations.

If Piaget admits—as Furth has declared—that organisms have implicit or explicit options to operate at different stages of thinking, dependent upon the area of activity with which they happen to be concerned at the particular time, the emphasis upon the principle of equilibration is weakened if not abandoned. Any concurrent or closely successive operations at different developmental levels ought to create a state of conflict which ought to be equilibrated. Such an equilibration, on the other hand, can only mean a progression toward the higher and later developmental level of operation. In other words, the option for multilevel operations contradicts Piaget's notion of equilibration since it reintroduces dialectical conflict; the emphasis upon equilibration would tend to resolve this conflict at the expense of the thinking at the earlier stage. My own modification recognizes dialectical conflicts and contradiction as a fundamental property of thought. At the levels of dialectical operations, the mature individual does not necessarily equilibrate these conflicts but is ready to live with these contradictions; stronger yet, the individual accepts these contradictions as a basic property of thought and creativity.

Conclusions

The purpose of my discussion was to reintroduce dialecticism into Piaget's theory of cognitive development. According to my interpretation, Piaget's theory is founded upon dialectics but, successively, each higher level of operation represents a further alienation from this original mode of thinking. Dialectical operations represent mature thought to which an individual might progress from any one of the four stages in Piaget's theory, that is, without necessarily progressing first through all four stages in their proper order. This option for multilevel operations also implies that an individual might perform in one area of concern at one level of thinking and in another area at another level. The possibility of operating simultaneously or in short succession at different levels, by itself, implies contradiction and is dialectical in character.

The modification and extension of Piaget's theory to the level of dialectical operations is concerned with intrapsychic processes. At least two other revisions are suggested. First, the interaction between psychic activities and their biological basis needs to be explored more fully. Undoubtedly, Piaget's orientation is basically a biological one, but it is evolutionary–systematic rather than analytic–experimental. The modern version of Pavlov's reflexology comes closest in documenting such an approach by exploring an interactive, dialectical model which relates psychic activities to their biological and (in its narrower explication) material foundation. Second, the interaction between psychic activities and the cultural–historical conditions needs to be explored more fully. For Piaget, individuals, through their own activities, create their intellectual world. But the activities of and within the environment are disregarded, and the ceaseless efforts of mankind have produced widely differing cultural–historical conditions. These activities exert their effects upon the individual through their specific structures (that is, widely differing cultural–historical conditions) and through the participatory efforts of other individuals, such as parents, siblings, and teachers (who ought to be considered as active organisms as much as the child). A developmental theory emphasizing the interactions between psychic activities and cultural–historical conditions has been proposed by Soviet psychologists, notably Vygotsky, Luria and Leont'ev. A theory integrating both interaction systems and, thus, regarding psychic activities and development in their joint interaction with conditions that are both inner-biological and outer cultural–historical has been proposed by Rubinstein (see Payne, 1968; and Chapter 2 of this volume).

Hegel's dialectical idealism, from which most of our present interpretations were derived, has been followed and superceded by the historical and dialectical materialism of Marx, Engels, and Lenin. For two reasons it seems appropaite to wait and contemplate before one embraces these historical developments. First, Hegel's philosophy, especially his "Phenomenology of Spirit," provides an exceptionally rich source and a distinct model of the development of the mind both in regard to the individual and to society. To this author's knowledge, Hegel's theory has never been explored for the purpose of psychological interpretations. Second, Hegel, much more than the dialectical materialists, has preserved the conception of an active developing organism, or more precisely, he has proposed a developmental model in which activities (labor) and products (material) remain in dialectical interdependence. It seems a regression, indeed, if we were to abandon this delicate notion too readily in order to obtain a naive material underpinning whose utility was recognized in a theory of labor, products, and economy, but not in a theory of a developing organism within a developing world.

4

The Relational Basis of Language

Most inquiries into early childhood development emphasize the undifferentiated state of the organism and its embeddedness in the environment. Development, subsequently, is considered as a differentiation of objects and, more basically, of the subject from the object. In accepting such an interpretation—and what choice is there?—it becomes apparent how inappropriate a stimulus-response theory would be. Stimuli and responses do not yet exist as separate conditions; they need to be differentiated before any acquisition based upon them can be explained. Similarly, associations cannot connect stimuli and responses according to their contiguity, frequency, or recency; everything is connected anyhow. The first task for children is to recognize some constancies in the flux of their sensory impressions and to practice some regularities in the shifts of their motoric expressions.

Many cognitive and philosophical psychologists have provided interpretations of early development similar to the one attempted here. Most notably, Werner (1926) has elaborated the early differentiation (and concurrent integration) of the child's experiences, and Piaget (1963), likewise, has explicated processes leading to schemata of perceptions and actions.

In focusing upon Piaget's work, I will compare his interpretation of cognitive development with the early acquisition of language and meaning. In both cases, children are confronted with a flux of events and their main developmental task consists in recognizing constancies in the flux of their impressions and invariances in the stream of their expressions. Only after these constancies and invariances have been recognized and practiced, can learning in the traditional sense be considered as a means for acquisition.

In spite of similarities in the goals of cognitive and language development, the task of recognizing constancies in the general physical environment and of invariances in the more specific sound and speech environment points toward basic differences which might have prevented any mutual benefit or consolidation of both interpretations. The former constancies mainly represent spatial structures (with the supplementary option of temporal shifts and changes); the latter invariances mainly represent temporal structures with the rather advanced technological option of fixating them in space through written transformations or on magnetic tape.

Of course, such a contrast overemphasizes the differences. The constancies of objects in space may represent stable states during short periods of time only; the objects change and move. Moreover, the observing subjects through their own movements create for themselves continuously changing impressions of these "stable" objects. Likewise for speech sequences, when persons perceive an invariant section (for example, a word), their percept will activate a conceptual field (Trier, 1931) or network (Quillian, 1967; Reigel, 1968; Riegel & Riegel, 1963) representing their past experiences related to this word. Thus, a spatial structure is brought into focus often identified with the semantic organization of the language. As subsequent units are perceived by the listener, other semantic structures are called upon blending into one another and modifying each other prospectively and retrospectively. The sequential progression across semantic structures represents that part in the organization of a language which has been identified with its syntactic order. Because of the sequential blending of the semantic structures, the distinction between both organizations, again, overemphasizes their differences at the expense of their similarities.

The above distinction, furthermore, holds only for an individual who has already acquired a fair amount of cognitive and linguistic experience. The young child has to generate, first, these semantic and syntactic orders. Of course, the language of the environment as well as the general physical surrounding already possess a high degree of segmentation and structure. These are either properties of nature (such as rocks, mountains, plants, animals, including the human organs for cognition and speech), or are structures that have been generated through human efforts (such as rooms, buildings, cities, social organizations, language). Students of learning and association have systematically neglected the structural properties of the world and pretended as if children were born into a random world of chaos.

Young children have not yet experienced these outer structures. Their development consists in recreating these outer organizations through their own activities and on the basis of their own inner structures. At the same time, these outer organizations will be induced upon them through the efforts of the groups of people around them. The groups not only include the people who are attending them, but the contemporary generation and, ultimately, all previous generations who laid the foundation and are continuously creating the physical and social world in which children grow. The children through their own activities also partake in changing this world, at least those sections that are experienced by the persons in his immediate social environment, that is, his parents, siblings, neighbors, etc. Indeed, children's activities might produce more dramatic changes in their parents, for example, than the parents are able to produce in their children.

In the following presentation, I outline the processes by which the children recognize and regenerate the invariant and organizational properties of language. In these efforts, children will conjoin and contrast recurrent segments of the messages presented to them. For example, a child might hear sequences such as "Drink your milk." "The milk is too hot." "We have to buy some milk." etc. After repeated exposure to such messages, the child recognizes invariant segments, for example, the word MILK. Using a visual analog, we might think of these statements as written upon strips of paper; the child would then bundle these strips together with the invariant segment at the intersection. As I will attempt to show, both the identification of meanings as well as the formation of classes can be explained on this basis.

In the second part of the following presentation, I discuss the acquisition of words, classes, class relations, and generally of the semantic and syntactic organization of language. The bases for these developments are contextual segments whose smallest units we will call simple relations. All of these acquisitions succeed through active operations by the child with and upon the relational information given. These operations consist in intersecting or separating, composing, or decomposing of relational information.

We are not able to explain much further how these operations originate in the child. But in the first part of my presentation, I will provide a general analogy for the language acquisition process by comparing linguistic operations with those in economy. By describing three

59

stages in the development of monetary systems, the barter system, the coinage system, and the debenture system, inferences about the origin of cognitive linguistic activities might be drawn. In extension of this discussion, I will delineate three levels in the origin, development, and study of language: The protolanguage, the token language, and the interaction language. Tangentially, I will also argue that the intellectual processes involved are roughly comparable to three stages of cognitive development as originally proposed by Piaget: The period of the sensorimotor activity, the period of concrete operations (including the subperiods of preoperational and concrete operational thinking), and the period of formal operations.

Comparison between Monetary and Linguistic Systems

The relationship between goods or merchandise and the labor or activities necessary to produce them has been regarded since the time of Marx (1891) as dialectical: Labor that does not produce something is futile; goods that are not produced by labor are miracles. In the following discussions I equate labor with the acts of producing or perceiving speech; merchandise with speech products (such as sentences, words, or speech sounds). Through acts of speech, a person increases the individual and collective repertoire of linguistic products. This repertoire is comparable to capital in the economic sense. Capital is only useful for the individual and society when it is productive, that is, when it is transformed into new labor, speech acts. Traditionally, linguists have regarded language as commodity but not as labor.

The Barter System and the Proto-Language

Our monetary system originated from the one-to-one bartering trade in simple hunting and farming societies. A social situation in which one participant exchanges a sheep or a pig against a certain amount of grain or wool seems to have few similarities with linguistic exchanges. The items traded do not have any representational or symbolic value but serve to satisfy directly the needs of the persons participating in the exchange. Basic similarities become apparent, however, once we realize that languages too are systems of social interactions in which not the objects but rather the labor that leads to their creation and possession is exchanged. Strictly speaking, objects do not play an essential role in such exchanges. Where would they come from, how would they be generated except through the efforts of the participating individuals? It is the labor involved in raising or catching the animal, in the seeding, tending, and harvesting the crop that is being exchanged. The exchange value is determined by the amount of effort, the diligence of the required skills, and the scarcity of the available resources (which, in turn need to be acquired and secured through the individuals' efforts).

Many linguists and, especially, psychologists look upon sentences, words, or speech sounds as building blocks or objects of language. But language is basically an activity which, in turn, serves to induce or to provoke activities in others. This comparison is similar, though not identical with de Saussure's distinction between *la langue* and *la parole* (1916). The former, characterizing the universal properties of language, represents the total repertoire of forms and the structure that has emerged through the efforts of mankind. Paradoxically, as Labov noted (1970), *la langue* has been studied by relying on the "linguistic intuitions" of one or a few individuals. A science of *parole*, though never developed, would have to deal with various speech acts in different social contexts.

Language as an activity reveals itself most clearly under primitive conditions comparable to those of the barter trade. Through grunts, cries, gestures, and manipulations [in Bühler's terms through "signals" and "symptoms" (1934)], one participant might induce the other to recognize a danger, to give assistance, or to coordinate activities. The sounds and movements might be recorded as objectifications of such a primitive language by the linguists, but these transcriptions provide only a distorted picture of the needs and intentions or the activities involved. These activities are meaningful in a given situation and in an immediate manner. In the linguist's description their meaning is bleached; they become abstract and rigidified (see Malinowski, 1923).

Already at this level, language as well as commercial exchanges rely on basic rules. The barter system presupposes property rights. If it is not granted, for example, that the sheep belongs to person A and the grain to person B, no stable exchanges, not even thievery, can take place. In Piaget's sense, this type of commercial activity is comparable to the level of sensorimotor operations. One item is exchanged against another item regardless of the particular shapes in which they happen to be found. Trade does not yet require a knowledge of conservation.

Similarly, protolinguistic communication presupposes the constancy of expression which once given can not be undone. In this sense they have immediate, existential meaning. Language at the protolinguistic level is bound to a given situation of high survival but of low symbolic value. Its increase in representational character can be compared to that occurring during the change from a barter to a coinage system.

The Coinage System and the Token Language

1. When changing from the barter to the coinage system, communities select one of their major commodities as a standard for exchanges. In agricultural societies a certain quantity of grain might serve this function, in stock-farming societies the horse, the cow, or the sheep. (In ancient Rome, the word for money, *pecunia*, derives from *pecus* denoting *livestock*.)

Shifts in standard commodities indicate the growing diversification of societies. This growth is determined by variations in geographical and climatic conditions. It has to be brought about, however, by the activities of generations of participating members. Through these activities, society progresses toward more advanced forms of manufacturing and industrial production, and at the same time, toward a division of labor. Such developments increase the significance of natural resources other than food crops, such as stone, wood, wool, coal, and—most important—metals. Because of their scarcity, compactness, and endurance but also because the resources can be easily controlled by the dominating classes of the society, metals soon became the exclusive standard for monetary systems.

The transition from the barter system to a coinage system is not necessarily abrupt (Cipolla, 1956). After one or a few items have been selected as standard commodities, the exchange continues to proceed as before. When metals are introduced to serve as standards, they continue, at first, to fulfill basic needs of everyday life. For instance, metals such as copper, bronze, or iron are not only used as currency but the coins also serve as standard weights, as well as provide the material for the production of tools and weapons. As the society advances, these common metals are replaced as standards for exchanges by others that are less readily available. Subsequently, smaller and lighter coins can be introduced whose mining, melting, and minting is more easily controlled and that do not serve essential functions for tool making. Their function is related to luxury and extravagance. For example, in the Roman Empire, bronze coins with a standard weight of 327.45 gm. were substituted by much smaller silver and gold coins. Whereas the amount of metal of the bronze coins had a direct, nonmediated value for the receiver, rare metals, such as silver and gold, lacked such utility. Therefore, refined rules about their use had to be established by the community; the value of the coins had to be guaranteed by the state through laws which set the standards, determined the metal composition, and regulated their distribution. At the same time, classes of persons, who succeeded in controlling the processing of these rare metals, could set themselves apart as the rulers of their society.

As coins lost their foundation upon the concrete value of commodities but gained in symbolic value, the economy expanded rapidly. At the same time, through the reckless manipulation of a few and through the uncritical trust of many, the changed conditions were selfishly exploited. The emerging histories represent unending sequences of catastrophies, inflations, and devaluations (Gaettens, 1955). Imperialistic expansions (from the Punic Wars to the War in Vietnam) always outpaced the growth of the economic and monetary systems. Since not enough metal could be secured, the silver or gold content of coins was drastically reduced. Subsequently, coins lost rapidly in value until the system had to be replaced at the expense of the working, wage, and salary earning population. In spite of these dire consequences, the coinage systems, in comparison to the barter system, offer many advantages which, in particular, shed some light upon similar implications for language systems.

2. Coinage systems, especially those based upon symbolic rather than pragmatic standards, allow for delayed exchanges, sequential exchanges, and multiple distributions. *Delayed exchanges* provide the possibility that the seller does not need to convert the items received immediately into other merchandise but may store coins of corresponding value until a better opportunity for a purchase arises. Such delayed reactions are of equal significance in the development of language systems. While the nonlanguage-using organism is closely bound to the here-and-now of a given situation, the use of a language, corresponding in abstraction to the coinage system, allows not only for more efficient communication but also for better storage, especially once a written code of the language has been invented.

In contrast to the barter trade, exchanges do not need to be limited to two persons interacting at a particular location; *sequential exchanges* are bound to result. A person who wants to buy a sheep but has no commodities that are of interest to the seller might reimburse him in coins; the seller, in turn, might approach a third person who is willing to dispose of the desired item. Frequently, the chain will extend over many more than three participants. Coins serve as efficient intermediary, provided that their value is sufficiently safeguarded by social agreements and rules. The social exchange of goods made effective through the invention of coins has implications similar to the invention of verbal

63

codes for linguistic systems. Once a coding system has been adopted, messages can be more reliably transmitted across long sequences of communicating persons than under the more primitive conditions in which utterances are spontaneously and idiosyncratically produced. In a more remote but also more significant sense, the composition of the messages themselves becomes sequential in nature. Linguistic tokens, such as sentences, clauses, words, or speech sounds, are ordered into strings. Nonlinguistically encoded action sequences are difficult if not impossible to transmit.

Once a coinage system has been introduced, *multiple distributions* of goods can be arranged easily. A person who has sold his sheep does not need to spend his earnings at the place of the trade but can distribute them across many vendors and purchase a multiplicity of items. Again the improvements of such operations in comparison to the one-to-one exchanges of the barter trade are comparable to those brought about through the development of language systems. In the most direct sense, a language user can transmit his message simultaneously to a whole group of listeners; in a remote sense, he has multiple ways of expressing his wishes or intentions and can partition his message into smaller chunks which are presented separately. This possibility is especially important for safeguarding the transmission of messages when individuals with varying linguistic skills are involved in the communication process.

3. The linguistic system that I have compared with the coinage system might be called a *token language*. It is founded upon basic forms or elements, such as words, syllables, letters, morphemes, or phonemes. Aside from determining its elements, the main goals in the analysis of such a system consist of the description of its syntagmatic and paradigmatic, that is, temporal–syntactic and spatial–semantic, properties.

A token language system lies half-way between the manifold of phenomena of the experienced world and the single token coinage system of the economy. Both systems are reductionistic. Languages use a large set of tokens, that is, words, to denote the many different objects, events, or qualities which we experience. However, every token denotes a whole array of similar items. For instance, the word CHAIR denotes many different objects. Moreover, the relations between tokens and the items denoted are of several different types, indicating actor–action, object–location, part–whole, object–class name, and many other relations. In comparison, the corresponding monetary systems consist only of one token (for example, the dollar) which designates (relates to) every possible item and condition in an identical manner. Because a large manifold is reduced to just a single element, elaborate forms of operations need to be implemented. This is done by relying on complex numerical properties of the system that capture the large variety of items and conditions by assigning to them corresponding variations in the quantity of tokens (e.g., dollars). The emerging structure represents an arithmetic formalism.

In comparison to a single token system, languages consist of many different tokens (frequently called *types*) and of many different kinds of relations between these tokens (words) and the denoted items (objects, events, or qualities). Manipulations with these tokens do not include operations of addition or multiplication but only those of order. By applying order rules recursively, a multitude of expressions can be generated; by applying them to different types of relations this multitude is enriched much further. The emerging structures are topologically rich and rely on cognitive operations that are mastered by older children only, for example, on decentration and reversibility. They remain concrete because the tokens (words) are thought of as building blocks reflecting directly the conditions of the real or phenomenal world. Just as the coins, these tokens, rather than the commodities which they represent or the labor which produces these commodities, may ultimately come to be regarded as the "true" objects of the world.

Tokens are selected and retained through social conventions which, moreover, determine the permissible rules of operations. They fail to express the activities and efforts that lead to their creation. As much as the further development of the monetary system advances to a full realization of the transactional character of economic operations, so does modern linguistics emphasize the interactional character of language. Whereas traditional linguistics consisted, essentially, of the delineation of linguistic forms and of the rules of their combinations, units such as words, syllables, or letters lose their significance in modern interpretations. What attains significance are clusters of relations representing the activities within and between language users.

The Debenture System and the Interaction Language

Due to ceaseless expansions and lack of constraint, economic history resembles a progression of catastrophies in which one monetary system after the other has been wrecked. At the terminal points of these progressions, the metal value of coins was reduced out of proportion to its original designation; the confidence in the system was lost, prices skyrocketed; and people were forced to return to the barter system in order to secure their daily needs. At least since the beginning of the eighteenth century, autocratic rulers began to make a virtue out of the pitiful state of their financial systems by abandoning the backing of the currency through silver or gold and by substituting hard coins by paper money.

The first well-documented case of such an innovation is that of John Law upon whose advice Louis XV introduced paper money in France. After a few successful years, the confidence in the financial system was lost, leading the nation one significant step closer to the French Revolution. At about the same time, Georg Heinrich von Görtz financed the military adventures of Charles XII in Sweden through the issuing of state certificates. After the King's defeat and death, the financial manipulations were violently attacked and Görtz was executed. Nevertheless, all leading nations have since then introduced paper money, and more recently, most have abandoned the full coverage of their currency by gold or silver or, at least, do not guarantee full convertibility. This shift represents the third major step in the development of monetary systems which we will call the *debenture system*.

It would be misleading to think of paper money only in terms of the common bills issued by national banks. Of course, these documents are of greatest utility for everyday commerce in comparison to all other certificates and, except for changes affecting the economy as a whole, remain fixed in their values. Similar in kind are bonds issued and guaranteed by national governments, states, and communities as well as by larger industrial and business organizations. Since their value fluctuates with the condition of the economy in general, and with the up and down of the money market in particular, these risks need to be compensated for by the payment of interests. Next in line, stocks fluctuate stronger than bonds. They are backed by commercial or industrial companies but rarely by the government itself. The last extension in the development of paper currencies consists in the utilization of personal checks. Here, each individual attains the role which formerly only a stable government was able to attain, namely, to guarantee the value of such transactions.

The last steps in the history of monetary systems, thus, represent another stage of operations and symbolic representations. Written statements become substitutes for standard units of rare metals which, in turn, served as substitutes for the items to be exchanged or as direct objects of trade. During the earliest stage in the history of trade, exchanges were tied to the given items and to the persons interacting in a particular locality. With the introduction of coins, exchanges could be temporally delayed, could be executed along extended chains of participants, and could reach simultaneously an array of different vendors.

Although this increase in flexibility led to advances in the volume of trade, the expansion remained limited because the total amount of rare metals backing the economic transactions increased only slowly. With the shift toward various forms of paper money, this limitation was abandoned, and the monetary system was explicitly tied to the sum total of activities in which a whole nation, an industrial complex, or lastly, a single individual was, is, or was to be engaged.

The explicit return to a standard set by the activities and labor of an individual or groups of individuals represents only a superficial shift. As emphasized before, the objects of trade have always been the efforts necessary for producing particular goods rather than the merchandise itself. Even the gold and silver accumulated in the treasuries of states represents, basically, the efforts and work by their people. Because of the static character of these financial units it appears, of course, as if the wealth attained had been once and for all removed from the activities that produced it. The deteriorations of such financial systems, whenever the growth in productivity failed to keep pace with the increase in monetary volume, show that such a stability is rather fictitious.

The apparent accumulative and static character of economies based on coins makes them closely resemble linguistic systems that emphasize linguistic elements, such as words, syllables, letters, morphemes, or phonemes, and fail to consider language as a system of activities and interactions. While the proto-economy of the barter trade implies too little symbolization to make it closely comparable to language, the intermediate system of coins, because of its elementalistic notions, is about equally inappropriate for such a comparison. An adequate understanding of language can be achieved only through comparisons with the debenture system which is based upon matrices of transactions rather than upon classes of fixed elements.

The power of commercial and industrial operations in modern economic systems is not so much determined by the amount of hard currency but by the diversification and the speed with which limited assets are transformed and retransformed. The worth of money is determined by its owner's ability to utilize it productively. Stored money is of lesser value and, indeed, lessening in value as a function of continuing inflation. While transformational operations also characterize the more advanced stages of the coinage system, it remains more firmly anchored to the amount of cash available to the operator. The opportunity of obtaining loans upon written declarations, of investing them immediately in new financial operations, of transferring the profits to cover commissions, and to obtain new resources for investments characterizes the effectiveness of the debenture system. In the extreme—and there exist numerous documented cases bordering on illegality—a financial operator might gain large profits without much or without any firm financial basis, only through quick transactions of fictitious capital. Through such transactions the debenture system has lifted itself from its foundation. It has become a pure system of interrelated activities. The cash that presumably buys these activities and the products that they generate has become of negligible importance.

In modern linguistics, beginning with Sapir, Jesperson, and the Prague School, the study of transactions has overpowered the study of forms. Already Jesperson emphasized that the purpose of a linguistic analysis is "to denote all the most important interrelations of words and parts of words in connected speech ... Forms as such have no place in the system [1937, pp. 13, 104]." More recently, this idea has been expressed in the transformational grammar of Chomsky (1965), in Piaget's (1963, 1970) cognitive developmental psychology, and in the structuralism of Levi-Strauss (1958). In Chomsky's theory, transformations relate deep structure components to the surface structures of languages. As for Piaget, the language-using individuals are actively participating in these transactional processes. These operations are confined, however, to the organisms. An interaction with external (for example, social) forces is deemphasized if not disregarded in both theories.

Undoubtedly, Chomsky's theory has profoundly shaken the traditional, elementalistic, and parallelistic views of linguists and psychologists with their undue emphasis upon external, physical stimuli and mechanical, physical reactions of passive organisms. Piaget, like Chomsky, has strongly emphasized the transactional character of psychological operations. He, indeed, seems to draw the final conclusion of such an interpretation by stating that "Transformations may be disengaged from the objects subject to such transformations and the group defined solely in terms of the set of transformations [1970, pp. 23-24]."

Both Chomsky and Piaget have stated their theories in mentalistic terms. While such an orientation has set them clearly apart from most American psychologists, they have failed to assign an appropriate role to the cultural–historical conditions into which individuals are born and within which they grow. The environment is regarded as passive. All learning and development is initiated and directed by the individuals. To attain their goals, they need information and material from the outside. There is no place in these theories, however, for an active role from the environment and for a codetermination of the individuals' development by other active organisms. It is at this juncture where a comparison with economic theories becomes most pertinent because these theories bypass and advance far beyond modern interpretations of language and cognitive development.

For a complete understanding of cognitive and linguistic operations, we have to consider two interaction systems. One relates these operations to their inner basis, to their physiological, biochemical foundation. The other represents the interactions with the cultural–historical environment into which an organism has been born. While the latter system is realized in theories of economic operations and in the symbolic interactionism of Mead (1934), the former system is expressed—though incompletely—in the theories of Piaget and Chomsky. An advanced synthesis of both interaction systems has been proposed by Rubinstein (1958, 1963; see also Payne, 1968; and Chapter 2 of this volume).

Rubinstein extended the first interaction system by relying on Pavlov's work. He introduced the second interaction system by relying on Vygotsky's (1962) work and, thereby, on the historical materialism of Marx, Engels, and Lenin. The psychic activities of an organism are seen as the changing outcome of these two interaction systems, one tying them to their inner material, biochemical foundation described in terms of relations within the nervous system and sensory and motor organs, the other tying psychic activities to their outer material, cultural–historical foundation described in terms of relations between individuals and society. Behavior is seen as an activity continuously changing in the process of interactions. It is not a thing-like particle that can be separated from these transactions. Language, likewise, is an activity, founded upon the two interaction systems. In particular, it serves to integrate nervous activities and cultural–historical functions. It should be studied as such a process rather than as a conglomeration of particles or forms which are the rigidified products of relational activities.

In order to carry Rubinstein's program to its systematic conclusion, it would be necessary to devise a theory and methodology of relations upon which the study of the interactions of the human language can be based. Such a task consists of two parts. First, a relational analysis has to be proposed that depicts the minor linguistic and cognitive activities or, in Rubinstein's terms, that explores the interactions between inner-biological and individual-psychological operations. In other words, the "reflexology" of Pavlov's first signaling system has to be supplemented by a "relationology" specifically designed to depict linguistic–cognitive operations. Second, a relational analysis has to be proposed that depicts the outer linguistic and cognitive activities or, in Rubinstein's terms, that explores the interactions between individual-psychological and cultural–sociological operations. The second task will be done in the next chapter, which is devoted to the study of dialogical interactions. The first task will be done in the following section of this chapter, where a brief sketch of a relational analysis of language and its acquisition is given.

The Relational Basis of Language

Psychologists studying language commonly regard defining the elements of an analysis as one of their most important tasks. Many settle quickly on words or syllables as basic units, if not on the infamous nonsense syllable. To linguists, however, words as well as syllables pose grave problems, and they have devoted tedious treatises to their analysis. The scholarly superiority of linguists is only superficial, however. If they do nothing else but choose different, although more sophisticated, elements for their analysis, such as morphemes or phonemes, they fail to overcome such particle models of language. Of course, once these units have been defined, the scientists will proceed to explain how they are arranged into larger sequences. In psychology, associations have traditionally provided the necessary bonds, and it was hoped that eventually science would be able to reconstruct the complexity of human experience. While in all these efforts elements were regarded as prior to their connections, I will argue for the priority of relations over elements. Such a shift in interpretation represents a renewed emphasis on the language users and on common, meaningful, phenomenal experience.

Extralingual Relations

Exchanged information consists of connected and never of isolated terms. Thus, if we explain the word ZEBRA to a child, we say "(A) zebra (has) stripes" or "(A) zebra (is an) animal" and even if we use nothing but the word ZEBRA we, most likely, point to a "real" zebra or to the picture of one. Thus we are invoking a special extralingual relation between a label and the object denoted by it, which I will call "ostensive relations." On some other occasions, we may utter single words like GO or STOP, expecting that the child will perform the requested actions. The role of commands and demands has received considerable attention in studies of classical conditioning by Pavlov and is basic to Skinner's interpretations of verbal behavior. However, these "intensive relations" have been as yet rarely considered in studies of language development. Finally, a third type of extralingual relations is invoked when persons utter, usually in an idiosyncratic manner, some words or sounds such as BRAVO, OUCH, etc., thereby indicating their emotions or feelings. Many theories on the origin of language, beginning with one proposed by Darwin, have focused upon such connotative or "expressive relations." However with few exceptions little attention has been given to this topic in studies of language acquisition.

All three extralingual relations (ostensive, intensive, expressive) are important for the initiation and control of psycholinguistic performances, but their significance decreases during the later periods of development. The vast majority of information consists of intralingual relations, that is, relations between different words. These relations are one step removed from their nonlinguistic basis.

Mutual Dependence of Elements and Relations

An apparent difficulty in relational interpretations is the circularity of the concepts of elements and relations. But the problem is not different from other intellectual explorations, for instance, those in analytical geometry, where a point (representing an element) is defined as the intersect of two lines (representing relations) and where at the same time, a line is defined as the connection between two points. Thus in both cases it becomes a matter of choice of where one enters the cycle and from what place one begins to unravel the issues.

Traditionally, an elementalistic viewpoint has dominated the natural as well as the social sciences. By disregarding the contextual implications, psychologists, thereby, have brought themselves into the unfortunate position of having eliminated meaning from their consideration, that is, those aspects that ought to be of greatest interest in their analysis of language acquisition and use. Elements in isolation are completely meaningless much like the ideal nonsense syllables of the psychological laboratory. On the other hand, relations, like the reflexes in Pavlov's view, are the smallest, though idiosyncratic, units of meaning. Since it is inconceivable that human activity can ever be completely without meaning (at least from the actor's own point of view), relations represent the immediate information given or produced; elements are constructed and derived.

Intersection of Relations

If relations are combined, two intellectual operations can take place: The meaning of the element at the intersection can be explored (that is, a word can be identified), and/or the free elements of the intersecting relations can be recognized as members of a class. Both processes involve an abstraction from the immediate information given, the relations. Both processes may occur simultaneously and instantaneously. However, if one of the elements or if the particular types of relations are unfamiliar to a person, considerable time might be required for completing these processes.

Two relations can be combined in no more than four different ways. The first combination aligns two relations opposite in directions. It represents a trivial loop or reverberation. If relations would combine in this manner only, for instance, if the word BLACK would always lead to WHITE and WHITE always to BLACK, then no relational structure would exist. Fortunately, psycholinguistic relations never combine exclusively in such a trivial manner, but always reveal sufficient variation in their arrangements.

Chaining	Stimulus equivalence	Response equivalence
$S_1 \to R_2; S_2 \to R_3$	$\begin{array}{c} S_1 \\ S_2 \end{array} \!\! \to R_{1,2}$	$S_{1,2} \!\! \to \begin{array}{c} R_1 \\ R \end{array}$

The three remaining combinations of two relations shown above are identical with the chaining, the response-equivalence, and the stimulus-equivalence paradigms (Jenkins & Palermo, 1964). The first attaches one relation at the end of the other. If nothing else but such chaining paradigms were prevailing, a language would consist of idiosyncratic strings. More likely, various chains will criss-cross each other, thus lending transient strength to the network of relations of which a language is made up. The last two paradigms, in particular, allow for the identification of the intersecting element and for the recognition of classes. In the response-equivalence paradigm, two relations diverge from a common left-hand term, leading from COW to DRINK and RUN. Both right-hand terms explicate the meaning of COW. In the stimulus-equivalence paradigm, two relations converge upon a shared right-hand term, for example, leading from COW and HORSE to RUN. Both left-hand terms explicate the meaning of RUN (see Quarterman & Riegel, 1968; Zivian & Riegel, 1969). If more than two relations are combined, considerable variation in the patterns results. The methodology for analyzing such networks has been considerably advanced during recent years (see Harary, Norman, & Cartwright, 1965; Sokal & Sneath, 1963).

Reductionistic and Discriminative Aspects of Language

When linguists explore an unknown language, they need to rely on extralingual relations. Except for the rare case of unequivocal proper names, there will always be a large range of items denoted by a common label but varying in many attributes. If this were not so, the language would be nonreductionistic. Only when numerous items are commonly labeled does a language become an efficient means for communication. Consequently, for any term, the linguists need relational information under numerous conditions in order to gain an understanding of the full range of its meaning.

Often, the linguists' task has been compared with that of children acquiring their first language. Such comparison would be simplistic, if we were to restrict it to information reduction through labeling. Concurrently with such performance, single objects, events, or qualities are denoted by different labels. For instance, a child might be called BOY, LAD, PAUL, SMITH, NAUGHTY ONE, etc. The choice of the label varies with the situation and depends upon the particular discrimination aimed for. An item might be called THING (if there are no other relevant items), BLOCK (if there are also beads and marbles), BLACK ONE (if there are red and white items), etc. The exclusion or disregard of attributes is often as important as the positive denotation of an item (Trabasso, 1970). Moreover, the discriminating use of labels makes their application more productive than when their function is exclusively reductionistic.

In terms of my interpretations, the reductionistic character of language is represented by relations diverging from the label and pointing toward the set of denoted objects, events, or qualities. The discriminative character, on the other hand, is represented by a set of labels converging upon a single object, event, or quality. Reductionistic and discriminative properties of language coexist dialectically. The same is true for the related issue of identifying the meaning of a word or of recognizing a class. The first implies the focusing upon a single term from which several relations diverge. The latter implies the focusing upon members of a distribution many of which might be linked to a single item (for example, their class name), all of which are linked to some shared items (for example, shared functions, parts, locations, etc.).

Criteria for Classes

Many psychologists regard the stimulus- and response-equivalence paradigms as sufficient conditions for the determination of classes. However, these two paradigms represent minimal criteria only because they imply that any two items elicited by a common stimulus or leading to a common response would form a class. They are also abstractions because in such simple forms they occur under laboratory conditions only. In concrete situations, a multitude of combinations are superimposed and embedded in one another, making up the complex network of the natural language and, thereby, strengthening the classes to varying degrees. But because of their abstractness, these paradigms, next to simple relations, may serve as units into which this network can be partitioned.

The superposition of the paradigms can be demonstrated by the example shown above. If children have learned that COWs DRINK, EAT, and RUN and that HORSEs EAT and RUN, they have formed a network of relations involving two semantic classes. COW is a stimulus for three response-equivalence paradigms involving the terms: DRINK/EAT, EAT/RUN, DRINK/RUN, respectively. HORSE is the stimulus for one response equivalence paradigm: EAT/RUN. Furthermore, EAT and RUN, respectively, are the responses for the two stimulus equivalence paradigms both involving COW/HORSE.

Undoubtedly, both the classes of right- and left-hand terms are more firmly established than when only a single response or a single stimulus equivalence paradigm was involved. The strength of classes might, indeed, be determined by enumerating the number of stimulus or response paradigms embedded in the more complex display (see Riegel, 1970). Once classes have attained a certain strength, a child might generate novel utterances without ever having been exposed to them before. In the example above, the child might realize that HORSEs DRINK.

Types of Intralingual Relations

Thus far I have discussed general procedures for identifying the meaning of words and for determining word classes, but I have not given any thought to the types of relations involved. Apparently, many types of relations are conceivable and, most important, will lead to different classifications. Thus, ZEBRA together with TIGER, CANDY-STICK, and BARBER-SIGN form a class sharing STRIPES as a common part or quality. On the other hand, ZEBRA will be categorized with ELEPHANT, NEGRO, and NILE, all of which are located in AFRICA. Thus, different relations lead to only partially overlapping categories. This result is the main reason why philosophers, linguists, and psychologists have failed, so far, to develop and to operationalize comprehensive semantic interpretations.

The above problems are further complicated by the mutual dependence of classes and general (class) relations. This difficulty is similar to the circularity in defining elements and simple relations. As I have argued, classes consist of those elements that share certain relations to outside terms, such as actor–action relations. On the other hand, we might conceive of a class of animals and of a class of actions that, in conjunction, define the general relationship between them. These two ways of looking at classes and general relations correspond to the alternative principles elaborated in mathematics by Dedekind (1893) and Frege (1903), respectively (see Chapter 1).

When considering developmental progressions, it seems unlikely that the recognition of general relations precedes the recognition of classes. Once simple relations are given, classes can be derived; once classes are derived, the general relationship between them can be apprehended. Such a general relationship does not represent anything more than the totality of all simple relations between the members of one class and the members of the other class. Similar to the concept of classes, no surplus meaning ought to be attached to the general relations between classes.

Relying on Piaget's interpretations (Inhelder & Piaget, 1958), I have previously (Riegel & Riegel, 1963) categorized general relations into three groups: (*a*) Logical relations between the words themselves and derived by verbal abstraction, such as synonymity, superordination, coordination, and subordination; (*b*) infralogical or physical relations based on the denoted objects, events, or qualities and derived by abstracting features from these physical items such as parts, wholes, locations, preceding, contemporaneous, or succeeding events; and (*c*) grammatical relations derived from the phenomenal (surface) structure of linguistic expressions and representing concatenations between the major parts of speech, that is, nouns, verbs, and modifiers.

The above list of general relations is neither exhaustive nor independent. It needs to be supplemented on the basis of more abstract considerations leading to the classification of relations into those that are: Symmetrical versus nonsymmetrical, transitive versus nontransitive, reflexive versus nonreflexive, etc. (Carnap, 1928, p. 21). Our list may also be supplemented by semantic relations discussed in Fillmore's (1968) case grammar and in the developmental studies by Bloom (1970).

Implicit and Explicit Relations

If we receive the abbreviated messages: ZEBRA → ANIMAL, ZEBRA → STRIPEs, ZEBRA → RUNs, we not only have four different words at our disposal but the implicit relational information of superordination, whole–part, and actor–action. The failure of a particle model of language to deal adequately both with semantic and syntactic interpretations is necessitated by the disregard for this relational information. Thus far, my discussion has been concerned with relations implied in meaningful combinations of words only (strictly speaking, all combinations of words are meaningful). An implicit relation is unique for the words which it connects; it is general if many words are combined in the same manner, that is, if the left-hand and the right-hand elements are members of two different classes.

The transmission of relational information would be insufficiently safeguarded if no other partially redundant clues were built into the natural languages. Thus, instead of the abbreviated messages listed above, we usually receive phrases like "The zebra is an animal" or "The stripes of the zebra" or "The zebra runs." In these examples, the auxiliary IS (used as a proper verb) plus the indefinite article AN explicate the logical relation of superordination; the definite article THE and the preposition OF explicate the infralogical relation of whole–part; only the grammatical relation of actor–action does not receive any further explication except for the inflection, *s*, marking the verb. I call these explicit clues redundant because they do not occur regularly in the "telegraphic" speech of young children. Apparently, implicit relational information is prior to its explicated form.

The significance of my last statement is underscored when we realize that many single words have inherent relational features. Such implicit relationality is most strongly exhibited among adjectives and adverbs whose role of modifying nouns and verbs necessitates this feature. Their relationality is further extended through the use of comparative constructions, such as TALL, TALLER, TALLEST, which make this part of speech an exceptionally rich topic for a relational analysis (see Clark, 1970; Huttenlocher & Higgins, 1971; see also Chapter 3, this volume). Also, verbs relating to noun subjects and/or to noun objects imply such relationality, for example, PUSH, PULL, GIVE, TAKE, etc. With the exception of professional and kinship terms, for example, FOREMAN, UNCLE, BROTHER, etc., such implicit relationality is not very common among nouns, however.

Compounding of Relations

With the discussion of explicit relations we have, finally, reached areas of inquiry traditionally explored as the foundation of language by linguistics. In contrast, my discussion did not begin with an elaboration of these abstract syntactic structures but was founded upon the concrete experiences and activities of the real child. Throughout, the order of the topics corresponded to the natural order in which a language is acquired: After sufficient relational information is obtained, the child may identify elements as well as classes. Next, explicit relational clues, such as the prepositions, will be utilized and the child will, increasingly, obey the proper sequential order of semantic classes. At this moment children are still not operating within the syntax of the linguists because they have not yet a sufficient grasp of the more abstract grammatical classes nor of the rules of their combination and transformation. They will be ready for these operations once the classes and class relations available to them have become sufficiently general. With few exceptions, semantic classes are subsets of grammatical classes and, without exception, semantics is prior to syntax.

If two or more elements co-occur regularly, the relations involved may begin to function as elements of a higher order. Such a stratification occurs, for instance, when words are compounded, such as YELLOW-BIRD, STORE-KEEPER, WINDOW-PANE, etc. These conditions can be depicted by bracketing, that is, (YELLOW → BIRD). Subsequently, a telegraphic sentence could be expressed as (YELLOW → BIRD) → SINGs, in contrast to the original formula YELLOW → BIRD: BIRD → SINGs.

The possibilities provided by such compoundings are not limited to words but lead us directly into questions of semantic and syntactic levels, strata, and hierarchies. The above example represents, indeed, the combination of noun-phrase, NP, that is, YELLOW → BIRD, with the verb SING. Instead of bracketing, Chomsky has preferred to depict hierarchical organizations by tree diagrams:

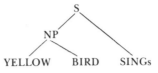

Thus, my example provides the important connection with the topic of syntactic structures and their acquisition during childhood (see McNeill, 1970a, 1970b; Slobin; 1971).

Relations of Relations

Despite their concern with language structure, psycholinguists have paid little attention to what we might call relations of relations or the logical connections of relations. Two relations, as discussed above, can be monotonically combined leading to the derivation of classes such as "animals" and "animated actions." They can also become a part of more complex expressions. For this purpose connectors need to be introduced. Mainly two types of function words serve such connective purposes: conjunctions and relative pronouns. In particular, symmetrical conjunctions (AND, TOO, ALSO, AS WELL AS, etc.) and relative (asymmetrical) pronouns (WHICH, WHO, and THAT) express—in analogy to our former distinction—logical relations of coordination and superordination–subordination as in the following examples:

Coordination:	(EAGLE → FLIEs) and (RABBIT → RUNs)
Superordination-Subordination:	(RABBIT → RUNs) which (EAGLE → HUNTs)
or	RABBIT which (EAGLE → HUNTs) → RUNs

Asymmetrical conjunctions (IF...THEN, BECAUSE, BEFORE, AFTER, etc.) and relative adverbs (WHERE, WHEN, WHY, etc.) generate infralogical relations between relations and represent spatial, temporal, causal and other physical conditions as in the following examples:

Spatial:	(HOUSE → BURNs) where (JOHN → LIVEs)
Temporal-Causal:	(CORN → GROWS) after (SUN → SHINES)
	if (EAGLE → FLIEs) then (RABBIT → RUNs), etc.

In spite of the lack of evidence, these logical and infralogical relations of relations are prior and of greater importance in the language acquisition process than any syntactic structures reflecting formal and abstract linguistic conventions. Since permutations within logical and infralogical structures produce, in most cases, changes in interpretations, such a "syntax" is more fundamental than the aspects of syntax commonly analyzed by linguists. Children will have to learn how to operate with logical and infralogical combinations; as a by-product they generate sentences that incorporate words according to their syntactic rules.

Psycholinguistic Systems

If instead of elements and simple relations we discuss classes and general relations, we shift from what Chomsky has called *finite state grammars* to phrase structure grammars. Of course, such an extension is not limited to syntax but, more important from our own point of view, holds for semantic systems as well. Instead of proposing simple relations such as RABBIT → RUNs, EAGLE → FLIEs, and of elaborating different types of combinations, I argue, now, in terms of semantic classes, such as "animals," "food," "toys," "animated actions," etc., and in terms of general relations which not only link but also define these classes. Since there are no nonoverlapping semantic classes, only the most formal and abstract features of the language, namely those of syntax, have been described in an unambiguous manner. But even here, multiple classifications often outweigh unique assignments. The ambiguities of semantic classifications may seem disturbing, but they also guarantee the richness of linguistic expressions and the creative potential of the language.

Rules for combining semantic or syntactic classes are more general than rules for chaining simple relations. While thus, the resulting semantic and syntactic systems are more powerful, Chomsky regards them as almost equally insufficient because they do not consider transformational operations. Although transformational systems might be still more comprehensive than the other models, it is well conceivable that various semantic and syntactic systems coexist in children and that large portions of their language skills might be sufficiently explained by systems of classes and general relations or even by transitional probabilities without invoking more complex operations.

Inversion and Negation

A language model based on classes and general relations accounts for the well-documented generative skills of children (Brown & Fraser, 1963; Stern & Stern, 1907; Weir, 1962), but it does not handle operations of intellectual shifts or reversals (Riegel, 1957), which recently have been discussed under the topic of deixis (see Bruner, 1972; Rommetveit, 1968). When we identify an object or a term, we always do so at the expense of others with which the target item is contrasted. Only during the very early stages of intellectual development, that is, during the sensorimotor period in Piaget's theory, does the child focus upon singular items. In most instances, the contrastive disregard of information (Trabasso, 1970) is as important as the positive identification of the item itself.

Recently, Olson (1970) has given a cogent analysis of this problem. By hiding a small paper star under blocks differing in several attributes, the verbal identification of the target item varies with the alternatives given. In one situation we might merely say that the star is under the block (if there is only one block within a set of other objects); in another we might say that it is under the black one, the round one, the large one, etc., depending upon the alternatives given. In the language of set theory, the identification of a concept A involves the recognition of its inverse A', both of which compose the superset B in the form $A + A' = B$.

The problem becomes more complex if the discrimination occurs along several dimensions at the same time. For instance, if children have to operate within the dimension of red vs. nonred and wooden vs. nonwooden, they might again discriminate red blocks or wooden blocks from all others by disregarding each time the second of the two interacting attributes. However, they might also be asked to form combinations, such as: red *and* wooden; red *but not* wooden; wooden *but not* red; *neither* red *nor* wooden.

Since psycholinguistic information is mostly positive, our discussion has been somewhat academic. Commonly, we describe an item by listing several, preferably, criterial features rather than by informing the listener what an item is *not*. For example, we tell a child that a "ZEBRA is an ANIMAL with STRIPES," rather than that "a ZEBRA is *not* a PLANT and does *not* have DOTS." We choose the positive strategy because complementary sets are often ill-defined and vary from situation to situation. Moreover, human beings seem to be better able to handle positive rather than negative information (see Bourne, 1970; Bruner, Goodnow, & Austin, 1956; Wason, 1959).

Due to the traditional emphasis upon cognition, the role of negative information has been insufficiently explored by psycholinguists. As soon as we focus upon language as a means for the initiation and control of nonverbal actions, motivations, and emotions, we will be impressed by the significant role of negation in the form of inhibition, repression, and denial. These noncognitive aspects of language provide important connections with other major areas of psychological inquiry, such as physiological, personality, and social research and theories. The concept of negative information also enters into consideration when we extend our discussion of classes to those of ordered relations. Within such models, negations of ordered or partially ordered subsystems represent the operation of transformation.

Transformations

In discussing transformations, it is useful to refer briefly to mathematics where this concept has been rigorously applied. Mathematical systems consist of sets of axioms defining possible operations with symbolic elements, such as numbers. As elaborated by Hölder (1901) and more recently discussed by Stevens (1951), Coombs (1964) and others, the simplest number system defines nominal scales that, when applied to observations, allow for the categorization of items in distinct classes to which, in turn, labels, such as words, letters, or numerals, may be assigned. Since there exists no order between the classes, the degree of transformation is almost unlimited and consists in the relabelling of the classes and their members. Differing from linguistics, however, logical or mathematical transformations keep the significant properties of the system invariant, that is, the classes remain the same even though their labels have changed. When additional axioms on the transitivity of the operations are imposed, ordinal systems are generated. Subsequently, logical or mathematical transformations, in keeping the order invariant, are more restricted than those applicable to nominal systems. Ordinal scales might be monotonically stretched or compressed, but the order of any two items may not be altered.

Unfortunately, linguists have used the term transformation in precisely the opposite sense. Linguistic transformations, in producing variance, gain importance as the system to which they are applied becomes more complex. In categorical systems, they lead to the identification of the inverse of classes. In ordered systems, such as various types of syntax, they imply rearrangements of these classes that, most often, require changes in interpretations. Linguistic transformations deal with the reordering of sequences of classes or at a lower level, of elements by which declarative statements are changed into questions, passive statements, negative statements, and vice versa or by which deep structure phrases are converted into surface structure expressions and vice versa.

Conclusions

With my brief reference to linguistic transformations, we have returned to the main issues of the first part of my chapter in which I tried to demonstrate that a purely transactional analysis is conceivable and that such an analysis has been successfully implemented in economics. Language, likewise, ought to be regarded as an activity and not merely as a system of particles or tokens, products or commodities. Such a conclusion does not contradict the analysis in the second part of this chapter where I emphasized the relational, transactional character of linguistic operations. In the following summary, I attempt, once more, to show the congruence of these two aspects of language development.

At the protoeconomic level, trade consists in the exchange of particular items on a one-to-one basis and is bound to a given situation. Such a system is concrete with little symbolic representation. But the items exchanged are not to be viewed as having thing-like, substantive character; what is exchanged are the activities and the labor necessary to produce them. Similarly, linguistic operations at this level involve extralingual relations between labels and objects, internal states, or—most important—actions. If a comparison with Piaget's developmental levels is attempted, the proto-economic and the protolinguistic systems are characterized by sensori-motor activities.

The next economic system is comparable to the level of concrete intellectual operations. It relies on standard commodities represented by concrete materials or objects (for example, gold or silver) and allows for a wider range and more flexible operations, such as sequential and multiple distributions of traded goods, as well as for advance storage and delayed actions. The conceptual danger of such a system lies in the tendency to regard its basic monetary units as fixed, universal entities. History has repeatedly shown that this apparent stability is easily shattered as the basis of activity (representing the labor and efforts by the participating people) is brought at variance with the standards of the system.

Traditionally, similar viewpoints have dominated psychology and linguistics, namely, the view that language consists of sets of basic units, such as words, syllables, letters, morphemes or phonemes, from which the more complex forms are derived. Thus, the view of language as an activity and a process is either disregarded or lost. Just as different currencies represent different monetary systems, so do different sets of linguistic elements represent different languages or dialects. Thus, there exists variability and between them (linear) convertability or (nonlinear, transformational) translation. The universal basis of different linguistic systems is represented by the protolanguage of the preceding level with its notion of the identity of operations. Correspondingly, the proto-economy of the barter system represents the universal features of the more-advanced trading operations based upon property rights. At the second economic level, more specific rules have to be implemented determining the standard, the order, and the distribution of exchanges. Likewise, at the second linguistic level, more specific lexicological conventions and syntactic rules of order are required.

Only at the third stage of development does an analysis of the economic system advance our understanding of linguistic systems to a significant degree. Monetary forms characteristic for this stage and represented by certificates, bonds, stocks, and checks, are representational units of exchange. They help us to realize that it is neither the object nor any particular material, such as rare metals, that is exchanged but the labor and activities of people producing these objects and operating with these documents. Transactions on such elusive bases require explicit rules of conduct of which only a minor portion concerns the specific relationship of these certificates to the objects of trade. Most of them deal with intraeconomic relations.

The conditions are similar in linguistic operations. Only when we realize that linguistic units, such as words, syllables, or letters, are mere abstractions from the stream of operations that characterizes language, do we gain a full understanding of linguistic systems. These operations constitute the information immediately given through the interrelating activities of communicating individuals. An understanding of these interactions can be gained only if these activities are studied as they are produced and perceived; the products of these interactions are rigidified objectifications that do not capture the constituting activities of languages.

5

The Temporal Organization
of Dialogues

Although dialogues represent the basis for communication, there have been only a few systematic inquiries into their temporal organization. Many philosophers (most notably Plato) and writers (most notably playwrights) have employed dialogues as a vehicle for explicating their ideas. Thereby they have elevated the art of dialogues to a high level of perfection, but, if they were concerned with the systematic analysis of the dialogue at all, their efforts resulted in practical suggestions to speakers and writers, that is, resulted in treatises on rhetoric.

Sociologists and psychologists, likewise, have paid little attention to the systematic analysis of dialogues. Only in their investigations of pre-lingual (Spitz, 1963a, 1963b, 1964) and pathological conditions (Hass, 1975; Watzlawick, Beavin, & Jackson, 1967) and in their studies of the psychotherapeutic process (Labov & Fanshel, 1977) have they engaged in directed explorations of dialogical interactions. These efforts were again guided by practical considerations. Finally, even among linguists, the study of dialogues has attracted little attention. There is, however, one notable exception. The Russian linguist and contemporary of Vygotsky, Voloshinov (1973), developed a theory of language which is explicitly based on the dialogue. Due to his early death, his work has remained in the form of a general outline of a theory, however, and it took the exceptional skills of his recent translators to provide a comprehensive integration (Matejka, 1973; Titunik, 1973).

The reluctance of social scientists (in particular linguists) to engage in systematic studies of concrete communicative interactions by human beings has been forcefully exposed by Labov (1970). It had led linguists in the past (in particular Chomsky, 1957, 1965, 1968) to devote all their attention to the study of language as an abstract system of signs and rules—*la langue* of de Saussure (1916)—rather than to the study of concrete forms of exchanges among individuals—*les paroles* of de Saussure. In their striving for scientific universality, modern linguists disregarded the most central part of their investigation: the individual, social human being. They disregarded that language has been created by men who, at the same time, have been created by language.

The reluctance of behavioral scientists to engage in systematic studies of concrete social interactions in language exchanges can be explained by their blind fixation upon individuals who are either seen in their ceaseless accumulation of sensory data (Locke, Hume, Mill) or in their mentalistic construction of ideas (Descartes, Leibniz, Kant) but whose engagements in social interactions are treated only as a secondary issue. The orientation of the behavioral scientists reflects a mood of inquiry that tries hard to simulate the paradigm of classical natural sciences and is closely tied to their particular viewpoint about the relationship between the subject and the object. This viewpoint conflicts sharply with the concept of the dialogue.

Subject–Object Relation

1. Classical natural sciences are founded upon a sharp segregation of the object from the subject and upon the attempt to eliminate the subject, that is, the observer or experimenter, from the context of the study. By adhering to these principles it became possible to formulate scientific descriptions in "objective" terms. Stimulated by the extraordinary success in classical natural sciences, this approach was translated into psychology during the second half of the nineteenth century through the experimental work and theorizing by Fechner, Helmholtz, Wundt, Donders, and many others.

Although "objectification" became the dominant theme for psychology, opposition and reservations were soon expressed, most notably in Brentano's "Act Psychology" and by the scholars of the Würzburg School. During the ensuing argument Wundt (1907) defended the classical natural science paradigm of the subject–object segregation. The criteria upon which he based his critique were all directed against the extensive form of introspection promoted by the scholars at Würzburg in their explorations of higher mental processes of thinking, problem solving, and concept formation. Most notably Wundt argued against the participatory involvement of the subjects in the study of their own thought processes and rejected the elaborated form of self-reports considering them as inappropriate for an "objective" description of these processes. While the procedures developed for this purpose by the scholars at Würzburg might have been doomed even before they were criticized by Wundt, he failed to suggest constructively any other methods and forms of analysis that would explore in a more appropriate manner the topics under consideration. His failure to do so merely reflects, of course, his uncompromising commitment to the paradigm of the classical natural sciences which is founded upon the subject–object segregation.

2. Modern natural sciences have begun to question the classical concept of the subject–object relation and, thereby, have assigned constructive significance to the participatory role of the subject. This shift is not only revealed in Heisenberg's formulation of the "uncertainty principle" but, more importantly, in his recognition that the whole field of science has been created by human efforts and can be understood only in the context of the whole history of these efforts. In criticizing the classical viewpoints of natural sciences, Heisenberg stated:

> Thus was formed the solid framework of classical physics, and thus arose the conception of a material world in time and space comparable to a machine which, once set in motion, continued to run, governed by immutable laws. The fact that this machine as well as the whole of science were themselves only products of the human mind appeared irrelevant and of no consequence for an understanding of nature [1952, p. 86].

Psychologists have not understood the implications of the intellectual revolution of modern natural sciences which, by recognizing the participatory role of the subject, has been primarily psychological in nature. Subsequently, natural scientists have looked in vain for assistance and support from the psychologists. Even when Rosenthal (1966) demonstrated the influence of the experimenter upon the conduct, analysis, result, and interpretation of psychological experiments, no major overhaul of their conceptual basis resulted but merely an increase in the complexity of the investigations: The experimenter became an additional variable to be studied or controlled in the multivariate analysis.

3. The traditional concept of the experimental task has not remained unchallenged in psychology (see Lewin, 1927, and the discussion

of his contribution in comparison to modern experimental analyses by Riegel, 1958), but most criticisms failed to provide constructive alternatives to the approach built upon the subject–object segregation. Most notably one of the first challenges of the traditional concept is due to Goethe (1900) who not only rejected the analytical approach to natural science (for example, the criticism in his phenomenological theory of color vision), but also the experimental methods upon which the analytical theory is based. He regarded the experiment as a mediator between the subject and the object rather than as a means for "objectification" that aims at eliminating the subject. However his discussion did not succeed in changing the course that the natural sciences were going to follow and that the behavioral sciences were going to copy. The outcome of this adoption was a paradoxical confusion of the terms. The subject was called the experimenter or observer, and the object of the experiments came to be known as the subject. In this disguise the subject had lost all of its distinctive characteristics, that is, the individual and social qualities of the human being. With this degradation the psychological experiment became alienated from its own topic.

4. The extent to which psychological thinking remained firmly rooted in the traditional concept of the subject–object relation is convincingly revealed in inquiries advocated by some of its most enlightened scholars, for example by Piaget. The following comments concern primarily the most influential period of Piaget's own career, his "structuralist period" (see Chapter 7, this volume), during which he elaborated his well-known stages in the cognitive development of the child (Piaget, 1950, 1952).

Piaget's experimental observations during this period of his work are derived by posing problems to children and asking directed questions in order to explore the details of their cognitions and the products of their intellectual operations. Omitted from the inquiry are situations in which the child rather than the experimenter poses a problem or raises a question. Thus at least one half of all cognitive operations is disregarded.

Piaget's one-sided preference for posing problems and asking questions restricts his interpretations to the child's operations with objects, such as clay balls, beakers, blocks, and sticks. He fails to take account of the child's operations with other subjects in the form of social, including dialogical exchanges. This restriction indicates Piaget's preference for balance and equilibrium that are achieved whenever the child finds a solution or answer in a particular task situation and that are developmentally attained whenever the child reaches one after the other stage or period of cognitive operations. If Piaget would have given equal attention to the problems raised by children as he has given to problems solved, he would have become concerned with the origin and creation of imbalances and disequilibria and would have transformed his studies of the child's operations with objects into performance dialogues between two or more active individuals. Piaget's theory of the monologue of mental development would have been transformed into a theory of the dialogue of human development.

5. The study of dialogues breaks in a radical manner with the traditional scientific description based on the subject–object segregation. In a dialogue both speakers are subject and object at the same time, and the relations established between them with each utterance are always reflective. These relations are not exclusively directed forward in time in a linear or causal flow but always relate backwards to their producers being forced in this direction by the presuppositions, intentions, and expectations which these relations imply. As a consequence, there is never anything objectifiable in the traditional sense or anything fixed in a dialogue; paraphrasing Heraclitus. *we never enter the same dialogue twice.*

The scientific study of dialogues has to follow two routes: (*a*) We have to derive a theoretical description of the temporal structure and temporal changes of the dialogue, and (*b*) we have to develop techniques of recording and forms of relational categorizations that would allow us to document on empirical grounds the temporal structures and changes derived in the first part of the exploration. While an increasing number of investigations has been published or is under way in exploring the second or "operational" topic[1], my attention will be exclusively directed toward a theoretical analysis of some basic properties and forms of dialogues.

[1]Two reviews of research related to dialogues have recently appeared, one has been published (Farwell, 1975), the other is an unpublished report (De Paulo & Bonvillian, 1975). Most of the studies reviewed have been concerned with the interactions between adults (especially mothers) and children. The following list includes only published reports: Blount (1972); Fraser and Roberts (1975); Holzman (1972); Lewis and Freedle (1973); Moerk (1972, 1974); Phillips (1973); Snow (1972). Five published studies have focused upon child-child language interactions with additional information on adults: Anderson and Johnson (1973), Berko Gleason (1973); Nelson (1973); Shatz and Gelman (1973); Weeks (1971). Ferguson (1964) made a cross-linguistic comparison of baby talk. Finally, there are some general interpretations of linguistic interactions and dialogues among children, some of these also include research results: Bruner (1975); Duncan (1972); Ervin-Tripp (1968, 1970); Harris (1975); Mishler (1975a, 1975b).

Situational Dialogues

A dialogue requires a shared code for communication between its participants. Such a code consists not only of linguistic signs and elements (for example, words or phonemes), but of relationships and rules which provide the basis for its temporal structure and make the occurrence and effective use of these signs possible (Riegel, 1970; see also Chapter 4). Moreover, the communication system utilized in dialogues presupposes some shared knowledge, ideas, feelings, and emotions between the participants. Although these components of communication are elusive, especially during the development of language, operative exchanges would not be possible without them. In sociolinguistics, these components have been captured by terms such as theme, topic, and register of exchange (Halliday, 1973); they also reflect the attitudes, opinions, roles, and biases of the speakers and listeners.

Although a "shared code" is a prerequisite for any dialogue, such a code does not preexist in the minds of the participants but is derived through developmental efforts. In particular, it arises through the dialogical interactions along other sequences of activities, that is, feeding, looking, touching, playing, etc. While the topic of the changing developmental context has to be further elaborated, at this moment it is sufficient to recognize that individuals entering into dialogues at various moments in their lives may differ widely in regard to these conditions. In order to engage in effective dialogues, they have to focus their attention jointly on some (though not on all) of them. If this were not the case, for example, if there were no agreement between the participants as to the theme or topic of their discussion, a dialogue would either degenerate into presentations of mere generalities and/or would move aimlessly from one issue to the next.

Monologues and Narratives

A dialogue can be graphically represented by a chain of relations linking the utterances of speaker A and B in their temporal order. Such a *dialogical chain* differs from a *monologue* or *narrative* in that there is a systematic alternation between the two participants. The complexity of both sequences increases if connections are going further back than to the utterances immediately preceding a given one, that is, from A_3 to A_1 and not only to A_2 in the narrative, and from A_3 to A_2 or A_1 and not only to B_2 in the dialogical chain.

Dialogical chain

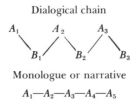

Monologue or narrative

$$A_1—A_2—A_3—A_4—A_5$$

In the graphical representations shown above, each A_i or B_i stands for one dialogical utterance presented by one of the two participants until interrupted by the other. Utterances may include several sentences, a single sentence, clauses, words, or merely expressive sounds, nods, or gestures. Each utterance has its internal structure and different utterances of a monologue or narrative are structurally related to one another. Labov and Waletzky (1967) have analyzed the structure of narratives or monologues in an insightful manner.

Narratives are commonly triggered by specific instructions. For example Labov and Waletzky initiated narratives by asking persons "whether they had ever been in a situation where they were nearly killed?" Usually this triggering question leads to no more than an affirmation or denial and requires further prompting until the narration gets on its way. During the course of the presentation, simple confirmations, expressions of doubts, nodding, and even the declining attention of the listener(s) keep the narrator in dialogical relation to the audience. Similar interactions exist between writers and readers although both are farther removed from one another than speakers and listeners in a dialogue and although their forms of interactions have been analyzed even less often in a systematic manner than the interactions between the participants in dialogues (for some references see Fieguth, 1973; Schmid, 1973).

Performance in "pure" monologues or narratives is a mere abstraction. Even isolated speakers rely on their vast experience with listeners in former dialogues in order to produce effectively. Monologues on stage, for example MacBeth's "is this a dagger which I see before me . . . ," commonly include as many questions as they include answers; the speakers, thus, express internal dialogues in an overt manner. In Mead's (1934) terminology, they interact with the internalized "me's" or with the "generalized me." The human being is never in complete solitude.

In contrasting the structure of narratives with the event sequences in the social and physical world which they describe, Labov and Waletzky (1967) demonstrate another important property of language. Even in the most simplistic stories reported by their informers, the social and physical scenes described consist of a multitude of coexisting conditions and events. The informer might, for instance, report that an unknown man approached him from a certain direction while he was engaged in a particular activity. The events in which both participants were simultaneously engaged led to a conflict. This conflict is the only event that was momentarily shared by both though again experienced from different perspectives. The main task for the narrator consists in channeling these coexistent conditions and events into the linear flow of the narrative. This task is achieved by interspersing short stretches of the events encountered by either of the two persons in an alternating manner. The effectiveness of the narration often depends, thereby, on extralingual means including the extensive use of intonation, pauses, and gestures that yield a dramatic version of the presentation. These qualities and props indicate that the narration is fundamentally a dialogue, not a monologue. Like the alternation in the dialogue of two speakers, the co-occurring events are interspersed in the linear flow of the narration.

Basic Properties of Dialogues

As the above example has indicated, a dialogue has temporal structure. The speakers alternate in their presentation and each successive statement reflects at least the one immediately preceding it. Restricting the range of successively incorporated statements to this extent represents a minimum requirement. The maximum would be attained if each utterance reflects all of the earlier statements. Each statement has to be consistent with the proponent's own previously expressed views and must represent an equally consistent or systematically modified reaction to all statements made by the other participant in the dialogue. Although they are not necessarily made explicit, each statement must also reflect basic issues of the theme or topic which are presupposed in the dialogue.

The simplest form of an exchange which can be called a dialogue is depicted below. Here the two speakers always relate their statements to the preceding ones by their opponent as well as to their own last statements. In other words, each statement is connected with the two preceding ones. Such a *simple dialogue* is characterized by a "depth" of two and has the structure of a *truss*:

Simple dialogue

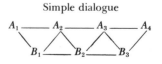

In *complex dialogues* connections span across more than two preceding utterances. In the example below the depth of the dialogue equals three:

Complex dialogue

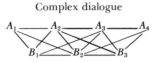

The *depth* of a dialogue can be determined by counting the number of converging or diverging relations for any A_i or B_i. Since the depth increases with the length of the dialogue, one should either eliminate the first statements of both speakers or compute an average value for the whole dialogue. Since the interaction of the two speakers may differ, separate evaluations ought to be made for A and B. In addition to the depths of dialogues, we might enumerate their *lengths* by counting the total number of utterances related to one another. By dividing the depth by the length, we obtain an index of the *density* of the dialogue.

The measurement of depth also allows for the determination of dialogue *boundaries*. Whenever the depth drops down and, in the extreme case, attains a value of zero, a boundary exists and a new *episode* or a new dialogue might begin. For such an evaluation we need to realize, of course, that the language exchange between two speakers represents only one, though the major form, of the interaction sequences to be considered. Aside from the dialogue, both participants will be engaged in numerous other activities, for example, playing a game, demonstrating a toy, taking a walk, correcting an essay, etc. Often boundaries will be determined by these nonlinguistic event sequences. For instance, a mother and her child engaged in a dialogue while going down a staircase might terminate their conversation at the moment when they open the door. At the inner-biological level, to use another example, a dialogue might be initiated in a state of hunger, it might continue while a meal is taken, but terminates as the food is eaten and the inner-biological status is altered. In particular Shugar (1972) has called attention to the interdependence of linguistic and nonlinguistic event sequences in dialogues.

The number of relations converging upon a statement indicates its integrative or *assimilative significance*; the number of relations diverging from a statement indicates its distributive or *accommodative significance*. Both terms are adopted from Piaget (1950, 1952). If a reflective coordination based upon assimilation and accommodation did not take place, dialogues would degenerate into alternating monologues in which both speakers merely follow-up on their earlier statements without reacting to the other speaker's elaborations. The other speaker's statements would, thus, appear as distractive interruptions and the only remaining dialogical property of such a performance would consist of the alternations between the participants. If these alternations cease also we approach conditions that Piaget (1926) has described as *collective monologues*. Comparable to the tuning of the instruments before the music begins, two or more speakers continue their productions uncoordinated on parallel tracks. Piaget regarded such behavior as a manifestation of "egocentric" speech in young children. Undoubtedly also the exchanges between adults often reflect such "egocentric" tendencies and, therefore, failures in communication. Both cases are shown below; each of them has a depth of one for both speaker A and B:

Collective monologue

A_1——A_2——A_3——A_4

B_1———B_2———B_3

Alternating collective monologue

A_1———A_2——— A_3———A_4

B_1———B_2———B_3

Dialectical Properties of Dialogues

In contrast to the chains of monologues, dialogues are composed of triangular subsections that, if different numerical subscripts can be assigned to them, represent what I will call *dialogical units*. Such units reflect the dialectical character of the communication process. The original statement represents a *thesis* which almost without exception will be denied, challenged, or modified by the utterance of the other speaker. The second statement, therefore, represents an *antithesis*. Even a simple confirmation by a nod of the head is a dialogical response and thus, a challenge to the first speaker who, in his/her second statement, will take notice of it and integrate this message in the form of a *synthesis*. But as this synthesis is uttered, the second speaker may object to it and propose a deviant interpretation that integrates his/her former statement (thesis) with that by his/her opponent (antithesis). The contradictory relationship between any two statements makes the empirical description of dialogues as difficult as it is. Traditionally, we are used to categorizing observations by their similarity but not by their divergence. For the analysis of the dialogue we have to do both.

The relationship between thesis and antithesis may vary widely. But even mere repetitions of the thesis, as employed on occasion in Rogerian psychotherapy, imply an antithetical challenge. However, such a challenge can not be comprehended within the overt exchanges between the two individuals but has to be located in the conflicting experience of the listener who is forced into a double reflection about his/her own statement—once when it was uttered and once when it was thrown back by the other therapist. The result is an inner-dialogical process which may lead the person to improved self-awareness. In this case too, the condition forced upon him/her and the apparent solitude that results reflect the dialogical character not only of the overt exchange but of each listener's internal thought processes as well.

The dialectical process that constitutes a dialogical unit makes us also aware of the reflective character of all dialogical interactions. The thesis provokes and anticipates the antithesis; the antithesis modifies and reinterprets the thesis. None can be thought without the other. And what holds for the thesis and antithesis also holds for their relationships to the synthesis. Thus, each utterance in the dialogical exchange represents a thesis, an antithesis, and a synthesis at one and the same time— dependent upon which of the triangular subsection in the truss one focuses upon. All adjacent statements are interdependent. Consequently no arrows but only lines are used in the diagrams. If unidirected arrows are used, they signify the flow of physical time in the dialogue (Riegel, 1977; see also Chapter 8, this volume).

If a statement never becomes a part of some outer or inner dialogue, it is of no interest at all and bare of any meaning. It becomes significant only if it is incorporated into a dialogical temporal structure, regardless of whether such a structure emerges immediately or months later. A statement in complete isolation is like the sounds in the wood occurring in the absence of any listener. One might question with Wittgenstein the existence of the sound, but as one begins to think about these sounds, they enter into an inner dialogical interaction and, therefore, gain meaning regardless of whether they "really" exist or not. All reality lies in the dialogical, or rather in the dialectical process.

Incomplete Dialogues

In a successful dialogue each speaker assimilates the other person's statements and accommodates his/her own productions so that they elaborate and extend the preceding viewpoints. If this were not the case, the dialogue would either degenerate into alternating collective monologues or would converge into a repetitive cycle in which each speaker merely repeats or reaffirms what has been said before. Such repetitive cycles would be indicated in the diagrams by any triangle with identical numerical subscripts. Like the subsections in the truss of a bridge, repetitive or recursive operations are necessary for the stability of dialogues. Strings, on the other hand, provide transitory threads. But a dialogue can not subsist on recursive productions alone or on strings that are not interlaced. The cycles have to be broken through "contrastive operations" (Riegel, 1974) by which the topic is either moved into new divergent directions or converges upon (is integrated with) previously made arguments.

Piaget identifies "pure" accommodation with imitation, and "pure" assimilation with play. The application of these concepts is even more appropriate for the analysis of dialogues than for the study of a single individual's cognitive operations. For example, pure accommodation or imitation occurs in dialogues if one speaker merely confirms, perhaps in modified phrasing, what the other participant has been saying. This case is at least partially identical with the production of repetitive or recursive cycles. Pure assimilation or play, on the other hand, is comparable to alternating collective monologues. In this case the speakers reinterpret idiosyncratically any previous statements and, without concern for alternative viewpoints, reiterate their own interpretations.

Several intermediate conditions or incomplete dialogues are conceivable that demonstrate various degrees of assimilation and accommodation. In the first of the following cases, A always assimilates the statements made by B but not his/her own preceding statements. Consequently, A changes always his/her position in reaction to B but does not remain consistent within himself/herself, whereas B participates appropriately in a simple dialogue. In the second of the following cases, B always and exclusively accommodates to A, whereas A participates appropriately in a simple dialogue. The structure of the following incomplete dialogues resembles a *saw*:

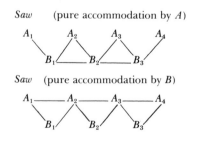

Saw   (pure accommodation by A)

Saw   (pure accommodation by B)

A second type of an incomplete dialogue occurs when one of the two speakers engages in a monologue—identified by Piaget as pure assimilation or play—while the other interacts in the form of a simple dialogue. The structure of these incomplete dialogues resembles a *ladder*:

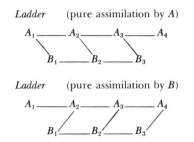

If one considers all properties of language, including phonetic, syntactic, cognitive, and affective characteristics, the communicative basis for any two speakers ought to be rather extensive. But if one considers only the criterial properties, that is, those that make a difference to the participants in the dialogue, then the shared basis might be rather small. In particular, pure accommodation or imitation by both speakers would produce maximum overlap between their messages. In the extreme case, the dialogue would degenerate into repetitions of shared generalities. In pure assimilation or play, on the other hand, both speakers introduce large amounts of new information with each of their statements. As a result the communicative exchange may become overloaded and may degenerate into alternating collective monologues.

My comparison of incomplete dialogues with pure assimilation and pure accommodation also reveals that successful dialogues are dependent on the active participation of both the alternating listeners and speakers. This proposition needs no amplification in regard to the speakers, but it does perhaps in regard to the listeners. The listeners have to engage in active selections and interpretations of the statements received in order to make them congruent with (assimilate) the content of former messages and, in particular, with their own former statements. Such reinterpretations prepare the listeners for their own rejoinders whether confirming and elaborating or rejecting and restricting the other speakers' statements. Thus rejoinders are already initiated at a time when the participants are still listening, long before they utter the first words of their replies. The synchronization or transformational coordination of their actions with their overt speech acts as well as the synchronization of both speakers' statements in the alternations of a successful dialogue represent the fundamental basis of individual and social developments.

Developmental Dialogues

Comparisons of dialogical performances with single children's imitation and play can be extended to interactive social games. For example, peek-a-boo, throwing and catching a ball, rhyming and rope skipping, Simple Simon says, or the more complex performances in a real stage play reveal all the properties of dialogue. In particular, social games often resolve into synchronized temporal structures quite similar to those describing the development of language. The resulting comparisons are helpful because the rules of social games are often more precisely specified than those of language. Experimental explorations of the structure of children's games and their impact upon language acquisition have recently been conducted by Greenfield, Nelson, and Saltzman (1972), Harris (1972, 1975), and Sutton-Smith (1976).

Comparable to the distinction between "primitive" and "scientific" dialectics (Lawler, 1975), development in general and the development of language in particular relies at the beginning on an intuitive understanding between the speaker and the listener, most likely between the mother and her child. With increasing experience in linguistic–cognitive operations the dialogue becomes explicit. Eventually a person might be clearly aware of its conditions and might consciously select certain topics, registers, or modes of expression and might apply effective ploys.

Mother–Child Dialogues

The linguistic environment consists at first of the caretaker (most often the mother) and the child. If both the father and the mother participate actively in the upbringing of the child, a higher degree of dialogical variation results exposing the child to a larger manifold of interaction patterns. If there are other family members (siblings, grandparents, relatives, or aides), the degree of alternation increases further although, during the early months, such changes might be experienced as distractive, annoying, or even as frightful by the child rather than as interesting and beneficial. During later stages of development, however, alternations in dialogical interactions are the prerequisite for successful and rapid expansion of the child's communicative skill.

Language originates in the social dialogue between the caretaker and the child. The dialogue is not limited to vocalization but includes the whole network of behavioral and social interactions as well as the changing physical context within which they take place. In the past most investigators of early language development (Braine, 1963; Brown & Bellugi, 1964; Brown & Fraser, 1963, 1964; Miller & Ervin, 1964) studied the spontaneous production by children, taking due account of the adult participants but without elaborating their contributions in detail nor studying the mutual determination of both the child's and the adult's languages. By calling attention to the physical conditions and events that accompany children's speech and often represent the only means for disambiguating ambiguous expressions, Bloom (1970, 1973) extended the frame of reference but still failed to focus upon the dialogical nature of the child's and the mother's interactions by which they jointly construct their developments.

Already during the first three months of life, infants are able to respond differentially to friendly or hostile voices as well as to exaggerated (baby talk) and normal intonation (Lieberman, 1967). Sound production at this age is essentially limited to crying that, according to Bell and Ainsworth (1972), serves communicative functions. Therefore responding to it usually does not lead to more crying but to different kinds of behavior. Consistent with these explorations, Lewis and Freedle (1973) studied the development of the communicative network between the mother and her child beginning a few weeks after birth.

Lewis and Freedle recorded the mother's and the child's activities in natural interactive situations and analyzed contingent verbal and nonverbal behaviors. In all instances, the vocalizing–vocalizing contingency was strongest regardless of whether the mother or the child initiated the interaction. However, their communication consisted of more than just vocalizations.

> A mother's smile may follow or a mother's look may precede an infant's vocalization. Likewise an infant's smile may follow or an infant's cry may precede a mother's vocalization. The network is a complex web wherein the repertoire of each member actively interacts with the other. Vocalizations (infant and mother) therefore may not be the only relevant data in understanding the unfolding process of meaning and language acquisition [1973, p. 28].

The development of the dialogue between a mother and her child depends heavily on shared extralingual knowledge, actions, and emotions. Shortly after birth the necessary synchronization of their activities is determined by their joint physiology which, though disrupted, continues for a while to function in unison (like Leibniz' perfectly synchronized clocks). But temporal coordination will increasingly depend upon the mother's and the child's experience and selective actions. After just a few weeks the child's and the mother's operations have already become finely tuned to one another. The child, let's say her son, begins to look at the mother's face; when she moves, he follows her with his eyes. Most important, when she speaks, he might look at her mouth; when she stops speaking, he might vocalize and switch his attention from her mouth to her eyes. Supportive evidence for these interpretations has been provided by investigations of social interactions (Jaffe, Stern, & Peary, 1973; Kaye, 1976a, 1976b; Moss, 1967; Rheingold, 1961; Sameroff, 1975).

Early in life the dialogues between mother and child are bound to be out of balance. Like the experienced musician, the mother has at her disposal a large repertoire of signs, rules, topics, and roles. The child has virtually none of these acquired forms of communication available. Thus the mother will have to be highly restrictive in her interactions with the child; she retreats to the mode of "primitive" dialogues. Only on a few occasions does she engage in directed attempts of naming objects or giving instructions to the child. Most of the time and independent of her conscious interactive efforts, she will talk and sing along, and eventually the child will follow her activities and participate in them.

In analyzing the acquisition of speech sounds, Baldwin (1895) observed that the child utters a great variety of sounds, some corresponding, others outside of the phonemic range of the adult's language. Either incidentally or by intent, these sounds might signal information to the adult who, in turn, selectively interprets the utterances of the child. Thus a rather diffuse sequence of sounds might be reinterpreted and reuttered as MAMA. The child listening to this modified feedback will make his own production congruent with it. Although limited in scope and quite rationalistic in its interpretation, Baldwin recognized clearly the interactive basis of language and language development.

Synchronization

The sign system shared between mother and child is at first private to both of them. As development advances, more signs become congruent with those used in the linguistic community. In this development, the mother functions as an intermediary between her child and society.

Thus the developmental dialogue is more than an exchange between two individuals. Through the mediation of the mother, society and history participate in the dialogue. Likewise in a nondevelopmental dialogue, let's say between two adult speakers, each of them may represent a particular societal group with its particular assumptions, preferences, and goals. Communication between the two speakers is possible only because both of them and the groups which they represent are part of the same larger society and, thus, share a common and more fundamental communication system.

The remote interactions between authors and their readers have been described in a similar manner in recent investigations by Marxist structuralists (see Fieguth, 1973; Mao Tse-Tung, 1968; Riegel, 1975b; Schmid, 1973). The authors' performances are not merely dependent upon their personal feelings and knowledge but are also determined by the values and ideas of the reader in contemporary society as developed from the cultural history and reflected in the philosophy and ideology. The authors' task consists in transmitting to the reader the values and ideas that have been generated in the society. The authors' task is achieved through the authors' participatory efforts in cultural history. Thus the author, like the mother, functions as an intermediary between the knowledge-seeking individuals and the values and ideas of the society.

Most important in the authors' as well as in the mothers' task is the synchronization of their efforts with those of the readers and the children, respectively. Neither the readers nor the children should be overburdened or underburdened. Information has to be given at the right moment, in the right amount, and of the right kind. This is achieved in dialogical interactions with the information seeker. The authors may become too abstract and remote; they may progress too fast or lag behind. The mother, in a more concrete sense, has to speak as she tries to influence her child, but she has also to listen and change her own activities in accordance with the development of her child. Here, more than in the author's case, the synchronization of two time sequences, that is, the development of the child and the development of the mother, is of central importance. This process of synchronization is the most important issue in any developmental description and theory.

The Social Nature of Dialogues

Investigators influenced by the theory of transformational grammar disregarded the significance of parental speech in language development. They assigned no more significance to it than the role of providing linguistic material which could be used by children to test their own hypotheses about languages. This argument was based on the belief—introduced by Chomsky (1957)—that adult speech is too ungrammatical to enable the child to learn the language from it. As McNeill stated (1966), adult speech to children is a "random, haphazard sample, in no way contrived to instruct a child on grammar (p. 173)." Rather than recognizing that such observations provide a decisive argument against their claim for the significance of grammar in language learning, the transformationists retained their preference for such an interpretation by naively postulating the unlearned availability or "innateness" of grammatical properties.

For a considerable period of time the observational basis of such viewpoints has been severely criticized. For example Labov (1970) stated:

> The ungrammaticality of every speech appears to be a myth with no basis in actual fact. In the various empirical studies that we have conducted, the great majority of utterances—about 75%—are well-formed sentences by any criterion. When rules of ellipsis are applied, and certain universal editing rules to take care of stammering and false starts, the proportion of truly ungrammatical and ill-formed sentences falls to less than 2% [p. 42].

Both Waterson (1971) and Halliday (1973) agree with this conclusion.

Although it has been recognized that during early development the language of the mothers or caretakers changes as much as, or even more than, the language of their children, almost all investigators have focused their attention upon the isolated child. Within the research tradition initiated by Roger Brown, however, some explorations of the influence of adult language upon children have been made by Cazden (1965). Brown, Cazden, and Bellugi-Klima (1969) have systematized some possible types of interactions in the following manner:

First, if a child utters an incomplete sentence the adult may *expand* it:

Child: *Dog barking*
Adult: *The dog is barking.*

It is not certain, of course, whether children using such utterances apprehend the modification introduced by the adult. If children react to the adult's statement, they rarely include the expanded material (Ervin-Tripp (1964); they rather reproduce their original utterance, often in a still more reduced form. Their failure to expand is related to their failure to imitate. According to Slobin (1968), children do not imitate more than they produce spontaneously. Only function words are occasionally added and new grammatical forms might appear first in imitation. For example, the child might delete the definite article from the adult's expanded utterance and say "dog is barking."

Second, adults may *model* the child's statements, that is, respond as in a conversation without repeating much of what the child has said:

> Child: *Dog barking*
> Adult: *He must be hungry.*

Modeling represents an important though incomplete case of a dialogical exchange. For an understanding of the adult's statement, a transfer from the noun to the pronoun has to take place. If a child succeeds in doing so by adding another utterance, for example "dog hungry", the dialogical unit will be closed (see Table 5.1). Thereby the child will have reached a higher level of performance.

Third, *echoing* occurs when the adult requests some clarification:

> Child: *I ate the XXX*
> Adult: *You ate the what?*
> Child: *Cookie.*

Echoing involves a longer sequence than expanding or modeling. Although echoing might include a complete dialogical unit, it often remains uncertain whether children relate their last to their first utterance. Table 5.1 shows an example in which dialogical closure is not yet achieved.

Fourth, in *prompting*, as in echoing, the adult requests some additional information. This interaction represents a focused form of questioning for eliciting specific answers:

> Adult: *What did you eat?*
> Child: (no reply)
> Adult: *You ate what?*
> Child: *Cookie.*

Prompting represents a fairly long, though not complete, dialogical sequence. It remains incomplete because the child fails at first to respond to the adult's question. In comparison to echoing, prompting, as represented in Table 5.1, is initiated by the adult.

Brown (1973) combined the last two forms of interactions under the heading "occasional questioning." Ervin-Tripp (1970), likewise, has added the form of "question and response" to the list of techniques by

TABLE 5.1
Simple Patterns of Linguistic Exchanges

Description	Structure	Example
Expansion	M over C_1—C_2	C_1: DOG BARKING M: YES, THE DOG IS BARKING C_2: DOG IS BARKING
Modeling	M over C_1—C_2	C_1: DOG BARKING M: YES, HE IS VERY UNHAPPY C_2: DOG IS UNHAPPY
Echoing	M_1—M_2 over C_1, C_2	C_1: I ATE XXX M_1: YOU ATE WHAT? C_2: COOKIE M_2: YOU ATE A COOKIE
Prompting[a]	M_1—M_2—M_3 over C_1, C_2	M_1: WHAT DID YOU EAT? C_1: (no reply) M_2: YOU ATE WHAT? C_2: COOKIE M_3: YOU ATE A COOKIE
Summons–Reply	M_1—M_2 over C	M_1: JOHN C: YES M_2: LUNCH IS READY
Question–Answer	M_1 over C_1—C_2	C_1: WHERE IS MY COAT? M_1: WHERE DID YOU PUT IT? C_2: I DON'T KNOW

[a]The prompting paradigm is frequently used by parents to induce a question–answer dialogue. For example, M_1: WHERE IS THE BALL? C_1: (no reply). M_2: HERE IS THE BALL. C_2: BALL.

which some adults make their children produce answers and by which they try to induce question-answer strategies upon them. All of these interrogative frames play a decisive role in the developmental differentiation of dialogues.

Developmental Levels in Early Dialogues

In summarizing the development of dialogues, several levels of interactions will be proposed. This interpretation assumes—as McLaughlin (1963) has assumed in his description of cognitive development—that the child will operate with an increasingly larger number of relations at one and the same time and thus, will become able to engage in dialogical exchanges of greater and greater complexity. When we focus upon the details of the dialogical structures, the addition of a single relationship constitutes a qualitative leap in development. But when average results are obtained for several children and/or for several situations, these stages will disappear and a smooth developmental curve will be obtained. In the following summary the focus is upon the detailed structures of the dialogue. For simplicity this description is limited to the interactions between mother and child, and furthermore, all relations intrinsic to the mother's operations will be disregarded.

At Level O only prelingual relations are operative. The child "looks" at the mother attentively (rather than merely "seeing" her) but does not yet follow her with the eyes as she moves away (Piaget, 1950). Soon afterwards such an interactive tracing begins to take place (see Table 5.2).

Level 1 is characterized by a single demand on the part of the child or the mother. Unless the mother's request results in a physical movement or a verbal reply, it remains uncertain whether the child comprehended the instruction. If such an action is performed by the child, a simple string of social actions results which would meet already the standard of the next higher level of dialogical interactions. If, on the other hand, the child initiated the action by its demand, it can be safely assumed that the mother will have comprehended the child's request.

At Level 2 two relations are combined. The outcome could either be the monological chaining of two relations, a binary exchange in the form of a summons (from the mother to the child followed by a reply) or an appeal (from the child to the mother followed by her reply).

Level 3 performance includes the basic dialogical unit composed of three relations. The other two configurations consist of strings, one initiated by the child and the other by the mother in which the utterances alternate between the two participants. Since the analysis of these exchanges does not indicate the cumulative retention of information beyond each of the preceding utterances by the mother, they do not fulfill the minimal requirement for a dialogue, that is, they do not incorporate a dialogical unit.

Performances at Levels 4 and 5 do not necessarily result in complete dialogical exchanges. However, this deficiency is merely due to the omission of the mother's intrinsic dialogical relations from Table 5.2. If these relations are added, the incomplete dialogues, shown for Level 4, would consist of two dialogical units that are either initiated by the mother or by the child. At Level 5 the dialogical interactions incorporate one unit, and at Level 6 two dialogical units based upon the child's utterances are incorporated. If the intrinsic relational connections were also indicated

TABLE 5.2
Developmental Levels of Dialogical Relations

| | Relations | | | | |
| | Receptive | Productive | | | |
Level			Description	Structure	Examples
Prelingual events					
0A	0	0(1)	Looking	M with dashed C	"Looking instead of seeing"
0B	0	0(2)	Following	$M_1 \cdots C \cdots M_2$	"Making an interesting sight last"
Monadic events					
1A	1	0	Demand	M — C	M: SIT DOWN C: (sits down)
1B	0	1	Demanding	M — C	C: COOKIE M: (hands out a cookie)
Diadic strings					
2A	0	2	Monologue	C_1—C_2—C_3	C_1: HERE CAR C_2: HERE TRUCK C_3: HERE AIRPLANE
2B	1	1	Summons	M_1—M_2 with C	M_1: PETER C: YES M_2: (hands him a cookie)
2C	1	1	Appeal	M	C_1: COOKIE M: HERE IS ONE

exchanges

	Code			Type	Dialogue
					M: WHAT DO YOU WANT?
					C_2: COOKIE
	3B	2	1	Other-initiated exchange	M_1: HERE IS YOUR COAT
					C_1: PETER'S COAT
					M_2: PUT IT ON
					C_2: PUT ON
	3C	1	2	Self-initiated exchange	C_1: COAT
					M_1: PUT YOUR COAT ON
					C_2: WHERE GOING?
					M_2: WE ARE GOING TO THE STORE
Tetradic half-dialogues	4A	3	1	Other-initiated half-dialogue	M_1: PUT YOUR COAT ON
					C_1: WHAT COAT?
					M_2: YOUR RAINCOAT
					C_1: RAINCOAT
	4B	2	2	Self-initiated half-dialogue	C_1: MAMA
					M_1: WHAT DO YOU WANT?
					C_2: COOKIE
					M_2: HERE IS ONE
Simple dialogues	5	3	2	Other-initiated dialogue	M_1: WHERE IS YOUR COAT?
					C_1: UPSTAIRS
					M_2: GO AND GET IT
					C_2: GET IT
					M_3: WATCH YOUR STEPS
	6	4	2	Self-initiated dialogue	C_1: MAMA
					M_1: WHAT DO YOU WANT?
					C_2: COOKIE
					M_2: HERE IS ONE
					C_3: 'NOTHER ONE

(continued)

TABLE 5.2 (*continued*)

	Relations				
Level	Receptive	Productive	Description	Structure	Examples
Complex dialogues					
7	5	2	Complex dialogue		C_1: COOKIE M_1: NO, YOU CAN'T HAVE A COOKIE BEFORE LUNCH C_2: HUNGRY M_2: WE WILL BE EATING SOON C_3: LUNCH SOON
8	6	2	Complex dialogue		C_1: COOKIE M_1: NO, YOU CAN'T HAVE A COOKIE BEFORE LUNCH C_2: HUNGRY M_2: WE WILL BE EATING SOON C_3: LUNCH COOKIE

for the mother and not only for the child, a simple dialogical truss would result.

The last qualitative shift in dialogues is produced at Level 7. Here, relational connections begin to reach farther back than to the last two utterances (one by the child, the other by the mother). After Level 7, the complexity and depth of the dialogue continues to increase further, but no additional structural shifts can be inferred on the basis of the methodology proposed. It is safe to assume, however, that dialogues at the adult level reach far back into the dialogical sequence and frequently pick up information that has been exchanged on much earlier and often disconnected dialogical occasions.

Conclusions

The study of dialogues represents a concrete case of the investigation of dialectical development and change. It is concrete because it lends itself to observations and detailed descriptions (see footnote 1). The study of dialectical development and change represents the more general case which is not limited to communicative exchanges based on language. Like the study of dialogues, a dialectical interpretation analyses changes both on a situational or short-term basis as well as on a developmental or long-term basis. These changes are interactively determined by at least two temporal sequences which—in terms of the general classification introduced in Chapter 1—represent either inner-biological, individual-psychological, cultural–sociological, or outer-physical progressions. Short-term changes and long-term developments result from the synchronization of any two and indirectly of all of these progressions. Taken separately these sequences are mere abstractions.

A dialectical interpretation of development and change does not emphasize stages or plateaus at which equilibrium is achieved. Development and change rather consist in continuing modifications. Critical leaps occur whenever two sequences are in conflict, that is when coordination fails and synchrony breaks down. These conflicting or contradictory conditions are the fundamental basis for development and change. Stable plateaus of balance, stability, and equilibrium occur when a developmental or historical task is completed. But developmental and historical tasks are never completed. At the very moment when completion seems imminent, new questions and doubts arise in the individual and society. The organism, the individual, the society, and even outer nature are never at rest, and in their restlessness they are rarely in perfect synchrony.

Synchronization denotes a balance structured in time (Riegel, 1977) which can be understood only if the state of imbalance is taken into consideration at the same moment. Balance and imbalance determine each other, and their relationship changes continuously. In this sense a dialectical interpretation of development and change is comparable to orchestral compositions. If there were only two instruments and if both were always playing in unison, they would merely increase the sound volume of the melody. Orchestral arrangements are built upon synchronized deviations which allow different instruments to interlace the theme in a multifarious manner.

Temporal structures of dialogues, likewise, are generated by the agreements and disagreements found in linguistic exchanges, but they are commonly codetermined by other conditions at the cultural–sociological or outer-physical level. The dialogue between a mother and her child, for example, might be initiated, facilitated, restricted, and/or terminated by events that take place as both leave the room, go down the staircase, and enter the street. Temporal structures at the cultural–sociological level often appear as "objective" or "normative" constraints to the single individual or to the dialogue partners. The most important of these constraints is the concept and measurement of time iteself that, like meter and rhythm in music, imposes conditions upon the producer and the listener which appear as firm, objective, and absolute to them. Creative advances in history have always shown, however, that a break with these traditions is not only possible but often necessary in order to deepen our understanding of language development and change (see Riegel, 1977).

6

The Recollection of the Individual and Collective Past

If you were to ask a young man about his own development, he would probably present a story like the following one: He was born in a small town in Illinois where his father was an accountant. He has one sister and two brothers with whom he got along, except for occasional squabbles. His friend, Jack, lived next door and entered elementary school with him. His first teacher was awful, and the later ones were not much better. So he was glad when he entered Junior High. The next year his friend moved away, but he had, by now, several other good companions. The following year his family moved into a new house, and a year later his father lost his job. He is now attending the last year of High School and has already been accepted at an Engineering College. He plans to go on to Graduate School and to move to a bigger city.

Surprisingly, developmental psychologists have rarely if ever explored these retrospective memories and the prospective hopes that, nevertheless, everyone brings to bear when they think about their own past and acts in the future. Instead, developmental psychologists have preferred to study abstract performances, attitudes, or behaviors that, more likely than not, are of little concern to the individuals who are constantly reviewing their own growth of activities—the changes of situations and their plans for the future. Developmental psychologists have failed to recognize that most objectified performances and products are experientially empty for the individuals and determined by their lived and experienced past. Developmental psychologists have also disregarded that all individuals, here and now, live with this knowledge all the time; they may care little about their performance and behavior unless understood within the context of their experienced past.

Historians, on the other hand, rely on recollections of the interpreted past. Of course, their attempts are much more systematic than those of common individuals who are casually searching through their memories or retrieving their experiences. Historians will utilize whatever means available, such as archives, books, treatises, documents, and advice by other experts, in order to reconstruct the past as accurately and comprehensively as possible. While they attempt to improve the precision of their reports, these efforts are hampered because the events to be reconstructed and interpreted are rarely experienced by the historians themselves, but are made known to them through the mediation of other historians. The source material may have been transmitted over long chains which threaten the authenticity of the reports to the same extent in which the abstractness of psychological variables distorts the meaningfulness of developmental interpretations.

Having thus sharply contrasted the approach used by historians with that preferred by developmental psychologists, we ought to recognize that transgressions have been made and combinations have been sought. Historians have encouraged the use, whenever possible, of objectified data as collected by archivists and actuaries. The historical methodology on the other hand, has been extensively applied in clinical studies and treatments. In particular, psychoanalytical explorations attempt to reconstruct persons' lives in order to detect major choice points at which fateful turns were taken and, thereby, to enable the patients to reprocess their lives in a different and, hopefully, more successful manner (see, Erickson, 1968; Riegel, 1973d; Wyatt, 1962, 1963). By restricting the analyses to particular cases, these explorations lack the cross-individual and cross-social systematizations that developmental psychologists are aiming for. The following inquiries into the past of individuals and of society attempt to reach such levels of generality.

Developmental Recollections

The method on which much of the following interpretations are based is exceedingly simple (see Riegel, 1973a, 1973b). It consists of asking persons, usually in groups, to write down past events or, in the cases to be reported here, the names of persons which they can re-member within a limited time period. In one of the present studies, 26 undergraduate students in psychology at the University of Michigan, 18 males and 8 females, ranging in age from 19 to 25 years (average age 20.8 years), wrote down as many names of persons they had met during their lifetime (relatives, friends, acquaintances) as they could recall dur-ing a 6-minute period. The students marked the end of each one minute interval by a line and were allowed to use any abbreviations as long as they were able to identify the persons thus denoted. After the comple-tion of the task, they indicated the year at which they had met for the first time each of the persons reported and marked—if listed—their own mother, father, sisters, and brothers. Furthermore, they recorded their sex, birthdate, the years during which they attended various types of schools, and the names and the years of birth of their sisters and brothers.

Figure 6.1 shows the average number of persons recalled as a func-tion of successive school years. Since the students differed somewhat in age, school rather than chronological ages were used in this comparison. In a few cases some years had to be discarded, especially between high school and college, but by and large, the 26 records could be aligned without any difficulties within an age span of 21 years.

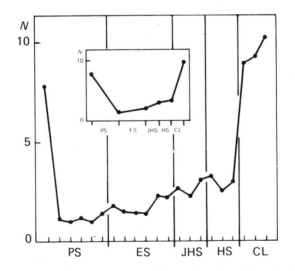

Figure 6.1. Average number of persons recalled as a function of time (in school years) of first acquaintance. Preschool (PS); Elementary School (ES); Junior High School (JHS); High School (HS); College (CL).

The results resemble a serial position curve in which the serial order represents the students' school age. Recency had a strong effect, that is, persons met late in life were recalled much more often than those met earlier. A primacy effect was also revealed, that is, persons met during the first year of life were recalled more often than those met during the intermediate years.

In analyzing recall strategies, two possibilities were studied: *clustering* and *recapitulation* (and its counterpart: regression). *Clustering* was determined by enumerating the differences in years of adjacently recalled persons. A zero-difference represents the strongest clustering and means that the two persons recalled were met within the same year. A total of 768 zero-differences were observed. The largest observed difference equaled 21 years but occurred only three times. If there had been perfect zero-clustering, that is, if all persons met within specific years were recalled within separate blocks, the total possible number of zero-differences would amount to the total number of responses, 1813, minus the average age of the students, 21, minus 1. (The latter figure, 20, represents the average number of transitions from year to year in the average length of the students' lives.) The number of observed over the number of possible zero-differences was found to be 43.9%. If, on the other hand, the recall of the 1813 persons had been completely random, there would be $1813^2 = 3,286,969$ possible combinations of names and $\Sigma a_i^2 = 275,354$ zero-differences, where a equals the average number of persons recalled within year i. Dividing the latter figure by the former indicates that 8.6% zero-differences could have occurred by chance combination. Since the observed percentage of 43.9 is far above this figure, a strong clustering effect by years of acquaintance was confirmed.

The *recapitulation* strategy (and its counterpart, the regression strategy) was tested by computing the median years of first acquaintance for the persons recalled in the successive 6 minutes of the recall period. As shown in Table 6.1, the median years for the first 2 minutes are low, thus suggesting the prevalence of the recapitulation strategy. But the changes over the remaining 4 minutes are rather irregular and were found to be insignificant. Therefore neither the recapitulation nor the regression strategy seems to be prevalent. However, additional support comes from an analysis of the recall of members of the immediate family: 73.1% of the students listed their own parents. Always, either both or neither of the parents were recalled. Since the mother (or the father) appears as the first response 19.2%, and during the first minute (including the first response) 53.8% of the time, whereas only 19.3% listed a

TABLE 6.1
Average Number of Persons and of Historical Figures Recalled and Median Years at
Which They Were Met for the First Time or at Which They Made Their Major
Contributions, Listed for Six Successive Minutes of Recall

	Minutes					
	First	Second	Third	Fourth	Fifth	Sixth
Persons	18.6	11.8	11.3	12.0	11.4	11.4
Years	1962	1962	1964	1962	1964	1963
Historical figures	12.8	8.1	7.7	7.4	7.2	6.4
Years	1840	1860	1850	1888	1825	1918

parent's name during the remaining 5 minutes, support for a limited
version of the recapitulation hypothesis is provided. Apparently the students, at the very beginning of the task, use this strategy but soon after
rely on clustering as an aid for recall. In addition, large sex differences
were observed. Males recall their parents 83.3% of the time, females only
50.0%. The females always named the mother first (100%); the males
chose randomly the mother (53.3%) or the father (46.7%) as the first
parent recalled. Siblings are named 90.0% by boys and 85.7% by girls.

The results of Figure 6.1 led to a hypothetical reconstruction of the
conditions under which individuals grow up. Two parameters were considered: The rate of physical-psychological mobility, α_i, at which an
individual explores his environmental possibilities, and the increases in
the environmental potential, a_i, denoted by the number of new persons
that enter into the life of an individual at various times.

As shown in Figure 6.2, an individual, born at time t_0, is being
exposed to a social environment with a_0 persons (parents, siblings,
friends, neighbors). During the early years the rate of physical-
psychological mobility, α_0, is rather small. The child is bound to the
immediate environment of his/her home and to the stimulation provided
there. During the following years, when the child is entering the various
types of school, successive expansions occur. Instead of staying close to
the home, he/she explores the block, visits the schoolmates, and travels
through the neighborhood, the town, and the country. While the rate of
mobility increases with age (α_i to α_n), the opportunity for social interaction also expands in ever bigger steps (a_1 to a_n). At first, in the
nursery or kindergarten, the child finds itself among other children.
The group size increases from the elementary to the junior and senior

high school. The high school graduates enter college with several hundred or thousands of other freshmen, all of whom they can potentially meet.

Figure 6.2 depicts the changes in the social possibilities of—what one might call—the "official child" regulated by educational policies and laws. Aside from this role, the growing individuals are exposed to various other social contingencies. They might engage, for instance, in religious, political, recreational, and occupational activities. Each of these settings provides for other, partially independent expansions. In conjunction, these settings will smooth the step-wise curve of Figure 6.2 and are likely to transform it into an exponential function, $y = 2^x + a_0$, that has been suggested as one potential model for historical growth [called a *branch structure model* (see Riegel, 1969)].

My discussion of the environmental potential for social interactions does not consider factors that restrict further growths during adulthood and old age. However, an interpretation of the recall process of the first study needs to emphasize that the experience of any event or person is subjected to forgetting. Utilizing one of the simplest interpretations possible, I propose that the decay or dropout from memory will be linear and that at a particular point in time the number of persons recalled will amount to 50% of those encountered at any point earlier in life. This point, measured in years, might be called the *half-life* of the specific experience to be recalled.

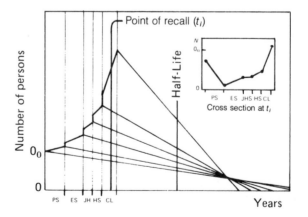

Figure 6.2. Model of the expansion of the social environment during school years and the recall of persons during the life span. Preschool (PS); Elementary School (ES); Junior High School (JHS); High School (HS); College (CL).

Figure 6.2 shows several forgetting lines originating at those points in time at which individuals enter new educational settings. Extrapolating these lines beyond the half-life provides for an inference congruent with "Ribot's law" that states that items learned last during the period of growth are forgotten first; childhood experiences are best retained, adulthood experiences least. More important for our present considerations, the free recall task of our students can be represented by the cross-section at t_i, indicated by a heavy vertical line in Figure 6.2. If we plot in a nonaccumulative manner the average numbers of persons predicted to be recalled by our students at t_i, we obtain the curve shown in the upper section of Figure 6.2. This curve is closely similar in form to the empirical data plotted in the upper section of Figure 6.1.

Undoubtedly the proposed model oversimplifies the growth of the social interaction potential and, especially, the forgetting process. For a more sophisticated model we might substitute the forgetting lines by Ebbinghaus' forgetting curves. Or we might replace the second stipulation on the half-life of experiences by the notion that only those persons will be retained in memory who are "related" to other persons encountered earlier and already incorporated into the memory structure of personal relations. The later a person enters into the cognitive–social structure of another individual, the less likely it will be that he/she becomes intimately connected. For instance, the members of the immediate family enter early and over a long period of time into the cognitive–social structure of an individual; later in life, for instance at college, hundreds of persons may enter, but only very few will become intimately connected to the structure or are introduced to his/her long-term friends and family. While the analysis of the clustering and the specific version of the recapitulation hypothesis provides some supportive evidence, supplementary information on the social interactions at various developmental levels (e.g., through sociometric studies) would be desirable.

My discussion served the purpose of contrasting "subjective" retrospective recall data with those that might have been obtained through "objective" face-value inquiries into social contingencies and their changes with the age of persons. The suggested mechanisms for forgetting and retrieval together with the interpretations on the changes of the social environment with the age of individuals predicted the observed recall surprisingly well. Therefore, it seems justified to make some comparisons between the flow of psychological and chronological time. Such an analysis will be based on another study in which individuals from three different age groups were engaged in the same task described above.

Age Differences

Twenty subjects each from three consecutive generations wrote down as many names of persons as they could recall during a 10-minute session. Most members of the youngest group (average age = 23.1 years) belonged to the same kin; the middle group (average age = 50.0 years) included their parents, aunts, and uncles; the oldest group (average age = 73.3 years) included their grandparents, grandaunts, and granduncles. Increasingly from the youngest to the oldest generation, the groups had to be supplemented by persons unrelated to the kin. After the completion of the recall task, the individuals listed behind each name the years at which they had met these persons for the first time.

An analysis of the results is shown in Figure 6.3. Here, the ordinate indicates the number of persons recalled. The abscissa indicates the years at which these persons were met for the first time. Since the aver-

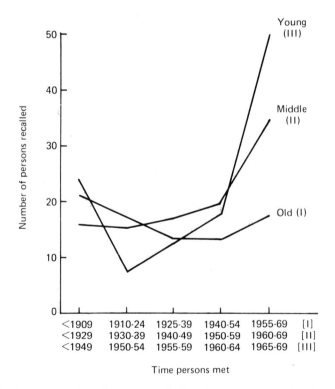

Figure 6.3. Average number of persons recalled by three age groups, plotted against time of first acquaintance.

age age of the three groups, I, II, and III, were related in ratios of about 3:2:1, the scales were compressed accordingly. Thus, along the abscissa, three different age scales are used.

As in the preceding study, the youngest group (III) shows a very strong recency effect and a less strong primacy effect; the curve is J-shaped and the data points are almost bisected by the influence of these two factors. The middle group (II) reveals a strong recency effect, but the primacy effect has disappeared; the curve has the shape of an inverted L. For the oldest group (I), the primacy effect reappears slightly, while the recency effect has almost disappeared; the curve resembles a straight line. Thus, in their retrospective perception the oldest individuals attend to all five time periods most evenly; the names of persons recalled are almost equally spread over the individuals' full age range. The retrospections of the middle-aged group as well as those of the youngest group are dominated by persons recently met. The youngest group also pays considerable attention to persons encountered very early in life.

According to these results, retrospective perception varies with age. If we consider the number of persons recalled per chronological time period as an index for the intensity of time experience, we would have to conclude that psychological time flows faster for the young and the middle-aged individuals the closer the period recalled is to the time of testing. The further backward in time these individuals go in their search for names, the more often events and persons seem to have faded away. The oldest individuals, however, live more intensely with their intermediate and their remote past; compared to the young and middle aged, recently met persons are of lesser significance. Young individuals split their attention between the very early and the very late periods of their lives; the intermediate years are experienced with low intensity; time seems to flow slower here.

All these interpretations are based upon subjective recall scores. Since the number of persons recalled will also be a function of the number of persons met, and since this number, as I have already shown in the preceding study, might vary systematically with the age of the individuals, the present data and interpretations need to be supplemented by "objective" records of changes in the social environment over the life span, more specifically, in the number of new persons encountered during the course of life.

In summary, my interpretations attempted to show how we might reconstruct the cognitive–social development of individuals and match it against their recall of past events. In the following study I will extend this comparison to the study of historical growth.

Historical Recollections

While I did not elaborate in detail the psychological determinants which transform and explain the relationships between the "objective" records and the individuals' recollections, with sufficient persistence these transformation matrices could be successfully derived. The pre-requisite for their analysis—as I have shown—consists of information about the expansion of the sociophysical environments of the developing individuals and not only an inventory taken at one time. In contrast to psychology, the derivation of transformation matrices is either not possible at all in historical studies or only in a very limited sense. The events and the time periods which most historians explore lie far back in the past. Objectified documentation is available on a selective basis only and, in most cases, has passed through the hands of many generations of intervening or interfering participants. If the methods and data of developmental psychologists could help us to explore the transformational processes through which information is changed and could help us to reconstruct those portions which might have been lost in the course of their transformations, important inferences about the process and fallacies of historical reconstruction might be drawn. Some of these implications have been discussed in recent attempts to develop mathematical models of development and history (see Goffman, 1966; Kochen, 1969; Rashevsky, 1968; Riegel, 1969, 1976b; van den Daele, 1969). Rather than describing these possibilities in abstract terms, the following study demonstrates some of the problems which I am trying to clarify.

I asked three groups of American students (freshmen, seniors, and graduates) to write down in 10 minutes the names of historical figures influential in military, political, or governmental affairs. The results, shown in Figure 6.4, reveal some striking similarities and differences to those on the recall of personal acquaintances shown in Figure 6.1. First, we find again a strong recency effect by obtaining the names of a large number of political figures who entered history less than a few months prior to the study. Second, the primacy effect has almost completely disappeared. The earliest accumulation of names occurs for the time of the American Revolution, most notably because of the frequent listing of George Washington. The absence of a steep early accumulation is easily understandable because history lacks an initition or zero point comparable to the birth of the recalling subject. American students compensate for this lack by considering arbitrarily the appearance of George Washington as the beginning of history, the "birth of a nation." Third, Figure 6.4 shows the occurrence of sharp spikes, the first representing

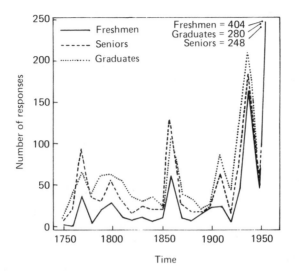

Figure 6.4. Number of persons influential in political, military, and governmental affairs, named by three groups of 30 students each, during 10-minute periods.

the time of the American Revolution, the others coinciding regularly with major catastrophies, the outbreaks of wars. It is this issue that should attract further attention.

The view of history as a progression of catastrophies raises some doubts about the validity of such historical constructions. Although one would readily admit that the names recalled are to be considered in their symbolic values, that is, they stand for the actions and deeds performed by the persons named, it is more important to recognize that we ought to accept the names listed by the students in the way they are given, not because they describe history as it "really" was. Rather, they reflect, in one way or another, the students' view of the historical past. Only this is of interest for our present purpose as well as for the purpose of any historical description. There may very well be other aspects to history which, eventually, need to be explored, but as long as these are not revealed through historical perceivers, they are of no value for debate.

For further explorations, I compared the records of the American students by their degree of education and, presumably, their historical knowledge (freshmen, seniors, and graduates). I expected that the more advanced students would show the spiking effect less strongly and would fill the gaps between the spikes more evenly with the names of historical figures not engaged in warfare and uprisings. Unfortunately, this expectation was not clearly confirmed. Although the spikes of the graduate students' records are less marked and although one of the most formative periods in American history, the period at the beginning of the nineteenth century, is more evenly filled with names of historical figures, the differences between the student groups were not strong enough to provide convincing support for this expectation.

Next I asked two other groups of American students to list important persons in the areas of music, literature, and painting, hoping that I would obtain a similar distribution of names over historical time as observed for the political leaders shifted, however, by one-half phase. In other words, I expected the peaks of the former task to coincide with the valleys of the present task. As shown in Figure 6.5, these expectations were, again, not clearly confirmed. When inspecting the distributions of the names of musicians and painters, distinct peaks were observed for historical periods intermediate between wars, that is, 1870, 1880, and 1920, thus confirming the distributional shift interpretation. For writers, however, large accumulations of names occur at 1810, 1860, and 1940, that is, at periods of military instability. Of course, the latter group includes political and historical writers whose activities might coincide

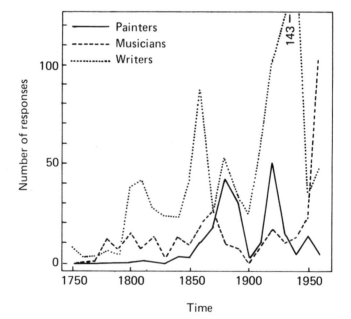

Figure 6.5. Number of persons influential in painting, music, and literature, named by 30 seniors during a 10-minute period.

with periods of tensions and wars. Moreover, many of the different paint-ers, musicians, and writers listed are from countries other than the United States and their activities extend beyond the national events and boundaries. At least in regard to the wars of the nineteenth century, they are less clearly influenced by the disturbances and changes in priorities brought about in this country.

After my first two attempts provided some suggestions but no defi-nite conclusions regarding either selective biases in the recollection of historical names as a function of educational levels or the distributional shift as a function of military–political versus artistic–scientific domina-tions, I finally analyzed the most likely source of these biases, namely, the professional writing of political history. The results of Figure 6.6 were obtained from an analysis of an advanced high school book, "A History of the United States," by Alden and Magenis (1962).

Figure 6.6 shows the number of lines given to each of the decades after 1750 in a summary of historical events, as well as the number of pages greater than two on which the names of particular historical fig-ures appeared in the index of the book. The results show more clearly than the listing of the names by the students that the dominant emphasis given by the writers of this book relates to military interventions and wars, rather than to contributions in arts, sciences, education, and wel-

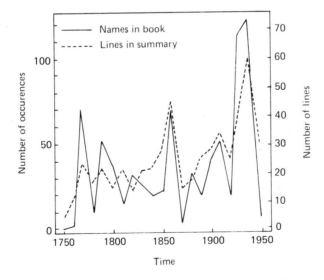

Figure 6.6. Number of lines in a summary of names appearing in a book on American history.

fare. Very marked spikes are observed for the time of the American Revolution, the Civil War, and World Wars I and II.

Historical Interpretations

My comparison—as incomplete as it may be at the present time—reveals some of the general problems of historical inquiry. History is always perceived and interpreted history. In history, we do not know, how it "really" was.

Let us consider the famous example of Caesar crossing the Rubicon during his march on Rome in the year 49 B.C. This event must have been quite accurately reported. After all, if a few days earlier Caesar was found to the north of the river and a few days later to the south, he could not have avoided the crossing unless he made a swing around it either far to the west or to the east through the Adriatic. But regardless of how accurate the "facts" were recorded, the description is insufficient to give them the status of an historical event. Only the interpretation of these steps by the historical perceiver who views them as leading to civil war and to the downfall of the earlier form of Roman government transforms these "facts" into historical events. Perhaps Caesar himself was aware of the potential interpretation. Perhaps later admirers projected this interpretation into the insignificant need of passing a small river in order to reach the destination, while Caesar himself remained unaware of the potential implications of this event. Perhaps the crossing was glorified in much the same way in which Washington's crossing of the Delaware, at a time when his army was in anything but a superb state, was glorified in the famous painting.

Our inability to learn "how it really was in history" should disturb us as little as our failure, according to Kant, to recognize "the thing as such." As shown in Figure 6.7, "history as it really was" is hidden behind a series of interpretive filters provided through the selective preservation of information by archivists, the insufficient scrutiny of scholars, the driving brevity of teachers, and the unchallengeable apathy of students. But even if we were able to look behind all these filters, we would not find what we were hoping for because the events themselves, in their numerosity and in their details are uninteresting to the present-day observer. They are without historical meaning.

Denoting these interpretations as selective filters is misleading, however. A filter presupposes something behind it, something which is

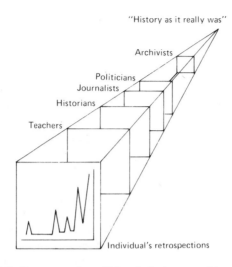

Figure 6.7. Representation of historical schemata of interpretations.

being filtered, but recognized in some of its grosser features. But all that we will find behind an historical filter is another filter and another filter. It might be better, therefore, to compare these selective interpretations with a Sudarium, for example with the holy veil of Saint Veronica, which when laid upon the face of the dying Christ preserved his image forever. Every interpretation derived by looking at or looking through the Sudarium, thereafter, imposed the image of Christ upon the events under concern.

A discussion of filters or Sudaria makes us aware of two alternative views of history. The first insists upon the need for recognizing the "facts" behind historical interpretations. This view has been called "objective." It aims for and depends upon "the historical thing as such" which—it is insisted—makes historical interpretations possible at all. Filters, in this case, select essential issues from unessential details. The other interpretation, which I shall call "constructive," is aware that it can be concerned only with the interpreting Sudaria and their relationships to one another. The systematic study of their transformations and of the invariant properties sustaining these transformations would represent a most advanced study of history or rather of the "science of the science of history," of metahistory.

Developmental Science as Action

With the recognition of the constructive viewpoint, we apprehend the future dimensionality of history. As already observed in the fictitious report of the development of an individual in the introduction, his interpretations are directed by and include wishes, expectations, and hope. Similar implications for historical changes are convincingly demonstrated by the studies described above. If these show that our interpretations of history are dominated by apocalyptic views, emphasizing warfares and catastrophies at the expense of welfare, arts, and sciences, we have also gained insights and access to alternative conceptualizations. By exploring these options, by discussing them with our students, and by presenting them to larger audiences in the form of essays or books, we thereby generate and implement a new Sudarium, a new interpretation of history, a new conception of men and their development. As emphatically claimed by Lynd (1968), the recognition of new interpretations and the awareness of former viewpoints should lead us to implementation or enactment of history. The historian should participate in creating history.

It is perhaps of little surprise that developmental psychologists have shown little appreciation of the forward surge of knowledge. Like the former-day historians, they have continued to restrict their task to the description of "development as it really is." Endless and mostly futile efforts have been invested in the refinement of methodologies and the increasing abstractness of theoretical constructs. Little did developmental psychologists apprehend that the most important part of their concern ought to be the changes in experienced and lived development both from an individual and societal point of view but not the mere description of "objectified" performances across chronological age.

For all too long, psychologists committed themselves to a belief in fixed capacities, such as general intelligence. This view, which has been refuted by Hunt (1961), did not even take developmental changes into account. Developmental psychologists have not kept us waiting, however. Soon, they began to promote their view of a fixed developmental order that was thought to lie beneath all observable changes and was to be detected, like a universal law, through increasingly refined methodologies and controls. This viewpoint too is now being replaced, at least among the students of life-span developmental psychology (Baltes & Schaie, 1973; Datan & Ginsberg, 1975; Goulet & Baltes, 1970; Nesselroade & Reese, 1973), by investigations that take both the development of the individual and that of the society into account. Earlier scholars pretended as if individuals were developing in a fixed social environment if not in a social vacuum.

But these advanced approaches would be as futile as the earlier simplistic investigations, if they were again searching for stable trends or universal developmental laws, now not only residing inside the organism but in the social surroundings as well. True advancement will only come when the sources and determinants of development are sought in the interactions between inner and outer processes. As organisms explore the world through their activities, they, at the same time, generate the world in which they grow. These outer conditions, which in their totality have been created through the ceaseless efforts of mankind, impose themselves, in turn, upon the organism. Development consists in dialectical interactions leading to the emergence and continuous changes of inner and outer structures in mutual determination.

It is at this point where my concluding remarks link up with the introduction. As much as the acquisition of advanced historical awareness begins to change history itself, so will an awareness of one's own development change the course of this development. Rather than apprehending our societal origin and our cultural history by the products generated, the viewpoint promoted here appreciates history by the activities which force it into new directions. Development of individuals, likewise, should no longer be apprehended by the products left behind (such as achievements and test scores) but by the critical awareness of past experiences which remain with the individuals and direct them toward their future. What we desire is neither a history of past failures (that is, catastrophies) nor a developmental psychology of petrified performances (that is, test records) but a science of the development of the individual and society based upon lived experiences and directed actions.

7

Adult Life Crises

Since the time that I was asked to discuss crises in adult life, I have felt uncomfortable about the topic. On the one hand, I cannot deny that incisive crises occur during adulthood and old age. On the other hand, I do not like the pathological and oftentimes fatalistic implications of this term. Searching through my vocabulary, I thought for a while that words such as developmental leaps, critical choice points, or existential challenges might somewhat better describe the condition under concern. Failing to convince myself of the preference for these substitutions, I began to realize that it would be necessary to devote large parts of this chapter to an analysis of the concept of crisis and its underlying philosophical model and ideology.

The concept of crisis is antithetically connected with those of equilibrium, stability, consonance, and balance. The notion of equilibrium as a desirable goal has thoroughly penetrated the thinking of behavioral and social scientists and defines crisis in a negative manner. Thus, the concept of crisis attains meaning as a disequilibrium only when viewed as a long-term condition, as an act of interrupting a state of tranquility, and as the shock of being thrown off-balance when viewed as a short-term imposition. But since contrastive states or events are closely interdependent, the concept of equilibrium cannot be understood without the concept of disequilibrium, and the concept of stability cannot be understood without the concept of crisis. What we ought to search for is not a better apprehension of each of these conditions alone but of their interpenetration. Stability and crisis ought not to be seen as negative and positive but as mutually dependent, though contradictory, conditions that only in their dialectical conjunction make development possible at all.

Contradictions and Development

In Chapter 3 I criticized the equilibrium model of development and, in particular, Piaget's theory as insufficient to account for changes during the life-span. Piaget emphasizes the removal of conceptual contradictions as the child's most essential development task. Similar arguments have been made for moral development by Kohlberg. Young children will be, at first, quite at ease when making contradictory judgments of, for example, the amounts of two clay balls: At one instance they might say that the balls have the same amount; at the next, that they do not have the same amount. But eventually children begin to feel uncomfortable with these contradictions; they experience conflicts. If they succeed in resolving the contradictions in a consistent manner, they lift themselves to the next higher level of cognitive operations, toward a new equilibrium. Finally, when the period of formal operational thought is reached, children's thoughts have become logically consistent, and they cannot be caught easily any longer in making contradictory judgments.

While scientific or scholarly debates among adults may continue to aim at detecting contradictions in the opponent's statements, mature thought and action cannot be based on such academic gamesmanship alone. The mature person achieves a new apprehension of contradictions. Contradictions are no longer regarded as deficiencies that have to be eliminated by rational thinking at all cost but in a confirmative manner as the basic source for all activities. In particular, they form the basis for any innovative and creative work. Adulthood and maturity represent the period in life during which individuals knowingly reappraise the role of formal, that is, noncontradictory thought, and during which they may succeed again (as the young children have unknowingly succeeded in their "primitive dialectics") in accepting contradictions in their thoughts and actions (scientific dialectics).

Crises and Development

The confirmation of contradictions enables us to propose an alternate interpretation of crises. Contradictions, doubts, and inner dialogues represent the very basis of individuals' thoughts and actions. Their social development likewise is founded upon conflicts, diagreements, and debates. Both these inner and outer interactions are functional and beneficial for both the individual's development and for that of the social group. Occasions may arise, of course, where the interactions are blocked or where the opposing forces are so strong that the individuals or the groups are unable to cope with them. Instead of constructive developments they might become subdued and the dialectical interaction thus destroyed. These conditions should be called crises or catastrophes in the narrower sense of these words. They represent pathological deviations from normal development

The normal course of life is partially determined by inner-biological factors that find expression in the normative age-grading system of any society (Neugarten & Datan, 1973). Thus, individuals become ready for leaving their parent's home and establishing their own careers or for marriage and having children. Physical maturation determines the boundaries of these normative events (Neugarten & Datan, 1973). None of them can properly be called crises, and even if they have such implications for the individual, the consequences are predominantly social in nature. Inner-biological crises do occur, however, in the form of accidents or illnesses at any time in the life cycle and in the form of increasing sensorimotor deficiencies during the later years of life. Unless these events lead to gross incapacitations or death, individuals will always attempt—even though their chances for success may not always be very bright—to overcome them through their psychosocial adjustments.

Besides inner-biological determinants, the occurrence of some outer-physical events such as earthquakes, floods, and droughts, may create catastrophes for the individual and society. Most of the efforts of society can be regarded as reactions against such catastrophes, trying to control or at least to predict them and, thereby, to improve the security and welfare of its members. Indeed, events become catastrophes or crises only in their interaction with social groups or individuals. Outer-physical events that strike organisms and, in the extreme, destroy their existence cannot be considered as crises or catastrophes unless they are experienced by the psychological individual or recorded by the sociological group.

As discussed in Chapter 1, the recognition of crises and catastrophes is brought about by the lack of synchronization between some or all of the four major dimensions of progression: (*a*) the inner-biological; (*b*) the individual–psychological; (*c*) the cultural–sociological; and (*d*) the outer-physical. In my discussion, I will focus primarily upon developmental stratifications that are determined by psychological or sociological conditions, rather than by biological or physical factors and their temporal synchronization or lack of it.

Preview

After the general development through the adult years has been described, I will consider the special case of a scientist. This progression is of interest because the scientist's development is closely dependent upon the concurrent development of a social group, representing his particular research orientation or discipline. Distinct developmental stratifications can be described for such a group, first, by determining specific participatory roles for the scientists at different stages in their development and, second, by comparing major revisions brought about through confrontations between various groups representing different paradigmatic orientations in the history of the scientific discipline. The first component determines individual changes in a specific manner, and, thereby, may provoke the occurrence of crises in the individual. The second component affects the groups as a whole and may provoke conflicts or in the extreme case the breakdown of the group. In particular, most individuals affiliate with only one group or paradigmatic orientation during their lifetime and thus benefit during its recognition and suffer during its decline or rejection. Only a few exceptional individuals might actively participate or even initiate the formation of several paradigmatic orientations. The summaries of the life histories of two such persons, Piaget and Wundt, represent almost ideal cases of the structural coordination between individual and societal progressions.

The history of conflicts between different paradigmatic orientations in sciences leads to the discussion of historical progression in general and of its crisis-generating impact upon the individual. As for the scientific paradigms, cultural and political progression is brought about by the sequential effectiveness of various subgroups. Through competition as well as cooperation they exert a dominant influence for limited periods of time only; soon afterwards they are replaced by other subgroups. The model to be presented applies to groups of scientists representing different paradigmatic orientations, to artists representing different styles, to individuals representing different political and economical interests, and to groups of groups, that is, to whole nations and civilizations. But it applies also to different cohorts or generations within any one, and across all, of these social groups. The resulting interactions of age strata and social groupings in their historical progressions determine crises in the development of society. The interactions in the developmental progression of particular individuals with the generational and historial changes in society determine the crises in their personal lives.

Contradictions and Crises in Adult Life

Former Interpretations

Occasionally attempts have been made to describe the progression during adulthood in terms of developmental stages, most often determined by psychosocial factors. These interpretations have frequently imposed an oversystematized order upon the life cycle. Although stages were described in eloquent terms (see, for example, the works by Roger Gould, Daniel Levinson, Gail Sheehy, and George Vaillant), all too often convincing arguments have been lacking on why a particular age span (for example, seven years) should receive exceptional attention and what would trigger the switch into more advanced forms of psychosocial interactions. But in this regard these interpretations are just as fallacious as Piaget's interpretation of the stages and periods of early cognitive development.

One of the earliest attempts to describe the development through the adult years was made by Charlotte Buehler (1933; see also 1968). Relying on biological and psychological investigations, on production and performance records, and most important, on autobiographical and biographical descriptions, Buehler described different styles of progressions and, corresponding to the three types of material used, she distinguished progressions which were dominated by biophysical performances, for example, those by manual workers and athletes, from those that led to productions and achievements, for example, businessmen, scientists, and artists, from those that revealed the contemplative integrations of the philosophers and writers. With a lessened emphasis upon developmental styles, her approach has been applied by Kuhlen (1959, 1964) and is retained in the extensive work by Lehman (1953).

While Buehler's interpretations focused upon differences in the style of developmental progression, one of the best known proposals of developmental stages for the human life span has been made by Erik Erikson (1963). Of the "eight ages of man" described in contrastive pairs, the last three cover adult development and aging.

Basic trust versus mistrust
Autonomy versus shame, doubt
Initiative versus guilt
Industry versus inferiority
Identity versus role confusion
Intimacy versus isolation
Generativity versus stagnation
Ego integrity versus despair

Erikson regards development as being constituted by the interaction of inner and outer forces. The dualistic determination implies

(1) that the human personality in principle develops in steps predetermined in the growing person's readiness to be driven toward, to be aware of, and to interact with, a widening social radius; and (2) that society, in principle, tends to be constituted as to meet and invite this succession of potentialities for interaction and attempts to safeguard and to encourage the proper rate and the proper sequence of their enfolding [1963, p. 270].

But development—it seems to me—remains insufficiently explained by postulating a "predetermined" order of enfolding. We need to know the determinants of the shifts which constitute this order.

In place of such an explanation Erikson introduces the concept of "initial steps" which he elaborates in the following manner:

We claim only that psychological development proceeds by critical steps—'critical' being a characteristic of turning points, of movements of decision between progress and regression, integration and retardation. . . . This indicates (1) that each critical item of psychological strength discussed here is systematically related to all others, and that they all depend on the proper development in the proper sequence of each item; and (2) that each item exists in some form before its critical time normally arrives [1963, p. 270–271].

While all these statements strike a resonable note, they fail to explain why the organism grows and moves from stage to stage; they merely describe a proper order of development.

In summary, Buehler has provided us with the notion of individual styles in the progression through the human life cycle. Erikson has emphasized the interdependence of individual and cultural development, but neither of the two has given us a comprehensive interpretation of why human beings develop and age. Neither the individualistic notions of achievement, power, creativity, and self-actualization, as implied in Buehler's theory (1933, 1968) and elaborated by Kuhlen (1964), nor Erikson's concept of "critical time" and "critical steps" provide sufficient explanations. In contrast to these attempts, the following outline considers the occurrences of asynchronies or crises along four dimensions of progression as causes of development. In addition to individual-psychological and cultural–sociological changes, the lack of synchronization with inner-biological and outer-physical events is regarded as a major determinent of development. Moreover, the occurrence of events along these dimensions will have to be considered in detail, because only such a study can inform us how crises are generated and asynchronies are brought about.

Adult Development

In following the earlier interpretations, a sequence of events can be described, some of which might have crisis character. While the occurrences of the latter can be explicated, we know much less about biological determinants. Since, at the present time, biological shifts can neither be pinpointed nor their sequential order explained with precision, we direct most of our attention to the outer-physical and cultural determinants. Such emphasis has the further advantage in that it might lead to sociological modifications. Although the possibilities for constructive changes have rarely been implemented, their discussion will be directive for future designs and planning.

If we consider various conditions affecting individuals during adult life, we may come up with the list shown in Table 7.1. After leaving school or college, individuals may enter their first occupational career, be drafted, or get married. While the attainment of an occupational role is primarily dependent on social conditions that, in turn, are the reflection of cultural standards at a particular historical time, service in the army is (at least so far) biologically determined so that in this society it applies primarily to males. The marital role requires sexual maturity of both partners. But in all these instances the separation of biological from sociological determinants is hard, if not impossible, to draw.

As determining events at the second developmental level, we have listed the birth of the first child coupled with a complete or partial loss of the wife's job, a change in the job, or promotion of the husband. The

135

TABLE 7.1
Levels and Events in Adult Life

Level (years)	Gradual changes				Sudden changes
	Males		Females		
	Psychosocial	Biophysical	Psychosocial	Biophysical	
I (20–25)	College/first job Marriage First child		First job/college Marriage	First child	
II (25–30)	Second job Other children		Loss of job	Other children	
III (30–35)	Children in preschool Move Promotion Children in school		Children in preschool Move Without job Children in school		
IV (35–50)	Second home Promotion Departure of children		Second home Second career Departure of children		
V (50–65)	Unemployment Isolation Grandfather Head of kin		Unemployment Grandmother Head of kin	Menopause	Loss of job Loss of parents Loss of friends Illness
VI (65+)	Deprivation	Incapacitation Sensorimotor deficiencies		Widowhood Incapacitation	Retirement Loss of partner Death

child can not be born unless a social or, at least, biological marriage has taken place; a job can not be lost or changed unless it has been held before. As obvious as these conclusions may seem, they need to be emphasized because they represent the very markings which structure the progression of the adult's life. They play an important role for both the recollection of minor events at a later date (such as an accident, the purchase of a household item, a birthday, or a party), as well as for the temporal markings of what the individual might perceive as a crisis in his life.

The determining events at the third developmental level include the birth of other children coupled with the execution of specific parental roles during their preschool years, especially by the mother, changes in job, promotion, move to a larger house, to a different location in the country, etc. The delineation of a developmental level corresponding to and determined by the children's preschool years, strictly speaking, is possible only for families with single or very few children, narrowly spaced by birth over a short time period. This limitation indicates, once more, the cultural–sociological determination of distinct periods in the adult life. Most of them can be identified only for members of small nuclear families in industrialized settings. Agricultural societies with elaborated kinship traditions do not allow for chunking the life span into distinct periods founded on determinants other than biological ones. As described by Margaret Mead (1928), large kins experience closely spaced arrivals of children which do not allow for the sectioning of the life span by generational shifts or career alterations.

In contrast to the events marking the two preceding levels, the following ones are spread over a longer and more variable time period. During the fourth developmental level, the children attend elementary school and, thus, the mother may prepare for or begin her second career. Few changes except those of promotion or shift in assignments may be experienced by her husband. This holds also for the fifth level that is characterized by the departure of the children from home in preparation or in search of their own adult development and career. Undoubtedly, these events affect profoundly their parents. If these departures are accompanied by—what is becoming increasingly likely—the death of one or both members of the older generation, the status of the adult with whom we are concerned is even more drastically altered. Both husband and wife may now attain the top position among the living members of the extended family, with their own children ready to marry and grandchildren to be expected. At the fifth developmental level, individuals also become increasingly vulnerable to dismissal, unemployment, and disease. Not only the death of the parents, but of the partner, friends, and relatives may create personal crises; these incidents are now occurring in greater number and with greater likelihood.

While most of these events are brought about by uncontrollable outer-physical circumstances or are due to unavoidable inner-biological changes in the adult himself, one of the most decisive final affronts, retirement, is not caused by increasing inner or outer deficiences but by conventional regulations. Mandatory retirement provides the last insult to the adult person and initiates his progressive social deterioration.

In summary, the early levels of adulthood are strongly influenced by social determinants. This has been indicated by listing several critical events on the left-hand side of Table 7.1. Late adulthood and aging are more strongly influenced by inner-biological or outer-physical conditions, by the occurrence of crises and catastrophies. Since most of these events can not be prevented and since the individual's reactions to it might be very limited, a person might be forced to accept a fatalistic viewpoint. The individual's attitude will fluctuate between despair and stoicism, with the latter being the more constructive philosophical stance. Nevertheless, the most devastating event to come, retirement, represents a social intervention and thus is susceptible to changes through constructive alterations of policies and laws.

Career Development

In the preceding section we described a general sequence of levels in adult development which are partially influenced by cultural–sociological and partially by biophysical conditions; they occur either in the form of gradual changes or suddenly in the form of crises and catastrophies. Throughout, I have emphasized the interdependence of the determinants as well as the form of changes (most often gradual changes are triggered by sudden alterations, e.g., when entering college, when being drafted, when a child is born, etc.). Because of the possibility for constructive modifications, I paid special attention to the cultural–sociological determinants of the various episodes in the adult life. In pursuing this topic further, I describe in the present section an ideal sequence of structural changes that provide for a more effective use of the adult's knowledge and abilities and will enable him to lead a more successful and gratifying life. Since few data and records are available on this topic, I retreat to the description of career development in an area best known to the present author, academic careers. As shown in Figure 7.1, I describe again the progression in the form of five distinct developmental levels.

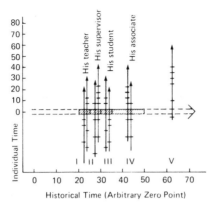

Figure 7.1. The changing roles of a scientist participating in one paradigmatic orientation at different historical times. Each heavy vertical line represents one developmental level in the individual's career, i.e., I: from 20 to 25; II: from 25 to 30; III: from 30 to 35; IV: from 35 to 50; V: from 50 to 65 years. The thin vertical lines represent the careers of persons with whom he is affiliated (see also note to Figure 7.2).

The foundations of an academic career are laid during the under-graduate and graduate years, at the first developmental level. Although teachers may not always be convinced of the impact of their teaching, and students may not always be convinced of the sense of their learning and its influence upon their future careers, there can be little doubt that formative directions are established and fundamentals are laid. This result might not be achieved so much through the specific content of lectures, discussions and readings but through the impact of the basic mentality and theme exhibited at a particular institution at a particular time. Through this influence, the philosophic-scientific images of the young cohort of scholars are formed, and a paradigmatic orientation (in the narrowest sense of Kuhn's term [1962]) is created, which the new co-hort will implement by failing to question it any further and by using it as a basis from which the explication of a new orientation can proceed during the coming years.

We could select many examples for demonstrating our case. Let us consider the recent conception of life-span psychology with its recognition of the interactive changes in the individual and in society as pro-moted at the West Virginia Conferences. Those of us who have lectured on this subject and have tried to implement it through their presentation at scientific meetings will often have felt a sense of helplessness when recognizing the sluggishness and tardiness with which new issues are

apprehended by the listeners (for example, child psychologists). Undoubtedly, the audience was often enthusiastic, but as soon as they re-
returned to their routine jobs, their enthusiasm disappeared like a dream
about faraway places. Occasionally, there was active resistance to the new
conception. After all, the life-span conception questions many past
achievements by demanding that they be placed in a much broader
conceptual framework, namely a framework that does not only take
account of individual but also of societal changes. No wonder, therefore,
that members of the dominating older cohorts failed to listen or became
resistant.

The reactions of the students were quite different. While some of
the older graduates might have been already too firmly committed to an
earlier orientation, the younger students accepted the new viewpoint on
a matter-of-fact basis without much quarrel. Their attitude may even
have raised doubts in the mind of the teachers whether they did not
emphasize the issue too repetitiously, boring their listeners as a result.
Stated in a confirmative manner, the younger students accepted the new
orientation and were ready to implement it as a self-evident form of
thinking and, eventually, to go beyond it. For their teachers, in comparison, the apprehension and realization of this orientation was the result
of a long struggle that at the time of their lectures, appeared still as incomplete to them and beset with many unresolved difficulties.

The activities of young scientists during the second level of their
academic careers aim at their establishment as an instructor and researcher. The demands upon them are heavy. They will have to teach a
variety of courses, not all of which are close to their own interests. They
may join an existing laboratory and use facilities made available to them,
thereby, engaging in work that is not necessarily close to their own interest and liking. Nevertheless, through their teaching, research and writing
they will try to reveal their unique orientation in confrontation to the
existing one and in cooperation with other young scientists with the same
paradigmatic conviction. This orientation might be based, for example,
upon the concepts of a life-span psychology and sociology. They do not
propose this orientation but rather presuppose it, develop it further and,
therefore, establish it firmly within behavioral sciences and developmental psychology. Only the application of a paradigmatic orientation by
subsequent cohorts of scientists leads to its full acceptance and victory
within a particular discipline.

In proceding through the third level of their academic career, our
psychologists are well-established, most likely, as associate professors.
They have become effective teachers lecturing on topics close to their

fields of specialization. They have published a number of papers explicating their unique orientation, though many of them have not received the attention that they feel these publications deserve. They have obtained research grants and succeeded in establishing their own laboratory sections with a few students, assistants, and doctoral candidates. These are the most effective years in the young scientists' careers during which they propose and explicate their own paradigmatic orientation in deviation from the one to which they were exposed during their undergraduate and graduate years.

At the fourth level, our scientists have firmly established themselves. They are full professors, are in charge of their own laboratories and research teams, are nationally known, and often are sought as speakers at colloquia and conventions. They mainly lecture in seminars, but continue to teach undergraduate classes because these efforts assist them in writing an advanced text on the topic of their specialization. Through textbooks their scientific theme becomes confirmed and accepted outside the narrow professional quarrels and debates. They serve on governmental, professional, and university boards, are chair-persons of their departments or of scientific committees. Their recognition is widespread and their influence is strong.

At the fifth level of their career our scientists have slightly retreated from their research activities. They still run their laboratories or programs, but devote most of their time to administration. If they write, they contribute chapters to specialized books or prepare new editions of their texts. They might continue to serve as chairpersons of their departments or have accepted other administrative duties in the university or in professional organizations. Their activities have not decreased but are rather channeled into managerial and representational tasks. Their influence continues to remain strong and might even have increased within the administrative structure. They have become more remote from their original activities—from teaching and research. They see students less often, and even their assistants interact with them only through intermediaries.

The role and status of the behavioral scientists remains unchanged until their retirement. But even this event does not affect them as strongly as it does most other persons in the larger society. They continue to serve on committees and accept honorary assignments. Although rarely found in the laboratory, they continue to write and might even increase the volume of their production both in amount and scope. While the scientists continue to fulfill gratifying roles throughout their later years, their life is affected by all those gradual or sudden events which place a heavy buden upon any aging individual. Before they die, they might have completed their *Reminiscence* as, indeed, Wilhelm Wundt did when he was 88 years old.

Breaking of Paradigmatic Crises by Exceptional Individuals

This sketch of a scientist lists a few of the major events in the life of a fortunate person in order to show the coordination of the individual's progression and the changes in the social group. The sketch has been intuitive since records and systematic interpretations are lacking. These limitations are even more severe if one were to describe the developments for other careers, most of which offer far fewer opportunities for promotion and variation. Generally, once a particular occupational role has been accepted, the holders remain tied to it for the rest of their lives or until their retirements, with gradual increases in their salaries being the only benefit that they can expect. Of course, each occupation allows for some changes. These possibilities ought to be elaborated more forcefully, and once alternatives have been recognized they ought to be implemented through programmed job arrangements in order to generate the most gratifying career development for the participating members.

Thus far I have considered a developmental sequence in which the individual fulfills, essentially, only one basic theme—the attempts of scientists to build a new paradigmatic orientation upon that of their teachers and, thus, to serve as historical catalysts of generational consciousness in their scientific discipline (Neugarten & Datan, 1973). In comparison to the one-paradigm scientists, persons may have the vision and power to embrace more than one orientation. They may, for example, quickly depart from the original paradigm that was imprinted upon them during their student years and lead the successive cohort of young scientists to a new orientation. But a few years later they may aim already at the development of other ideas thereby alienating themselves from their former friends, colleagues, and students. Still later, they might develop a third orientation. There are at least two well-known psychologists whose careers can be described in terms of multi-paradigmatic progressions: Piaget and Wundt.

The careers of both of them give dramatic demonstration of how the individual's generativity catalyzes a new paradigmatic consciousness and how in the further course of their own progressions the very orientations which they have created in society prevent them from moving successfully ahead. Society is being changed by the individual, but as it is changed it also changes the generativity of the individual. This holds both for the common and the exceptional persons. I focus upon the latter because their contributions, especially in sciences, are more visible. The formers' participatory actions are mainly expressed by their conforming or nonconforming in particular roles, attitudes, and values. Any deviation from them represents a step, though a small one, in generating a new mode of living and a new historical consciousness.

Piaget

As shown in Figure 7.2, three periods can be distinguished in Piaget's career and work. After receiving his training as a biologist and deciding to direct his intellectual efforts to the study of the growth of knowledge, he settled upon child psychology as a pragmatic route for investigating these problems. The first period in his career can be denoted as *functional* and is best represented by his book on the "Language and Thought of the Child" (1923). In contrast to his later approaches, he analyzed intellectual development in close conjunction with the child's acquisition of language, stressing the lack of communicative functions in the language of young children. This interpretation led to the well-

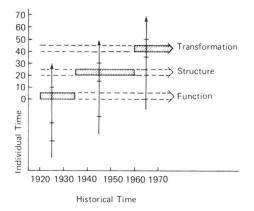

Figure 7.2. The changing roles of one eminent scientist, Jean Piaget, participating in three paradigmatic orientations at different historical times. This figure corresponds to a two-dimensional time representation occasionally used in physics. The vertical vectors represent "world-lines" for the individual at different historical times; the horizontal vectors represent "world-lines" for society at different individual times (see also note to Figure 7.1).

known controversy with Vygotsky [(1962); see also Piaget's separate preface to the English translation of Vygotsky's book, (1962)] about the social basis of language and cognitive development as well as to excessive research in the United States (see, for example, McCarthy's review, 1954) which through mechanistic distortions brought the first wave of enthusiasm for Piaget to an early end.

In the meantime Piaget had further developed his perspective. He deemphasized the functional and social aspects of language and elaborated his theory of stages in cognitive development. These activities covered the late 1930s, 1940s, and 1950s and aimed at structural descriptions of the child's logical operations at successive developmental levels. Beginning with interpretive-clinical observations covering the six stages of the sensorimotor period (Piaget, 1936), considerable experimental attention was given to preoperational (2 to 7 years) and concrete operational intelligence (7 to 11 years) (Piaget, 1947). The fourth and last period of formal operational thinking has been explored in theory but less thoroughly in his research investigations. Here, and to a lesser extent for the earlier stages, Piaget's work culminated in theoretical constructions of how the child's thought ought to operate. Piaget's work during the second period in his own development can appropriately be called *structural*. It has been supplemented by extensive studies of perception and perceptual development which have not yet received the full attention of American investigators since only a few have been translated into English (see Piaget, 1961).

In pursuing further his theoretical analyses, Piaget has since then moved forward to what might be called his *transformational* period. While previously, he maximized the differences between the "logics" of children at successive developmental levels, he became more profoundly concerned with the changes from one into the other, with the problem of invariances in transitions, with transformations. His interpretations—oddly enough published in a book entitled "Structuralism" (1968)—have attracted considerable attention, but it is doubtful whether they will influence psychology as deeply as his earlier work. In part, this expected lack of broad success is determined by the difficulty in translating his ideas into operational routines for the American psychological laboratory and by Piaget's disinterest to provide such translations.

Conceivably, Piaget might still enter into another stage of his career. He might integrate, perhaps from a developmental–historical perspective, much of his former work and lend it an authoritative and *absolute* character. In part, this is indicated by his growing concern with "Genetic Epistemology" (1950, 1970). But primarily my speculation is based upon biographical reports about developmental changes of famous philosophers, for example, Schelling and Aristotle (see Jaeger, 1923). It finds further support in Lehman's (1953) comparisons between the intellectual productivity at different periods during the life span and between different disciplines and art forms which show a general shift from creative achievement and empirical work to theoretical analyses, logic, history, and metaphysics.

Wundt

A better documented case for a scientist's constructive participation in several paradigmatic orientations as well as for the collective disregard of his progressing contributions is that of Wilhelm Wundt. As shown in Figure 7.3, Wundt was born in 1832 and entered the University of Tübingen in 1851 where he stayed for one year only before he moved to Heidelberg for four years. Part of his last year of study, 1856, was spent in Berlin where he was influenced by Johannes Mueller, Magnus, and du Bois-Reymond.

The following decade, the 1860s, is described by Boring (1957) as "presystematic." Nevertheless, Wundt laid the foundation for his later

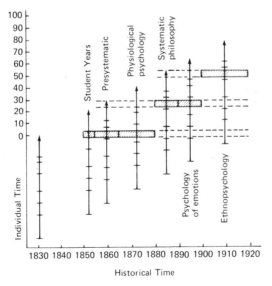

Figure 7.3. The changing roles of one eminent scientist, Wilhelm Wundt, participating in three paradigmatic orientations at different historical times (see notes to Figure 7.2 and 7.2).

145

work during this time. Between 1857 and 1864 he was Dozent (Assistant Professor) in Heidelberg, at the same time as Helmholtz was there and, presumably, under his influence. In 1858 Wundt published the first section of his book entitled "Beiträge zur Theorie der Sinneswahrnehmungen," which was completed in 1862 and has been regarded by Titchner as a blueprint of his lifetime work. Also during this period, he published in 1863 his "Vorlesungen über die Menschen und Thierseele." This book includes a brief outline of his "Ethnopsychology," a topic and program of investigation which was to lay dormant for several decades until Wundt started extensive writings in it at the beginning of the twentieth century.

Wundt revealed his first paradigmatic orientation during the period from 1865 to 1880. He elaborated and presented his work on perceptual-motor processes with an emphasis on sensory elements and their compounding into complex units. Although much broader and more comprehensive than later critics have made us believe, Wundt was never able to shake off the impressions that he created during these years—the impressions of promoting psychophysiological elementalism. This paradigmatic orientation is most distinctly represented by his two-volume work, entitled "Grundzüge der Physiologischen Psychologie" which appeared between 1873 and 1874. Also during this period, he became Ausserordentlicher Professor (Associate Professor). In 1874 he moved for one year to Zürich and in 1875 to Leipzig where he opened his Psychological Laboratory in 1879.

The following decade was almost exclusively devoted to philosophical writings. In 1881 he started the journal *Philosophische Studien* (although it included predominantly psychological reports and was later renamed in this sense). Between 1880 and 1883 he published two volumes on logic, in 1886 one on ethics, and in 1889 a book entitled "System der Philosophy." He concluded the decade by serving as the Rector of the University of Leipzig.

The 1880s can be regarded as a preparatory period for the expounding of his second paradigmatic orientation. This work led to his three-dimensional theory of feelings, first elaborated in his "Grundriss der Psychologie" of 1896. In contrast to the earlier psychophysiological and psychophysical theorizing, Wundt tried to establish psychology systematically on a more independent basis. Although the extensive theorizing and research on his theory of emotions or feelings created a considerable stir during Wundt's time, later psychologists (at least of the post-Titchner period) paid little attention to his work. Wundt remained branded as an introspective elementalist.

A similar disregard was shown by psychologists for his extensive writing in ethnopsychology from the first two decades of the twentieth century until his death in 1920. This approach—as already outlined in his "Vorlesungen" of 1863—was to supplement the experimental methods promoted by the two earlier paradigmatic orientations. By analyzing the customs, habits and languages of society as objectifications of the human mind, a second route for the study of psychology was to be provided. Experimentation is analyzing the mind from within; ethnopsychology analyzes the mind (more precisely, its products) from without. Both approaches are necessary and supplement each other. But in spite of the significance that Wundt assigned to it and in spite of the extensive debates and controversies that ethnopsychology created among anthropologists, linguists, and historians, present-day psychologists are hardly aware of this contribution and of Wundt's two-prong attempt for a comprehensive integration of the behavioral and social sciences. Only renewed historical interest in Wundt's work during the most recent years (see Balance, 1973; Blumenthal, 1970, 1973; and Brinkmann, 1973) has given him some delayed recognition.

The Individual and Society

Undoubtedly, the lives of Piaget and Wundt have been also subjected to the alternating conditions and constraints which affect the individual's life cycle for a person less productive in scientific or intellectual affairs. Wundt, for example, moved steadily through all the administrative duties of a scientist establishing himself. He founded and directed his laboratory, served as chairman, Dean, and Rector of the University, participated actively in various scientific organizations, and even ran for and held a political office. Thus, both sequences, that of Wundt as a creative, ever-moving scientist and that of Wundt as a skillful researcher and administrator, ought to be integrated to provide a comprehensive picture of his career and the criterial points in its development.

The descriptions of these two scientific careers were introduced to indicate how, in exceptional cases, the individual may break out of the paradigmatic orientation that is imposed upon and restricts the development of the "normal man" including the "normal scientist." This comparison enables us to elucidate the interactive progression of the individual and society in the following manner: Historical progression is constituted by generational shifts and by the substitution of one cohort of leading individuals by the next. The individuals, through their developments, change but they make their main contributions during a limited time period only, most likely, around or just before mid-adulthood. During the earlier periods they either prepare themselves; during the later periods they rigidify their paradigmatic orientation, the scientists, for example, by writing textbooks and chapters and by their administration of laboratories and departments. The shifts in roles and, in particular, the experienced lack of success to continue in contributing in modes of earlier developmental periods might be considered as crises in adult life. Only a few exceptional persons, for example, Piaget and Wundt, succeed in providing an array of different conceptions to the community.

The individual, especially the creative individual, produces social changes; but as they are brought about, the modified conditions change the individual. The individual might have been the spokesman for a new paradigmatic orientation; as this conception becomes obsolete and is submitted by a newer orientation, a crisis is generated reflecting qualitative shifts in the interactions between the individual's and society's development. Crises generated by the individual might become a revolution in society, for example, scientific revolutions. Crises generated in society are, in all cases, traceable to individuals' actions; they might be experienced as catastrophes. In the preceding sections I have looked at the individual and, finally, at his interaction with the social group. In the following section, I analyze cultural–sociological changes and catastrophes.

Structural Stratifications in History

In several recent investigations (Riegel, 1972b, 1973d, 1976b; see also Chapter 6), I was struck by the apocalyptic view of history exhibited by most individuals. When students were asked to recollect the names of historical figures, they produced many more names of persons who were instrumental in coping with major historical catastrophes, such as revolutions and wars. Few names were given for the more peaceful interludes, although many of their representatives produced important changes in economic, social, educational, and scientific domains. These findings are depressing, but one will have to realize that they give adequate expression of events decisive for the contemporaries who suffered through them, as well as for later generations of individuals who merely heard about these events but were, nevertheless, influenced because their parents feared their repetitions.

In my earlier interpretations (Riegel, 1976b), I emphasized perceptual-constructive aspects in historical progression. Human beings through their actions generate events which might converge into catastrophes; in their perception of history, they focus upon these events rather than upon the tranquility of intermediate stages. Similarly for the development of individuals; through their participatory actions, they create changes, for example, accept jobs, marry, have children, move to another location. When they reflect about their development in retrospect, they perceive their past as structured sequences marked by these "disruptive" events. Unless seen as an object, neither historical progression nor individual development are experienced as a process of continuous changes but always as a progression in qualitative leaps. These leaps, experienced as crises or catastrophes, are brought about by the lack of synchronization in either inner-biological, individual-psychological, cultural–sociological or outer-physical progressions.

The Family

Considering first the smallest subunit, the family or kin, I disagree with the traditional view expressed in Galton's study of "Hereditary Genius" (1869). By analyzing the family trees of famous people, Galton tried to show that superior productivity is genetically inherited since it occurs disproportionately more frequently within certain well-known families than in others. Disregarding the likelihood that this observation is determined by cultural–sociological factors of upbringing, education, and intellectual milieu rather than inner-biological, genetic components, the domination of such families or kins is temporally restricted. Although strong, supportive data do not seem to be available except from family biographies, such as "Buddenbrooks" by Thomas Mann, different clans replace each other in the course of history of growth, stability, and decline. These changes in significance create crises for its members as much as its competition with other clans causes conflicts in society. Major catastrophes arise if a particular clan succeeds in dominating others and the society in general for an extended period of time. In these cases of aristocratic or monopolistic dominations, only warfare or revolutions succeed in restructuring the society for the benefit of other subgroups and its individual members.

The present discussion of historical progression regards the family or the clan as an extended cohort with an internal history that becomes significant for society during a limited period of time only. Overall progression is brought about by the replacements of different cohort clans during historical time. These families and clans represent subgroups of larger social, political, and geographical units that, in turn, have their own internal history and replace each other in succession. Finally, the analysis leads to the histories of states and nations.

The Nation

Different social groups or nations undergo profound changes generating upward and downward mobility that peaks at different historical periods. The political–cultural history of western Europe can be written, for example, as a sequence in which different political groups attained their domination in ordered succession. The late Middle Ages were dominated by the remnants of the Frankish empire, especially in western and southern Germany. Their influence was replaced by the Italian city–states during the early Renaissance of the fifteenth century and by Spain and the Netherlands during the later periods up to the sixteenth century. In the meantime, France gained increasing recognition and became the dominating power during the seventeenth century even though several other nations, most notably England, Austria, Russia, and Sweden, entered into ambitious conflicts. England dominated the European scene of the nineteenth century until in renewed competition with Germany and France, all of these nations began to lose out to the United States.

The sequence described might appear as simplistic. It depicts alternations in political domination which are not necessarily synchronized with the cultural progression in the arts and sciences. Indeed, cultural progressions often seem to lag behind political advances. During the height of the Spanish empire, for example, artists, craftsmen, and scientists had to be imported from foreign countries in order to express the power and prestige of the state through their creations. During the eighteenth and early nineteenth century when Germany was anything but a political power, music, writing and painting reached a never-before-achieved height, and the sciences began to make decisive advances.

The Arts

While political history attains its consistency by the geographical cohesion of the supportive groups, arts and sciences have always broken through these barriers and cannot be firmly tied to particular places, groups, or nations. What provides cohesion to these domains of human activities are the common mentality of the participants, the universality of their theme, and the accumulative advances in knowledge and technology. In the history of arts, for example, the early periods of activities centered upon architecture. Only after basic needs for shelter and storage were secured did it become possible to add decorative refinements and sculptures. The art of painting required further technological advances and fulfills basic biological needs of the individuals to a lesser extent. Materials, tools and media had to be developed before painting could become a dominating mode of artistic expressions. When studied in greater detail, the history of painting reveals a close dependency upon scientific concepts, going as far back as the planar murals of the Egyptians. During the Renaissance, the history of painting can be described as a sequence of advances in projecting the three-dimensional space defined by scientists and philosophers upon the two-dimensional canvas. Boring (1957) described how step-by-step all the perceptual cues are mastered until during the Baroque period, the artists engaged in dynamic overrepresentation of space in action. Modern art both playfully and compulsively denied the very cues laboriously acquired during centuries of artistic traditions. Finally, music, first created for ceremonial and devotional purposes, later realized in stage performances, required a high degree of abstraction and the development of sophisticated instruments and refined transcription systems before it could become a dominant mode of artistic expression.

The Sciences

Although artistic styles differ widely, there exists an intrinsic logic which determines their historical progression. Cohesion of this type is still more characteristic for scientific efforts. In the history of physics, for example, the study of mechanics had to precede that of thermodynamics, which had to precede that of electromagnetics, which, finally, had to precede that of nuclear physics. Although I do not wish to promote an accumulative model of growth (guided by the conception that the more you do the closer you get toward the detection of "the truth"), sciences are founded upon the ceaseless efforts of many individuals over many generations contributing step-by-step to the stock of universal knowledge. But in Kuhn's sense (1962), development of sciences is also determined by changes in style (e.g., experimental versus clinical analysis), breakthroughs in technology (e.g., the measurement of the speed of nerve conductivity, the development of microelectrodes), and confrontations of scientific paradigms (e.g., behaviorism versus cognitive psychology). Finally, scientific knowledge does not only progress by paradigmatic leaps, but the different orientations are related in structurally complex manners, reflecting coexisting competition and progressive differentiation and integration (see Riegel, 1969, 1976b).

The Individual and Society

The example from the history of three-dimensional representation in painting has demonstrated the interdependence of arts and sciences. This interdependence prevails throughout history: All arts are also sciences, and all sciences are also arts. Historically, this relationship changes in a systematic manner. Following Spengler's (1912–1922) analysis, during the early periods of the history of a civilization, arts dominate over sciences. Later on the relationship is reversed. At the point of reversal, arts and sciences find both balanced and dichotomized expressions; this condition typifies the "classical" period of a cultural–historical progression.

In concordance with these historical shifts, society demands different kinds of persons to represent different historical times. Early in history the artist and craftsman will outweigh the scientist and technician. During the classical periods a balanced orientation is demanded. Later in history the preference goes to the scientist-technician. Groups who fulfill the required conditions best prevail as leaders; all others fade into the background until their time arrives. Individuals who do not fulfill the demands of their time attain lesser significance and may experience their lot as personal crises. But individuals can change their affiliation. By taking such actions they may create history. And even though these steps may be experienced as crises, they lead to a new consciousness and a new sense of freedom.

Extrascientific Bases of the Concept of "Crises"

The contrastive distinction between continuous and discrete models of growth (Riegel, 1969, 1972b; van den Daele, 1969; see also Chapter 2) redirects our attention toward issues raised in the early part of this chapter. If we look at the history of sciences as a continuous accumulative growth process, crises are offensive disturbances. If we look at the history of sciences as a progression through discrete leaps, crises are necessary steps in the advancement of knowledge. Both interpretations fail to detail the reasons and causes of crises, and thus, we need to extend our interpretation further. By arguing that crises are generated at the interface between different dimensions of progressions—especially, through interactive changes along the individual-psychological and the cultural-sociological ones—we specify not only the advancements in sciences but in political history as well. Thereby we are also able to return to the discussion of crises in the life of common man.

The concept of crisis and its significance for individual and cultural development are historically determined. As shown in Chapter 2, in Western philosophy and sciences at least two orientations can be distinguished. One conceives development as a progression by qualitative leaps and structural reorganizations. It represents the continental European way of thinking and, since the catastrophies interpretation of natural history by Cuvier (1769–1832), has been implied in the interpretations of development by Rousseau, Pestalozzi, Spranger, Piaget, and Velikovsky (1950, 1955). The other orientation interprets development as a continuous accumulation of pieces of experience or information and deemphasizes structural reorganizations. In the words of a modern exponent of the theory of evolution: "Present continuity implies the improbability of past catastrophism and violence of change either in the lifeless or in the living world; moreover, we seek to interpret the changes and laws of past time through those which we observe at the present time [Osborn, 1917, p. 24]." This orientation originated in Britain and through the works of Lyell, Darwin, and Galton, gained dominant influence in the United States in biology and in the behavioral and social sciences. As I have argued in Chapter 2, the origin of these two orientations can be traced to different economical and political ideologies and needs to be extended by a third or dialectical viewpoint which subordinates both interpretations as one-sided.

For the concept of continuous growth, crises do not play an apparent and significant role development. Although the directions of their changes are not always clear, individuals strive toward greater success by accumulating experience in the same way as the merchant accumulates wealth. However, crises are significant in a deeper sense. More than in any of the other two interpretations, they appear as shocks and disruptions of the process of steady expansion and enrichment. Crises are unpredictable in this case because neither inner-biological nor cultural-sociological sequences are interactively considered. There is only one crisis predictable from such a point of view, namely, the final shock when individuals realize that they do not compete effectively any longer with younger persons, when they recognize that they are losing the struggle for survival in competition with the younger persons.

In contrast to this orientation, the continental European viewpoint gives positive recognition to crises which, thereby, lose their deleterious character. In Piaget's theory of cognitive development, for example, the transitions between different periods of cognitive operations can be considered as constructive crises. The different forms of operations are not compared as being qualitatively better or worse; all serve their appropriate function at appropriate developmental time. When extended into cross-cultural and cross-generational comparisons, such concepts could lead to a positive interpretation of developmental shifts.

Conclusions

The careers of common men and women often represent deficient forms of structural developmental progressions. The major events affecting individuals are arbitrarily induced upon them by social and legal regulations (e.g., departure from school, recruitment into military service, job appointments and dismissals, and, ultimately, retirement). Other changes are brought about by cultural–sociological or outer-physical catastrophes (e.g., economic depressions, inflations, revolutions, and wars, or droughts, floods, fires, and earthquakes). Only the inner-biological determinants seem to follow some predictable order, first revealing the individual's maturation, the birth of children, and later his increasing proneness to incapacitation, illness, and death. Most of these events appear as crises to the individual and as catastrophes to society. They reflect a lack of synchronization between the biological, psychological, cultural, and physical event sequences. The fatalistic viewpoint, in turn, is generated by our failure to consider these progressions simultaneously and, thus, to reach a more comprehensive understanding that would enable us to program and coordinate them more effectively.

Among the few favored individuals, the life-span of academic scientists allows for considerable structural variations and for sensible structural transformations during their developmental progressions. Since the structure of the scientific community and its historical changes are more variable and better understood than those of most other groups, I devoted much attention to the interactive development of scientists and their scientific disciplines or subdisciplines.

Scientists in the development of their careers tentatively explicate their paradigmatic orientation through their teaching and their affiliation with a few like-minded colleagues and students. As they advance, they establish their own "scientific communes" and disseminate their ideas through reports and papers until they crystalize in research routines and textbooks. The small team with which scientists affiliate represents the basis for their activities and success. But the more they advance, the more they will find recognition from other groups that, though geographically remote, become attached to one another by their shared knowledge and technology. Eventually, the larger group might come to represent a distinct paradigmatic orientation which through its achievements creates a new constructive interpretation of a scientific theme.

As one scientific cohort succeeds, it forces others into opposition and rejects earlier ones as insufficient. The resulting conditions create conflicts for coexisting orientations and crises for the preceding ones. These discrepancies exist between the groups but are created by individuals. They affect the individual members of coexisting groups who find themselves in earnest competition. The ideas expressed by representatives of former paradigms are regarded as outmoded and obsolete, although the individuals who represent them are not likely to accept such a judgment. If they do, they are faced with a personal crisis. For a while they will find some like-minded colleagues to lean on, but these persons might more successfully adjust to the changing conditions by moving forward in their individual career and retreating from the laboratory into organizing and administrative duties. Finally, only the staunchest supporters are left, and they are left in a state of crisis.

Crises can be resolved by structural transformations of the individual's development in concordance with social history. Ideally, one should outline a structural progression—as I have tried to do for the career of an academic psychologist—and implement such a model through the proper selection of assignments and allocation of resources. Such a design can be prepared only through careful observations of the changes within the scientific-social system. Therefore the study of historical progression has to be linked with the analysis of individual developmental patterns. One can only depict healthy individual development if one also describes the historical progression within which it takes place. And what holds for the scientists holds for any other woman or man in the array of other activities and occupations. Unfortunately—because their life styles provide lesser structural-developmental differentiations—their forms of operations are more difficult to describe. This should only induce us, however, to search harder and to become more determined to change their fate. Only when individual and societal changes are transformationally synchronized can the individual succeed in happiness and society in achievement.

8

The Dialectics of Time[1]

When I step out of my house in a clear night and look at the sky above me, I might accept its beauty as a sign for the existence of God or its stability as a sign for the law and order of the universe. But I might also start to reflect and realize that what appears as harmonious and stable to me is merely a transient abstraction. The light of some stars will have been emitted only a few minutes earlier, that of others hundreds of years ago, and some might have exploded and disappeared, only their light is traveling on. My own perceptual–cognitive position represents that point or knot at which all the different time-lines or world-lines originating from the stars interesect at this instance. These world-lines constitute a cone in front of me and represent the past; my own position represents the here and now. Behind me we might, with Minkowski (1970), extend the world-lines so that they form another cone representing the future.

[1]Invited address given by the recipient of the 1976 Robert W. Kleemeier Scientific Award of the Gerontological Society. A more detailed version appears in N. Datan & H. W. Reese (Eds.), *Life-span developmental psychology: Dialectical perspectives on experimental research,* New York: Academic Press, 1977. Pp. 3–45.

Since for all practical purposes, other observers in my neighborhood have the same perception of the sky, this form of parallel description has come to be accepted as the dominant mode of common sense as well as scientific analysis. Even if we describe events in time, we merely secure two or more timeless spatial descriptions and infer changes by comparison (e.g., the sky at 10 P.M. and at 11 P.M.). Time has hardly ever been a primary and independent mode of analysis; it has received secondary consideration only.

After having looked at the sky for a few minutes, I may step into my car and drive to the movie house. There I watch the movements and actions, and it would not occur to me to break the stream of events into a series of discrete, timeless frames of which the film is composed.

In our two examples, we have either attended to simultaneous or to sequential conditions. In our observations of the sky, we maximize the simultaneity of events; watching a movie we observe several interlaced event sequences. But most likely we do both operations at the same time: We search for a falling star and are disturbed by the moving cloud; we apprehend the simultaneity in which the movements of two actors are harmonized and interlaced (in a love scene) or disharmonized and out of step (in a gun fight). Thus within a short period of time, if not at one and the same moment, we attend to apparent stable states and experience the flow of events.

Western science has been written in spatial or—as linguists would say—in synchronic terms (de Saussure, 1959). Even when temporal processes are analysed—and this is a dominant task for sciences—their description had to consist of comparisons of several timeless slates (e.g., cross sections of the fall of a body at various instances). There was no other option, because the logic underlying classical sciences is a logic of spatial structures or distributions rather than a logic of temporal orders or changes. As a consequence, science has been built upon abstract entities, such as qualities and competencies, rather than upon concrete events. Science has given one-sided preference to identity and equilibrium, rather than to their opposites—contradictions and crises. A science of development and change requires radical change in our basic conceptions. Such a science would have to be founded upon the notion of contradiction and tension between concrete events for which identity and balance are merely momentary states that immediately converge into the flux of new changes. The foundation for such a science has been laid in dialectical logic. Time is one of its most important and intriguing concepts.

The Concept of Change

Properties of Time

What objects are in space, events are in time. A young child does not separate stable objects from changing events (Piaget, 1970). It attends to objects only if the objects are in motion or if, through the child's own motions, the impression of such changes is created. Also for the mature person, the separation of stable objects and changing events remains artificial. Events involve objects, and objects are constitutive of events. Indeed, only through the conceptual separation of space and time did it become possible to regard objects (being in space) as independent from events (being in time) [Cassirer, 1923].

One of the basic properties of temporal descriptions, *simultaneity*, is comparable to the notion of equivalence and identity in spatial descriptions and formal logic. Simultaneity in space is determined by the coexistence of objects. Especially the early Greek concept of space was dominated by this notion, and thus, space was negatively defined as that domain that is not filled by coexistent substances or objects, i.e., space was regarded as a void (Jammer, 1954). In western philosophy and sciences, the concept of substance became subordinated to that of space (and so was time). Substances and objects were regarded as being located in space. As the example of the stars in the sky has shown, coexistent objects (or our perceptual impressions of them) define simultaneity as the intersection of world lines. Such a point has no temporal extension; time collapses upon timeless instant. Simultaneity of this kind is not concerned with movements through time or changes over time. If such a punctilism is all that an analysis of time would yield, the resulting description would again be formulated in the spatial terms of classical natural science and philosophy into which time enters only secondarily through comparisons of different timeless slates. Within these slates, all objects (or our perceptual impressions of them) retain their identity, everything is fixed and stable, nothing alters or changes.

Simultaneity provides temporal markings if the interaction of at least two event sequences is being considered, for example, the handling of the stop watch and the event observed. If we wish to determine whether two performances extend exactly over the same duration or whether two children are exactly of the same age, we have to consider simultaneity twice, namely, the simultaneity of the birth and the simultaneity of the measurement here and now. In drawing inferences from such observations, we impose the ordered relation between start and measurement and thus move conceptually beyond the topic of simultaneity. We become concerned with the second basic property of time, its *directionality*. Relational time is constituted by the sequence of ordered events.

When we contemplate about the past various events will appear in our memory. These events are neither haphazard collections nor are they merely organized in terms of their simultaneity. The events appear in their movements and temporal order. Moreover, such a directional or relational organization does not occur as a single series but within different temporal orders illustrated, for instance, when we alternately reflect on our career in school, our vocation, our family, our friends, the political, or economic situation, etc. The interactions between these sequences provide temporal markings in the stream of events.

The idea of different event sequences criss-crossing each other but converging upon the momentary state of the reflecting observer is comparable to that of projective space. It is also comparable to the Minkowski cones. During later periods of history and childhood, such a relational notion of time is substituted by the concept of absolute time (Piaget & Inhelder, 1956). Piaget regards the operation of "decentering" as a prerequisite for this transition. If the child succeeds in looking at the past (as well as into the future) from various "angles" or points of view, this transition will have been achieved. Already the idea that different time sequences might be partially independent of each other and might intersect at only a few event points or "knots" prepares the children for this transition. The transition is achieved when they succeed in seeing the past (or the future) from the perspectives of others. If they recognize, for example, that what appears as an intense period with many temporal markings to them is but an insignificant set of events to their parents, or that what appears well-timed to them might appear as tardy to their teachers.

Aside from an increased degree of decentering, the transition to an absolute time concept requires the notion of an ideal observer who is infinitely far-removed from the present either into the past or into the future and, thus, can decenter to an unlimited extent. The resulting concept of time is one-dimensional, uniform, and stretches positively and negatively into infinity. In contrast to the ideal observer, the temporal experience of any concrete individual counts for little and fills but an infinitesimal stretch of universal time. Now, the individual has ceased to take an active part in the construction of time but is subordinated to it in alienating manner. In compensation, time has become quantifiable, even if the procedures employed remain somewhat arbitrary, that is, rely on selected periodic systems, such as the solar year, the lunar month, or the swing of a pendulum.

As relational time is comparable to a single intrinsic event sequence represented, for example, by a monophonic melody, absolute time is comparable to a single extrinsic standard, such as the meter and the bar lines on the score sheet. Both concepts are integrated by a dialectical interpretation. Dialectical time is comparable to polyphonic music in which various monophonic sequences are interwoven and in which temporal markings are generated by the harmonies and disharmonies of such a composition. Absolute time also plays a role in such an arrangement, namely, as a selected monophonic sequence that serves as an extrinsic yardstick and may aid in the synchronization of the different voices or instruments in their joint performances. In comparison to relational time, which is intrinsic (absolute time is extrinsic), dialectical time is both intrinsic and extrinsic, neither one nor the other.

Types of Event Sequences

In describing event sequences, I will compare some of the interactions between and within four dimensions of change: Inner–biological, individual–psychological, cultural–sociological, and outer-physical. If we consider the interactions of any one dimension with any other, we obtain the 4 × 4 matrix shown in Table 1.1 (Riegel, 1976a). Here, the tentative labels attached to the 16 cells either denote interactive events with a negative (upper word) or positive (lower word) outcome. Interactions within any particular dimension, that is, for the cells along the main diagonal of the matrix, require special consideration.

Interactions of event sequences along the inner-biological dimension include the conflict between two fighting animals, the cooperation between mother and child when feeding, the mutual excitement of sexual partners, etc. At more elementary levels we might think of the coordination (or lack of it) between different body organs, cell clusters, single cells, cell bodies, and nuclei, etc. The individual-psychological interactions include those between husband and wife, parent and child, employer and employee, etc. At more elementary levels they involve subsystems within a single individual, for example, between the sensory and motor system, thought and speech, anxiety and motivation, or whatever categories psychologists are ready to propose. Further extensions are necessary for cultural–sociological and outer-physical interactions. The constitutive groupings of the former include the family, tribe, or nation;

union, party, or religious order; the neighborhood, community, or city; the age and sex group, generation, and many others. Equally wide is the distribution of outer-physical conditions. They include large scale external interventions, such as earthquakes, floods, and droughts, as well as physical processes within organisms on the organismic, cellular, molecular, atomic, and quantum levels (Riegel, 1976a).

By considering time in reference to these four dimensions, I draw the following comparisons: At the inner-biological level, temporal markings appear as developmental shifts from activity to passivity, excitement to satisfaction, growth to decay. At the individual-psychological level, they are experienced as conflicts and resolutions, doubts and decisions, movements and rests. At the cultural-sociological level, they are objectified by incentives and restrictions, conquests and defeats, expansions and retreats. At the outer-physical level, they appear as day and night, summer and winter, floods and droughts. By comparing all of these dimensions with one another, the individual psychological dimension makes us aware of temporal markings; the cultural–sociological dimension records events so that they can be transmitted to other people and to other generations. Because of their exceptional status, I will give special attention to these two aspects of temporal structure.

While the matrix of comparisons is exceedingly wide, there are no compelling reasons that all dimensions have to be considered at one and the same time and for one and the same purpose. Quite to the contrary, a selective restriction is necessary for any concrete analysis. But whatever the choice of restriction, temporal sequences are always generated by the interactions of at least two series of activities. The consideration of separate, single event sequences is an abstraction that prevents any meaningful interpretation of temporal structures.

Inner-Biological Changes

Biological Event Sequences[2]

Behavioral and social sciences have commonly neglected the temporal relations between the inner and outer environment of the organism. In seeking to describe these relations, Reichenbach (1958; Reichenbach & Mathern, 1959) adopted a definition from relativity

---

[2]Many thanks to Donna Cohen, School of Medicine, University of Washington, Seattle, for many ideas included in this section.

theory. Age of an organism is characterized by the location of its subsystems on different world-lines. Healthy development represents the synchronized movement along these world lines; pathological development represents lack of synchronization. Chronological time is the outer-physical standard for the analysis of world lines. Since it is arbitrarily measured by the clock on a linear scale, it is not necessarily a meaningful index of developmental processes.

Reichenbach's propositions differ from the traditional reductionistic analyses employed in the social, behavioral, and life sciences. These attempts are commonly based on a regress model and thus fail to explain development and changes. Certain changes in behaviors during adolescence, for example, are reduced to changes in endocrine functions which, in turn, are reduced to some central changes that trigger and perhaps control the chain of events. However, such an analysis still fails to depict how the changes in the controlling cells are brought about. Similar arguments are made for any other development—embryonic, postnatal, reproductive, post reproductive, etc.—and are applied to any system—tissues, skeletal, neuronal, glandular, etc.—and to any organ— heart, lungs, liver, cranium, etc. Proponents of a reductionistic analysis seek some conditions that precede an observed state and that are expected to "explain" it. But as one searches, there remains always the next question to find events preceding the one that was just explained, that is, there remains always the search for the "last" cause.

The insufficiencies of reductionistic explanations are most apparent when changes stretch over long periods of time, for example, when some biological or psychological modifications take place after another event, such as the birth of the organism. How can changes be preprogrammed so far in advance and how is the change implemented? Traditional interpretations lead to nothing more than sophisticated versions of "preformation" or "homunculus" theories and, thus, do not explain development and change. Satisfying explanations can only be expected from an interactional analysis in which temporal conditions are generated by the interdependence of several different event sequences but not by listing events along a single sequence in isolation.

If we consider living systems as composites of various subsystems, that is, cells, cell cluster, organs, organ systems, or some other functional groupings, their analyses will depend on their quantum, atomic, molecular, cellular, organismic, individual, cultural, or cosmic states. Development consists in a series of processes along several of these dimensions, with time marked by their transformations. For example, each row in Figure 8.1 may represent liver cells posited on their respective world lines. Each cell is dependent on others for the healthy functioning

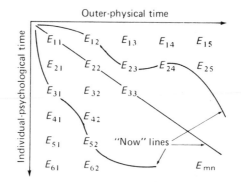

Figure 8.1. Two-dimensional time matrix with world-lines of events accumulating along several levels of analysis and with alternative "now" lines.

of the organ. Different cells, cell groupings, organs, or whole organ systems may develop at different rates determined, for example, by their metabolic conditions. The liver and lungs may be changing rather fast, while the heart may be changing in a negative direction relative to the lungs or neuronal tissues. Birren (1959) has suggested that there may be as many processes of development as there are cells, cell clusters, organs, etc.

By using a clock we can order various events in the form of the series, $E_{i1}, E_{i2}, E_{i3}, \ldots, E_{in}$. But the nature of these sequences would remain insufficiently explored if we merely impose a universal order on the events. We also need to consider other relations, which, as shown in Figure 8.1, might be represented orthogonal to the first. In the resulting two-dimensional system any instant of "now" is represented by the intersection of the time axes at some event E. Sets of E_{ij} constitute "now lines" which can assume many functional forms. A change in velocity of the event accumulation could, for example, result in curvilinear now lines.

Numerous examples demonstrate the synchronization of different event sequences along the inner-biological dimension. For instance, Piaget's (1950) distinction between *accommodation* and *assimilation* implies such a temporal coordination. In his explanation of adaptation and structural changes, Piaget considers accommodation as that process by which the organism makes adjustments in order to cope with the condition of the object. When eating, for example, the organism accommodates to the food by grasping, breaking, biting, chewing, salivating, and swallowing. At the same time the food is assimilated by being grasped, torn, broken, chemically altered, etc. Both types of processes complement each other; one can not function without the other and whenever the complementarity fails, for example, when the food is too hard, a conflict arises that searches for new solutions.

Many examples from the inner-biological level are interwoven with individual-psychological processes. In his discussion of cognitive development, Piaget uses the example of eating only to demonstrate the complementarity of accommodation and assimilation. An instructive example on the interdependence of event sequences at the biological and psychological levels has been provided by Schaltenbrand.

Schaltenbrand (1967) argues that all perceptions are brought about by the experience of contradictions. For example, three-dimensional spatial impressions are created "by the fusion of two pictures of the world which are not completely congruent, since both eyes see the objects at a different angle. We attain the conception of movement in a similar way. Here, too, pictures with a particular contradictory content are integrated into something new. The conception of movement is therefore similar in performance to the conception of three-dimensionality." Since our visual system can handle only a limited number of frames in a given time, a presentation at a slow rate will lead to the discrete experience of these contradictions in the form of jerky patterns. If the rate of presentation is high, the contradictory states are resolved into smooth movements.

Psychological Event Sequences

The coordination of event sequences at the inner-biological level is frequently confounded with psychological activities. The following example of dialogical exchanges focuses more strongly on psychological functions and represents one of the best demonstrations of the temporal coordination of two event sequences (Riegel, 1976a).

The development of dialogues during infancy can be traced through the changing relationship between a mother and her child. Prior to birth the two are firmly coupled with one another by their joint physiology. Though disrupted, this relationship continues to function after birth in unison like the two clocks in Leibniz' demonstration of *pre-established harmony.* But increasingly with age, coordination will depend upon the mother's and the child's experiences and actions. The child begins to look at the mother's face. When she moves, the child follows her with his or her eyes. When she speaks, the child might look at her mouth. When she stops, the child might vocalize and switch its attention from her mouth to her eyes (Lewis & Freedle, 1973). Thus, the development of dialogues is preceded by a finely tuned temporal coordination of activities.

The communication system shared by mother and child is at first private to both of them and depends on shared knowledge about extralingual objects and events, and about personal states and wishes. As development advances, the signs begin to be used in the absence of extralingual objects and events. As signs are related to signs they must become congruent with the language of the society. Otherwise no efficient communication could take place. As the child attempts to make its own expressions congruent with those of the society, one of the mother's most important tasks consists of the transmission of this information to the child. The success of this transmission depends on the synchronization of her efforts with those of the child. Information has to be given at the right moment, in the right amount, and of the right kind. The mother has to speak as she influences her child, but she has also to listen and change her own activities in accordance with the development of her child. The development of the child and the development of the mother are constituted by the synchronization of their activities. Synchronization also produces the temporal structure of their interactions, of their dialogues.

A dialogue has temporal structure not only because the speakers alternate in their presentations but also because each successive statement reflects the two immediately preceding it and those produced before. Every statement has to be consistent with the views previously expressed by its proponent and must also represent an equally consistent or systematically modified reaction to all statements made by the other participant in the dialogue. Thus, in the simplest form of a dialogue, the two speakers always relate their new statements to both the last statement made by the opponent and to that made by the speaker himself or herself.

As we have seen in Chapter 5, each speaker assimilates the other person's statements in successful dialogues and accommodates his/her own productions so that they elaborate and extend the preceding viewpoints. If this were not the case, dialogues would either degenerate into what Piaget (1926) has called collective monologues or would converge into repetitive cycles in which each speaker merely reaffirms what has been said before. As in the truss of a bridge, successful dialogues are composed of triangular subsections which I call *dialogical units*. Such units reflect the dialectical character of the communication process. The original statement represents a *thesis* which will be denied, challenged, or modified by the other speaker. The second statement, therefore, represents an *antithesis*. Even a simple confirmation by a nod is a dialogical challenge to the first speaker who will take notice of it and integrate this message in his or her next statement. But as this *synthesis* is uttered, the second speaker may object to it and propose a deviant interpretation which integrates his/her own former statement (thesis) with that by the opponent (antithesis).

The composition of the dialogical unit makes us aware of the reflective character of all dialogical interactions. The thesis provokes and anticipates the antithesis; the antithesis modifies and reinterprets the thesis. And what holds for the thesis and antithesis also holds for their relationships to the synthesis. Thus, each utterance in the dialogical exchange represents a thesis, an antithesis, and a synthesis at one and the same time—dependent upon which of the triangular subsection in the truss we are focusing upon.

Implications

Temporal organization is brought about by the synchronization of at least two event sequences, for example of two cells, two organs, two organisms, or two dialogue partners. While the biological examples might be consistent with the traditional forms of inquiry (though they are more complex since the observation of two rather than only one sequence of events is involved), the psychological example of the dialogue suggests a more radical alternative. Traditional inquiries (e.g., into language development) consisted of collecting samples of utterances from the child over a stretch of time. Typical forms of grammatical constructions were then abstracted from the data (McNeill, 1970a). Thus, as in cognitive developmental psychology, different stages in grammatical production were delineated in order to demonstrate the child's linguistic progress.

The orientation of the students of linguistic and cognitive development has been guided by the paradigm of classical natural sciences. In order to obtain "objective" data, performances were recorded by the investigator and, then, cast into a series of structural descriptions. As in the studies of motion in physics, changes were inferred from the differences between successive structures. Time did not enter as a primary concept into the analysis. In contrast to this approach, time and change are basic properties of the dialogue. The temporal structure unfolds itself through the interlacing of the two participants' activities. There is no desire to average each speaker's performances in order to describe typical stages in development; only differences in the degree and form of synchronization are of interest. As a further consequence, also the distorted view of the speakers' performances as the object of study for the investigator is abandoned. In dialogues, both speakers are objects and subjects at the same time, and the investigators function as a metasubject at a higher level of analysis. But their relationship to both dialogue partners is open to a dialogical analysis.

Individual-Psychological Changes

Temporality of Narratives

According to Wundt (1911–1912), the most fundamental problem of language consists in the transformation of sets of coexisting ideas into the sequences of linguistic expressions. This problem is not narrowly restricted to language and to the common contrast between semantic and syntactic organization but touches upon the simultaneity and sequential order of thought, upon the harmonic and contrapuntal structure of music, and upon the synchronic-logical and the developmental-dialectical analysis in sciences.

The problem of spatio-temporal transformation is also familiar to writers and historians. In particular Carlyle is credited with handling these difficulties in a most eloquent manner. As stated by Clive (1969)

> In ordinary narrative history, "A" occurs; then "B" occurs (possibly, but not necessarily, caused by "A"); then "C" happens, etc. This of course, is a false rendering of actuality, since not only do many other events transpire simultaneously, along with "A," "B," and "C"; but it is also true that "A," "B," and "C," like all historical events, are anchored in the past and have repercussions in the future. The historian's usual means of dealing with this basic problem is to make use of phrases such as "meanwhile," "at the same time," "while this was happening here, that was happening there;" and to spell out, in so many words, both the background and the aftermath of the events he is narrating.
>
> The trouble with these stylistic devices is that they completely fail to capture the historical *process*, in which nothing is stationary, and everything is constantly in motion and in flux, in which growth and decay proceed at the same time; in which events do not occur in isolation, but are related to each other in a constantly shifting network of interconnections. What Carlyle does is not to evade this problem, but to face it head on, by using linguistic literary devices to create the equivalent of living reality [p. xxxvi].

As I have mentioned in Chapter 5, the temporal structure of narratives has recently been analyzed by Labov and Waletzky (1967). Like

Wundt, these authors consider the task of narration as one of transforming a set of simultaneous states of events into a structure sequentially ordered within itself as well as transformationally related to the external conditions which it aims to describe. In particular, narratives coordinate sets of nonlinguistic events with a sequence of linguistic expressions. Often, the latter imposes a more restricted order upon the former that by themselves might be confusing in their temporal organization. In trying to maximize these transformational aspects in controlled tasks, Linde and Labov (1975) asked individuals to describe, for example, the layout of their apartments (coexisting spatial conditions) in narrative form (sequential description of spatial conditions).

The task of mapping sequences of external events upon linguistic expressions is comparable to dialogues in which one partner is missing. But there is a more basic similarity between narration and dialogical interactions. Narratives are produced only if there are listeners to listen or readers to read. These listeners and readers remain relatively passive and rarely interact with the producer of the story. But if a statement never becomes a part of some outer or inner dialogue, it is of no interest at all and bare of any meaning. It becomes significant only if it is incorporated into such a temporal structure, regardless of whether such a structure emerges immediately or many months later. A statement in complete isolation—to repeat it once more—is like the sounds in the woods occurring in the absence of any listener. One might question with Wittgenstein their existence but as one begins to think about these sounds, they enter into an inner-dialogical interaction and, therefore, gain meaning regardless of whether they "really" exist or not.

The Temporality of Memory

The preceding examples have given evidence for a concept of time that emphasizes event sequences, the temporal markings of which are generated by the interactions between two cells, organs, or individuals. In the following section, attention will be given to a single sequence of events. Nevertheless, the psychological experience of these events by the observer creates the effect of contrapuntal interactions, that is, the interactions between what was, what is, and what will be. The following section is addressed to the temporal structure of memory as recently explored by Kvale (1974) and as graphically represented by Figure 8.2.

The horizontal line indicates the world line of an individual recalling three events, *A, B,* and *C.* The vertical lines at *A* and *B* represent

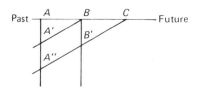

Figure 8.2. Retentionalizing of impressions.

some other world-lines depicting the changing state of the memorized events. The process of recollection at the time of events *B* and *C* is indicated by slanted now-lines. Most notably at the time of event *C*, the previous *B* appears in recall as *B'*, and the previous *A* appears as A". From *C*, *A* is now seen through the intervening *B'*. As stated by Husserl (1964),

> Retention itself is not an "act" but a momentary consciousness of the phase which has expired and, at the same time, a foundation for the retentional consciousness of the next phase. Since each phase is retentionally cognizant of the preceding one, it encloses in itself, in a chain of mediate intentions, the entire series of retentions which have expired [pp. 161–162].

Figure 8.2 utilizes a two-dimensional time plot. The horizontal dimension represents the remembering individuals who in interaction with other individuals and social conditions generate the occasions *A, B,* and *C* about which they retrospect at later occasions. The vertical dimension represents the experienced events as they are changed in interaction with other events experienced either prior to them or after they have occurred. The slanted now-lines represent cross sections through the memory at particular moments in time. Underlying the representation of Figure 8.2 is the idea that memory as well as the human being and society are in a constant state of change (Kvale, 1975, 1977; Meacham, 1972, 1975b, 1976, 1977a, 1977b; Reese, 1976, 1977) and through these changes earlier states can never be attained again. Every new experience alters the structure of the memory, every new event added onto the horizontal dimension extends the slanted now-lines over a wider and wider range.

The activities of an individual are determined not only by the interactions with co-occurring events and by the retentional interactions with events of the past, but also by the individual's attention.

> The unity of the present with the past is thus constituted by retentions, and at the forward end of the perceptual arc the protentions join the present to the

future. When listening to an enduring tone I more or less implicitly expect it to continue, to change, or to stop. This expecting consciousness is an integral part of the consciousness of the tone. In its most basic form, a protention is an empty intention with an open indeterminateness, constituting the formal basis for eventual more explicit contextual expectations of what is coming [Kvale, 1974, p. 16].

Implications

The approach advocated by Kvale is diametrically opposed to the efforts by experimental psychologists and to the goals of developmental psychologists. Experimental psychologists have studied abstract performances outside of their developmental and historical contexts. By testing the degree to which an individual could exactly reproduce the material learned in the past, they assumed an ideal permanence of the events and failed to recognize that such a performance would be abnormal indeed. Concrete events are in constant change and are modified by all events preceding them and by all events following them. Therefore, the individual can never and should never recall an event as it "really" was.

Developmental psychologists have attended to developmental differences and changes but have failed to recognize that the individual changes within a changing world. Like the experimentalists they disregarded that performance objectified here and now is experientially empty for individuals unless it is understood within the context of their experienced past and anticipated future. Neither experimental nor developmental psychologists have explored the retrospective memories and the prospective intention of individuals (Riegel, 1976b).

Writers, narrators, and historians, in contrast, are relying on recollections of past events. Thereby they are utilizing whatever means are available to them, that is, books, treatises, documents in archives or libraries, and advice by other experts, in order to reconstruct the past as accurately and comprehensively as possible. But their efforts are always hampered because the events to be reconstructed are rarely experienced by the historians themselves and, most important, are affected by the intervention of other historical events. The source material has often been transmitted over long chains which modify the sense of the reports to the same extent that the abstractness and idealized permanence of psychological variables distorts the meaningfulness of experimental and developmental interpretations.

Cultural-Sociological Changes

Individual and Societal Changes

Although developmental psychology and history have hardly influenced each other in the past, their interest in individual and cultural changes provides a common basis. This is most clearly seen in the study of modern developmental research designs.

As shown by Schaie (1965) and Baltes (1968), certain psychological variables, such as the amount of mobility and communication, may yield developmental gradients increasing in magnitude from generation to generation. If these increases are linearly related to age and if, furthermore, we assess age differences by the traditional cross-sectional method, that is, by testing samples from different age groups, the results might indicate a curvilinear increase in scores with age and a decline thereafter. Curves like these are familiar to developmental psychologists, yet they represent mere artifacts because neither the generation nor the time of testing (historical time) effects have been controlled as contributing factors.

The proper analysis can be best explained in reference to Table 8.1 which lists the age of three cohorts (born around 1850, 1900, 1950) over two times of measurements (1920 and 1970). Comparisons within the rows of the table represent longitudinal designs; those along the diagonals from the left-lower to the right-upper cells represent cross-sectional designs; a third design, the time-lag design, compares cohort differences at various times of testing within specific age groups, that is, within the two columns. As in the examples used before, Table 8.1 represents a two-dimensional time plot in which one dimension indicates the individual-psychological age and the other cultural–sociological time.

TABLE 8.1
Time of Cross-Sectional Testing (Now-Lines) in
Developmental Research Designs

	Age	
Cohort	20	70
1850	1870	1920
1900	1920	1970
1950	1970	2020

Cross-sections taken, for example, in 1920 and 1970 represent now-lines.

None of the three basic developmental designs measures in an unconfounded manner either age, cohort, or historical time (time of testing) differences. An inspection of Table 8.1 shows that results from cross-sectional designs (CSD) confound age (AD) and cohort differences (CD); those from longitudinal designs (LOD) confound age (AD) and historical time differences (TD); those from time-lag designs (TLD) confound historical (TD) and cohort differences (CD). These conditions can be summarized in the following equations:

$$CSD = AD + CD$$
$$LOD = AD + TD$$
$$TLD = TD + CD$$

If we solve these equations for any of the three right-hand terms we obtain the following results:

$$AD = \tfrac{1}{2}\,(CSD - TLD + LOD)$$
$$CD = \tfrac{1}{2}\,(TLD - LOD + CSD)$$
$$TD = \tfrac{1}{2}\,(LOD - CSD + TLD)$$

Thus, it is in principle possible to obtain estimates of the pure effects of age, cohort, or historical time differences, but such attempts will always have to rely on the joint utilization of all three basic designs. If this is being done, psychology may describe developmental differences or changes, sociology may describe cohort or generational differences, and history may describe changes with chronological time. But these disciplines should not remain in their isolation. Any understanding of their topics can be achieved only if their contributions are recognized in their complementary determination. Each alone produces abstract results and fictitious interpretations.

Implications

In the preceding sections, I explored only a few of the sixteen types of temporal interactions shown in Table 1.1. First, I compared event sequences at the inner-biological level which ranged from those in single cells, to cell systems, organs, organ systems, and whole organisms. Second, at the individual-psychological level, likewise, a wide range of event sequences could be compared. My discussion was limited, however, to exchanges between two persons in dialogues. Third, I called attention to the temporal structure of narratives within which different co-occurring events are transformed into the single sequence of oral or written presentations. Fourth, similar transformations are necessary in memory processes. This topic, in particular, calls attention to the ever-changing state of the experienced conditions.

Fifth, the analysis of historical changes led us away from the inner-biological and individual-psychological event sequences of the earlier sections. However, this separation can never be complete, and it is not surprising, therefore, that some of the most intriguing questions arise in the study of the interdependence of individual and cultural progressions. Sixth, the interdependence of these changes has been treated in a systematic manner in modern developmental research designs. As in all other examples, this analysis employs a two-dimensional time plot with one dimension representing individual and the other cultural development. In the following sections, I will generalize these comparisons by relying on an analysis of temporal structure of musical compositions.

Music, Time, and Dialectical Logic

Temporal Structure of Music

The organization of time is brought about by the interdependence of at least two event sequences. If these event sequences are sound waves, their particular interactions create the experience of beats and, thereby, of temporal order. Without this order we would merely hear a continuous sound which soon we would cease to register. Only when the stimulation is interrupted do we suddenly recognize the sounds again. Due to their differences in wave length, musical tones either create these interruptions by themselves in the form of beats or they are introduced by the composer through accent, rhythm, and pauses.

Since preceding sounds always reverberate—are in "holding" patterns—they blend into following ones (and vice versa) and thus, temporal impressions of consonance or dissonance are created even in the monophonic arrangements of simple melodies. As in Kvale's model of memory, events experienced in their temporality are modified in retrospection by those following them, as they are modified by those to follow. However the impressive development of music became possible only when during the course of its more recent history, different voices or instruments were interlaced with one another. In such polyphonic compositions different sequences, by interacting with one another, create temporal markings and provide temporal structure to the music.

We can look at polyphonic compositions in a perpendicular and in horizontal manner. In the former way, we would recognize a multitude of chords which are the elements of harmony; in the latter way, we would recognize several superimposed melodies.

> A choral conductor, if handed a new part-song and told he would have to begin to train his choir in it five minutes hence, would be likely to . . . mentally run through the music, noting how the voice-parts weave in and out, one ceasing for a moment and another entering, one holding a long note while others are engaged with a number of shorter notes, and so forth. On the other hand, the pianist who was to accompany the choir would be likely to look at the music as a series of successive handsful of notes, observing the nature of the groups of notes to be simultaneously sounded, the way in which these carried the music into new keys . . . , and so forth. In other words, whilst the conductor was engaged in *contrapuntal* exploration the pianist would be engaged very largely in *harmonic* exploration [Scholes, 1970, p. 441].

In polyphonic compositions, various instruments create musical event sequences which, by elaborating or supporting a basic theme, might occasionally be in unison, frequently in harmony, but most often in tension. Such a composition is comparable to the network of event sequences that characterize both the single individual's development as well as those of two or more individuals in their situational interactions. It is comparable, for example, to the individual's attempt to synchronize his wishes with his duties, his affects with his skills, his movements with his thoughts. It is comparable to the attempts by different individuals to synchronize their interests and tasks, for example, in the family, in school, at the job, in a club, etc.

Relational, Absolute, and Dialectical Time

According to one of the earliest philosophical viewpoints, space was negatively defined as that domain which is not filled with substances (objects); space was regarded as a void. Comparable to this concept, time could be regarded as that stretch which is not filled with events; thus, time would be negatively defined by events. However events imply action and, thus, reflect a higher degree of organization than substances in space. A concept of time based on series of events has been called relational. Like a musical theme or a passage in a narrative, relational time arises as a consequence of serial interactions between events. In a simple monophonic melody, for example, it is produced by the contrast between preceding and following sounds. The temporal structures of individual experiences and cultural representations, likewise, are based upon variations of event sequences. Since these event sequences are founded upon the movement of objects or substances in space, the relational interpretation compounds the three basic concepts of classical sciences and philosophy: Substance, space, and time. It relies on the notion of activity and movement as the most basic property of nature.

While relational time is intrinsically defined (not necessarily in the experience of the observer only but by the order of the events), absolute time is regarded as extrinsically defined and constitutive of nature; it regulates the rates of processes and is physically prior to events. In music, for example, it is superimposed by means of the clicks of the metronome during rehearsal and by the meter and the bar lines on the score sheet.

Finally, dialectical time is both intrinsically and extrinsically determined. It is comparable to polyphonic compositions and, thus, incorporates a diversity of monophonic or relational sequences. It also incorporates absolute time because it will rely on an extrinsic standard, for example, the clock or calendar, which assists in the synchronization of different event sequences. This yardstick represents one particular monophonic structure which has been elevated to serve as a uniform standard. Finally, the dialectical concept indicates that common and scientific experience of time involve at least the interaction of two-event sequences, for example, the phenomena observed and the measurement taken.

As the dialectical concept of time focuses upon changing interactions, it emphasizes concrete experiences and events. For example, it emphasizes the changing interdependence of the utterances by two speakers in a dialogue, of the activities of husband and wife in the family, or of the metabolic rates in the circulatory and neuronal systems. As these activities lead to the formation of conflicts and resolutions, questions and answers, disharmonies and harmonies, temporal markings are generated. Temporal markings, knots, or points of coincidence represent transitions in the sequence of changes. Harmonies and disharmonies represent momentary states in a flux of changes. They resemble simultaneous structures that lack temporal extension and are similar to semantic fields in distinction from syntactic orders. These harmonies and disharmonies merge into the temporal organization of melodies. The contrastive comparison between simultaneous spatial conditions and developmental temporal changes elucidates the basic properties of the dialectical concept of time.

Several other conditions demonstrate the contrast between relational and absolute time on the one hand, and dialectical time on the other. For example, a dialectical interpretation integrates the concepts of substance, space, and time as well as the concepts of absolute and relational inertia. As discussed by Fraser (1967) in classical physics inertia had an absolute character intrinsic to matter. Matter was thought to be identifiable without regard to the rest of the world. Like space and time it rather constituted a prerequisite for the structure of the physical world. But according to Mach, inertia may also be regarded as a relational entity if the interaction of local matter with all matter of the universe is taken into consideration. A dialectical interpretation would accept and integrate both viewpoints.

The analysis of inertia parallels the comparison between endogeneous and exogeneous biological clocks.

> The existence of a purely endogeneous clock could only be proved in an empty universe without history, the existence of a purely exogeneous clock could be proved only if it has no potentially rhythmic internal structure. In practice, the temporal nature of the biological clock must be conceived of as a relationship between its physical self and the world. For convenience, this relationship may be imagined as the fusion of two abstract clocks, an endogeneous and an exogeneous one. . . . [Thus] absolute and relational inertia, on the one hand, and endogeneous and extrageneous clocks, on the other hand, are conceptually similar pairs of abstraction. The inertial properties of real matter and the timekeeping properties of real biological clocks are neither of relational nor of absolute nature. . . . They may be better described as being both [Fraser, 1967, p. 835].

The contradiction implied in these comparisons can not be resolved in our two-valued Aristotelian logic. All that we can do is to contemplate about the "nature outside of us *or* about our own nature. The glorified formulation to discriminate between subject–object, true–false, body–mind, real–illusion, etc. compels us to perceive–conceive a dual and contradictory character of experience" (Fischer, 1967, p. 457). In our two-valued Aristotelian logic, we can not apprehend that something is both subject *and* object, true *and* false, body *and* mind, real *and* illusion at one and the same time. In order to develop such notions we have to adopt a multivalued logic, such as dialectical logic.

Formal and Dialectical Logic

Traditional logic, as well as traditional philosophy and science, have been exclusively concerned with nontemporal conditions. The concept of a nonchanging state of being, as originated in Eleatic philosophy, was thought to reflect the universal order of the cosmos. Traditional logic and mathematics are the remnants of the a-developmental and a-historical thinking of Eleatic philosophers.

Our sciences are founded upon traditional logic and deal, therefore, with spatial structures. Even when Galileo investigated the laws of gravity and Newton the laws of motion, they measured the spatial conditions at some time slices and inferred the temporal relations afterwards. But for an analysis of development and change, time should be given primary and not only secondary consideration. As cogently argued by Günther (1967), this is possible because

> the scientific development leading from Archimedes to Einstein was accompanied by a parallel trend—the history of dialectic logic. And dialectic logic poses an entirely different question. Its first concern is not the relation of time to Being, but the relation of Time to Logic itself. It can be shown that the discussion of Time on the basis of natural science remained incomplete and insufficient because it ignored the dialectic aspect [p. 397].

Dialectical logic, comparable to polyphonic musical compositions, is more than a counterpart to traditional logic. As much as the movements in music are built upon simultaneous slices in the sequence of changes, so does dialectical thinking presuppose traditional logical structures. Dialectical logic recognizes that it cannot exist without traditional logic. This recognition provides a more general basis to dialectical logic than available to traditional logic. Traditional logic fails to recognize such dependency and is bound to consider itself immutable. Dialectical logic represents an open system of thinking that can always be extended to incorporate the more restricted systems. Traditional logic aims at a single universal analysis. As a consequence it is inflexible and cannot apprehend itself; in particular, it cannot apprehend itself in the developmental and historical process.[3]

The development of dialectical logic, especially by Hegel, has not been commonly accepted in natural sciences (at least not in classical natural sciences) (Wundt, 1949) and, most surprisingly, it has received

[3]Similar limitations hold for existentialism and phenomenology. These philosophies too (with some notable exceptions, e.g., Gadamer, 1975, and M. Merleau-Ponty, 1962) regard "being" as primary and "becoming" (which the individual completes) as secondary. While there is a shared concern for the concrete experience of the individual, dialectics emphasizes human activities (rather than contemplations) in their interactional determination during developmental and historical processes. Thus dialectics goes only part of the way with Schaltenbrand's conclusion that modern man "instead of seeing his living existence, he sees himself as a kind of album-leaf in a herbarium, dried and pinned onto the

even lesser attention in the behavioral and social sciences. Since—as it has been demonstrated by Kosok (1976)—dialectical logic can be cast into a systematic language that makes it applicable to sciences and since dialectical logic is the mode of thinking that alone can deal appropriately with change, development, and history, such a disregard is regrettable indeed. Nevertheless, both the rapidly growing appreciation of dialectical logic in modern natural sciences and the similar, if belated, recognition of its significance in the behavioral and social sciences (see Datan & Reese, 1977; Riegel, 1975b; Rychlak, 1976b) indicate that a decisive change is taking place.

Conclusions

I have compared three concepts of time: relational, absolute, and dialectical. Relational time is constituted by the serial interactions of events. In a simple monophonic melody, for example, it is produced by the contrast between preceding and following sounds and sound groupings. While relational time is intrinsically defined, absolute time is regarded as constitutive of nature. It regulates the rates of processes and is prior to events. Thus, absolute time is extrinsically defined. In music, for example, it is superimposed by the clicks of the metronome during rehearsal and by the meter and the bar lines on the score sheets.

Dialectical time is both intrinsically and extrinsically determined. It is comparable to polyphonic compositions and, thus, incorporates a diversity of monophonic or relational sequences. It also incorporates absolute time because polyphonic music also relies upon an extrinsic yardstick that assists in the synchronization of the different instruments or voices. The dialectical concept indicates that common or scientific experience of time involves at least the interaction between two event

---

abstract scheme of the flow of time.... Because he considers time as a stretch, the present as zero, and events ordered by deterministic laws, he has no time to exist. Consequently, he can see himself and the world only from a historical point of view. He is, so to speak, already dead and his future is, also, already dead (p. 643)." While dialectics would agree with the notion that time, as conceived in classical natural sciences, "evolves from the codification of events interfering with living presence, or is created by acts of the present [p. 641]," it does not subscribe to the view that living presence is itself timeless. Quite to the contrary, dialecticians maintain that the living presence is experienced as movement and action that create and within which is reflected the living past and the anticipated future both of the individual and society.

sequences, for example, the phenomena observed and the measurement taken.

As the dialectical concept of time focuses upon changing interactions, it emphasizes concrete experiences and events. As these lead to the formation of conflicts and resolutions, questions and answers, disharmonies and harmonies, temporal markings are produced by the synchronization of these sequences. Harmonies and disharmonies represent momentary states which merge into the temporal organization of melodies. The contrastive comparison between simultaneous (spatial) conditions and developmental (temporal) changes elucidates the basic property of the dialectical concept of time.

References

Alden, J. R., & Magenis, A. *A history of the United States*. New York: American Book, 1962.

Anderson, E. S., & Johnson, C. E. Modifications in the speech of an eight-year-old as a reflection of age of listener. *Stanford Occasional Papers in Linguistics*, 1973, *3*, 149–160.

Balance, W. *The Grundzüge revisited: A review for contemporary psychology*. Paper presented at the 81st Annual Convention of the American Psychological Association, Montreal, 1973.

Baltes, P. B. Longitudinal and cross-sectional sequences in the study of age and generation effects. *Human Development*, 1968, *11*, 175–171.

Baltes, P. B., & Schaie, K. W. (Eds.) *Life-span developmental psychology: Personality and socialization*. New York: Academic Press, 1973.

Bavink, B. *Ergebnisse und Probleme der Naturwissenschaften*. (6 Aufl.). Leipzig: Hirzel, 1940.

Bell, S. M., & Ainsworth, M. D. Infant crying and maternal responsiveness. *Child Development*, 1972, *43*, 1171–1190.

Berko Gleason, J. Code switching in children's language. In T. E. Moore (Ed.), *Cognitive development and the acquisition of language*. New York: Academic Press, 1973.

Bertalanffy, L. von. Comments on Professor Piaget's paper. In J. M. Tanner & B. Inhelder (Eds.), *Discussion on child development* (Vol. 4). New York: International Univ. Press, 1960. Pp. 69–76.

Bickford, B., & Looft, W. R. More on more: The mythology and actuality of children's understanding of relational terms. *Journal of Genetic Psychology*, 1973, *123*, 139–143.

Birren, J. E. Principles of research on aging. In J. E. Birren (Ed.), *Handbook of aging and the individual*. Chicago: Univ. of Chicago Press, 1959. Pp. 3–42.

Bloom, L. *Language development*. Cambridge, Massachusetts: MIT Press, 1970.

References

Bloom, L. *One word at a time: The use of single word utterances before syntax.* The Hague: Mouton, 1973.

Blount, B. G. Parental speech and language acquisition: Some Luo and Samoan examples. *Anthropological Linguistics,* 1972, *14,* 119–130.

Blumenthal, A. *Language and psychology.* New York: Wiley, 1970.

Blumenthal, A. *Wundt's psycholinguistics.* Paper presented at the 81st Annual Convention of the American Psychological Association, Montreal, 1973.

Boring, E. G. *History of experimental psychology* (2nd ed.). New York: Appleton-Century-Crofts, 1957.

Bourne, L. E., Jr. Learning and utilization of conceptual rules. In B. Kleinmuntz (Ed.), *Concepts and structure of memory.* New York: Wiley, 1970. Pp. 1–32.

Braine, M. D. S. On learning the grammatical order of words. *Psychological Review,* 1963, *70,* 323–348.

Brinkmann, W. *The background: Wundt at Heidelberg.* Paper presented at the 81st Annual Convention of the American Psychological Association, Montreal, 1973.

Brown, R. *A first language.* Cambridge, Massachusetts: Harvard Univ. Press, 1973.

Brown, R., & Bellugi, U. Three processes in the child's acquisition of syntax. *Harvard Educational Review,* 1964, *34,* 133–151.

Brown, R., Cazden, C. B., & Bellugi-Klima, U. The child's grammar from 1 to 3. In J. P. Hill (Ed.), *Minnesota symposium on child psychology.* (Vol. 2). Minneapolis: Univ. of Minnesota Press, 1969. Pp. 28–73.

Brown, R. & Fraser, C. The acquisition of syntax. In C. N. Cofer & B. S. Musgrave (Eds.), *Verbal behavior and learning.* New York: McGraw-Hill, 1963. Pp. 158–197.

Brown, R., & Fraser, C. The acquisition of syntax. In U. Bellugi & R. Brown (Eds.), The acquisition of language. *Monographs of the Society for Research in Child Development,* 1964, *29* (No. 92). Pp. 43–78.

Bruner, J. S. Nature and uses of immaturity. *American Psychologist,* 1972, *27,* 687–708.

Bruner, J. S. The ontogenesis of speech acts. *Journal of Child Language,* 1975, *2,* 1–19.

Bruner, J. S., Goodnow, S. S., & Austin, G. A. *A study of thinking.* New York: Wiley, 1956.

Buck-Morss, S. Socio-economic bias in Piaget's theory and its implications for the cross-cultural controversy. *Human Development,* 1975, *18,* 35–49.

Buehler, C. *Der menschliche Lebenslauf als psychologisches Problem.* Leipzig: Hirzel, 1933.

Buehler, C. The developmental structure of goal setting in group and individual studies. In C. Buehler & F. Massarik (Eds.), *The course of human life.* New York: Springer, 1968.

Bühler, K. *Sprachtheorie.* Jena: G. Fischer, 1934.

Carnap, R. *Der logische Aufbau der Welt.* Hamburg: Meiner, 1928. [*Logical structure of the world.* Berkeley, California: Univ. of California Press, Berkeley, 1967.]

Cassirer, E. *Substance and function and Einstein's theory of relativity.* Chicago: Open Court, 1923.

Cazden, C. B. *Environmental assistance to the child's acquisition of grammar.* Unpublished doctoral dissertation, Harvard University, 1965.

Chandler, M. J. Relativism and the problem of epistemological loneliness. *Human Development,* 1975, *18,* 171–180.

Chomsky, N. *Aspects of the theory of syntax.* Cambridge, Massachusetts: MIT Press, 1965.

Chomsky, N. *Syntactic structures.* The Hague: Mouton, 1957.

Chomsky, N. *Language and mind.* New York: Harcourt, 1968.

Cipolla, C. M. *Money, prices, and civilization in the Mediterranean world.* Princeton, New Jersey: Princeton Univ. Press, 1956.

Clark, H. H. Comprehending comparatives. In G. Flores d'Arcais & W. S. M. Levelt (Eds.), *Advances in psycholinguistics.* Amsterdam: North-Holland Publ., 1970. Pp. 294–306.

References

Clive, J. (Ed.). *Thomas Carlyle: History of Frederick the Great.* Chicago: Univ. of Chicago Press, 1969. p. xxxvi.

Coombs, C. H. *Theory of data.* New York: Wiley, 1964.

Datan, N., & Ginsberg, L. H. (Eds.). *Life-span developmental psychology: Normative life crises.* New York: Academic Press, 1975.

Datan, N., & Reese, H. W. (Eds.), *Life-span developmental psychology: Dialectical perspectives on experimental research.* New York: Academic Press, 1977.

Dedekind, R. *Was sind und was sollen Zahlen?* (II Aufl.). Braunschweig: Vieweg, 1893.

De Paulo, B. M., & Bonvillian, J. D. *The effect on language development of the special characteristics of speech addressed to children.* Unpublished manuscript, Harvard University, 1975.

Donaldson, M., & Balfour, G. Less is more: A study of language comprehension in children. *British Journal of Psychology,* 1968, *59,* 461–471.

Duncan, S. Some signals and rules for taking speaking turns in conversation. *Journal of Personality and Social Psychology,* 1972, *23,* 283–292.

Erikson, E. H. *Childhood and society.* New York: Norton, 1963.

Erikson, E. H. *Identity, youth, and crisis.* New York: Norton, 1968.

Ervin-Tripp, S. Imitation and structural change in children's language. In E. H. Lenneberg (Ed.) *New directions in the study of language.* Cambridge: Massachusetts: MIT Press, 1964.

Ervin-Tripp, S. An analysis of the interaction of language topic and listener. In J. A. Fishman (Ed.), *Readings in the sociology of language.* The Hague: Mouton, 1968.

Ervin-Tripp, S. Discourse agreement: How children answer questions. In J. R. Hayes (Ed.), *Cognition and the development of language.* New York: Wiley, 1970.

Farwell, C. B. The language spoken to children. *Human Development,* 1975, *18,* 288–309.

Ferguson, C. A. Baby talk in six languages. *American Anthropologist,* 1964, *6,* 103–114.

Fieguth, R. *Struktur des literarischen Wandels: Struktur der Einzelwerke.* Unpublished manuscript, University of Konstanz, Germany, 1973.

Fillmore, C. J. The case for case. In E. Bach & R. T. Harms (Eds.), *Universals in linguistic theory.* New York: Holt, 1968. Pp. 1–88.

Fischer, R. The biological fabric of time. *Annals of the New York Academy of Sciences,* 1967, *138,* 440–488.

Flavell, J. H. *The developmental psychology of Jean Piaget.* New York: Van Nostrand-Reinhold, 1963.

Flavell, J. H. Cognitive changes in adulthood. In L. R. Goulet & P. B. Baltes (Eds.), *Life-span developmental psychology: Research and theory.* New York: Academic Press, 1970.

Flavell, J. H., & Wohlwill, J. F. Formal and functional aspects of cognitive development. In D. Elkind & J. H. Flavell (Eds.), *Studies in cognitive development.* New York: Oxford Univ. Press, 1969.

Fraser, C., & Roberts, N. Mother's speech to children of four different ages. *Journal of Psycholinguistic Research,* 1975, *4,* 9–16.

Fraser, J. T. The interdisciplinary study of time. *Annals of the New York Academy of Sciences,* 1967, *138,* 822–847.

Freedle, R. Dialogue and inquiry systems: The development of social logic. *Human Development,* 1975, *18,* 97–118.

Freedle, R. Logic, general systems, and human development: Preliminaries to developing a psycho-social linguistics. In G. Steiner (Ed.), *Piaget's developmental and cognitive psychology within an extended context, Vol. 7.* (*The psychology of the 20th century*). Zürich: Kindler, 1978.

Frege, B. *Grundgesetze der Arithmetik.* Jena: H. Pohle, 1903. [*The basic laws of arithmetic.* Berkeley, California: Univ. of California Press, 1964.]

References

Furth, H. G. *Piaget and knowledge.* Englewood Cliffs, New Jersey: Prentice-Hall, 1969.

Furth, H. G. Piaget, IQ and the nature-nurture controversy. *Human Development,* 1973, *16,* 61–73.

Gadamer, H. G. *Wahrheit und Methode.* Tubingen: Mohr, 1960. [*Truth and method.* New York: Seabury Press, 1975.]

Gaettens, R. *Inflationen.* Munich: Pflaum, 1955.

Galton, F. *Hereditary genius: An inquiry into its laws and consequences.* London: Macmillan, 1869.

Giorgi, A. Psychology: A human science. *Social Research,* 1969, *36,* 412–432.

Goethe, J. W. von. Der Versuch als Vermittler zwischen Subjekt and Objekt. In *Goethes Werke* (30. Bd. Schriften zur Naturwissenschaften, II). (K. Heinemann, Hrsg.) Leipzig: Bibliographisches Institut, 1900. Pp. 378–388.

Goffman, W. Mathematical approach to the spread of scientific ideas—The history of mast cell research. *Nature,* 1966, *212,* 449–452.

Goulet, L. R., & Baltes, P. B. (Eds.). *Life-span developmental psychology: Research and theory.* New York: Academic Press, 1970.

Greenfield, P. M., Nelson, H., & Saltzman, E. The development of rule bound strategies for manipulating seriated cups: A parallel between action and grammar. *Cognitive Psychology,* 1972, *3,* 291–310.

Griffiths, J. A., Shantz, C. A., & Sigel, I. E. A methodological problem in conservation studies: The use of relational terms. *Child Development,* 1967, *38,* 841–848.

Günther, G. Time, timeless logic, and self-referential systems. *Annals of the New York Academy of Sciences,* 1967, *138,* 396–406.

Halliday, M. A. K. *Explorations in the functions of language.* London: Arnold, 1973.

Harary, F., Norman, R. Z., & Cartwright, D. *Structural models.* New York: Wiley, 1965.

Hardesty, F. P. Early European contributions to developmental psychology. In K. F. Riegel & J. A. Meacham (Eds.), *The developing individual in a changing world.* The Hague: Mouton, 1976.

Harris, A. E. *Cognitive skills in verbal and nonverbal activity.* Unpublished doctoral dissertation, University of Michigan, 1972.

Harris, A. E. Social dialectics and languge: Mother and child construct the discourse. *Human Development,* 1975, *18,* 80–96.

Hass, W. A. Pragmatic structures of language: Historical, formal, and developmental issues. In K. F. Riegel & G. C. Rosenwald (Eds.), *Structure and transformation: Developmental and historical aspects.* New York: Wiley, 1975. Pp. 193–213.

Hefner, R., Rebecca, M., & Oleshansky, B. Development of sex role transcendence. *Human Development,* 1975, *18,* 143–158.

Hegel, G. W. F. *Phänomenologie des Geistes.* Frankfurt/M.: Suhrkamp, 1969(a). [*The phenomenology of mind.* New York: Harper, 1967.]

Hegel, G. W. F. *Wissenschaft der Logik.* Frankfurt/M.: Suhrkamp, 1969(b). [*Science of logic.* London: Allen & Unwin, 1929.]

Heisenberg, W. *Wandlungen in den Grundlagen der Naturwissenschaften.* Leipzig: Hirzel, 1942.

Heisenberg, W. *Philosophic problems of nuclear science.* New York: Pantheon, 1952.

Hölder, O. Die Axiome der Quantität und die Lehre vom Mass. *Berichte der Sächsischen Gesellschaft der Wissenschaften, Leipzig, Mathematische—Physikalische Klasse,* 1901, *53,* 1–64.

Holzman, M. The use of interrogative forms in the verbal interaction of three mothers and their children. *Journal of Psycholinguistics Research,* 1972, *1,* 311–336.

Hooper, F. H. Cognitive assessment across the lifespan: Methodological implications of the organismic approach. In J. R. Nesselroade & H. W. Reese (Eds.), *Life-span developmental psychology: Methodological issues.* New York: Academic Press, 1973.

Hunt, J. McV. *Intelligence and experience.* New York: Ronald Press, 1961.

Husserl, E. *The phenomenology of internal time consciousness.* The Hague: Nijhoff, 1964.

Huttenlocher, J., & Higgins, E. T. Adjectives, comparatives, and syllogisms. *Psychological Review,* 1971, *78,* 487–504.

Inhelder, B., & Piaget, J. *The growth of logical thinking from childhood to adolescence.* New York: Basic Books, 1958.

Jaeger, W. *Aristotles: Grundlegung einer Geschichte seiner Entwicklung.* Berlin: Weidemann, 1923.

Jaffe, J., Stern, D. N., & Peary, J. C. "Conversational" coupling of gaze behavior in prelinguistic human development. *Journal of Psycholinguistic Research,* 1973, *2,* 321–330.

Jammer, M. *The concepts of space.* New York: Harper, 1954.

Jenkins, J. J., & Palermo, D. S. Mediation processes and the acquisition of linguistic structures. *Monographs of the Society for Research in Child Development,* 1964, *29,* 141–169.

Jesperson, O. *Analytic syntax.* London: Allen & Unwin, 1937.

Jordan, P. *Physikalisches Denken in der neuen Zeit.* Hamburg: Hanseatische Verlagsanstalt, 1935.

Jordan, P. *Die Physik des 20. Jahrhunderts.* (5 Aufl.). Braunschweig: Vieweg, 1943. [*Physics of the 20th century.* New York: Philosophical Library, 1944.]

Kaufman, W. A. *Hegel: Reinterpretation, text, and commentary.* Garden City, New York: Doubleday, 1966.

Kaye, K. Infants' effects upon their mothers' teaching strategies. In J. C. Glidewell (Ed.), *The social context of learning and development.* New York: Gardner Press, 1976. (a)

Kaye, K. Toward the origin of dialogue. In H. R. Schaffer (Ed.), *Interaction in infancy: The Loch Lomond Symposium.* New York: Academic Press, 1976. (b)

Kochen, M. Stability in the growth of knowledge. *American Documentation,* 1969, *20,* 186–197.

Kominski, C. A. *The Muller-Lyer illusion and Piaget's test for the development of the conservation of space in a group of older institutionalized veterans.* Paper presented at the College of William and Mary, Williamsburg, Virginia, 1968.

Kosok, M. The systematization of dialectical logic for the study of development and change. *Human Development,* 1976, *19,* 325–350.

Krüger, F. E. *Uber Entwicklungspsychologie, ihre sachliche und geschicht-liche Notwendigkeit.* Leipzig: Engelmann, 1915.

Kuhlen, R. G. Aging and life-adjustment. In J. E. Birren (Ed.), *Handbook of aging and the individual.* Chicago: Univ. of Chicago Press, 1959. Pp. 852–897.

Kuhlen, R. G. Developmental changes in motivation during the adult years. In J. E. Birren (Ed.), *Relations of development and aging.* Springfield, Illinois: Thomas, 1964. Pp. 209–246.

Kuhn, T. *The structure of scientific revolution.* Chicago: Univ. of Chicago Press, 1962.

Kvale, S. The temporality of memory. *Journal of Phenomenological Research,* 1974, *5,* 7–31.

Kvale, S. Memory and dialectics: Some reflections on Ebbinghaus and Mao Tse-Tung. *Human Development,* 1975, *18,* 205–222.

Kvale, S. Dialectics and research on remembering. In N. Datan & H. W. Reese (Eds.), *Life-span developmental psychology: Dialectical perspectives on experimental research.* New York: Academic Press, 1977. Pp. 165–190.

Labov, W. The study of language in its social context. *Studium Generale,* 1970, *23,* 30–87.

References

Labov, W. & Fanshel, D. *Therapeutic discourse: Psychotherapy as conversation.* New York: Academic Press, 1977.

Labov, W., & Waletzky, J. Narrative analysis: Oral versions of personal experience. In J. P. Helm (Ed.), *Essays on verbal and visual arts.* Seattle: Univ. of Washington Press, 1967. Pp. 12–44.

Lawler, J. Dialectic philosophy and developmental psychology: Hegel and Piaget on contradiction. *Human Development,* 1975, *18,* 1–17.

Lehman, H. C. *Age and achievement.* Princeton, New Jersey: Princeton Univ. Press, 1953.

Lenin, V. I. *Philosophical notebook.* New York: International Publishers, 1929 (*Collected Works,* Vol. 29).

Leont'ev, A. N., & Luria, A. R. The psychological ideas of L. S. Vygotsky. In B. Wolman (Ed.), *Historical roots of contemporary psychology.* New York: Harper, 1968.

Levi-Strauss, C. *Anthropologie strcturale.* Paris: Plon, 1958. [*Structural anthropology.* New York: Basic Books, 1963.]

Lewin, K. Gesetz and Experiment in der Psychologie. *Symposion,* 1927, *1,* 375–421.

Lewis, M., & Freedle, R. Mother–infant dyad: The cradle of meaning. In P. Pliner, L. Krames, & T. Alloway (Eds.), *Communication and affect: Language and thought.* New York: Academic Press, 1973. Pp. 127–155.

Lieberman, P. *Information, perception and language.* Cambridge, Massachusetts: MIT Press, 1967.

Linde, C., & Labov, W. Spatial networks as a site for the study of language and thought. *Language,* 1975, *51,* 924–939.

Lynd, S. Historical past and existential present. In T. Roszak (Ed.), *The dissenting academy.* New York: Pantheon, 1968. Pp. 101–109.

McCarthy, D. Language development in children. In L. Carmichael (Ed.), *Manual of child psychology,* New York: Wiley, 1954, Pp. 492–630.

McLaughlin, G. H. Psychologic: A possible alternative to Piaget's formulation. *British Journal of Educational Psychology,* 1963, *33,* 61–67.

McNeill, D. Developmental psycholinguistics. In F. Smith & G. A. Miller (Eds.), *The genesis of language: A psycholinguistic approach.* Cambridge, Massachusetts: MIT Press, 1966.

McNeill, D. *The acquisition of language.* New York: Harper, 1970. (a)

McNeill, D. The development of language. In P. H. Mussen (Ed.), *Carnichael's manual of child psychology.* New York: Wiley, 1970. Pp. 1061–1161. (b)

Malinowski, B. The problem of meaning in primitive languages. Supplement I. In C. K. Ogden & I. A. Richards (Eds.), *The meaning of meaning.* New York: Harcourt, 1923. Pp. 296–336.

Mannheim, K. The problem of generations. In K. Mannheim, *Essays on the sociology of knowledge.* London: Routledge & Kegan Paul, 1952.

Mao Tse-Tung, *Four essays in philosophy.* Peking: Foreign Language Press, 1968.

Matejka, L. On the first Russian prolegemena to semiotics. In V. N. Voloshinov (Ed.), *Marxism and the philosophy of language.* New York: Seminar Press, 1973. Pp. 161–174.

Meacham, J. A. The development of memory abilities in the individual and society. *Human Development,* 1972, *15,* 205–228.

Meacham, J. A. Dialectic approach to moral judgment and self-esteem. *Human Development,* 1975, *18,* 159–170. (a)

Meacham, J. A. Patterns of memory development in two cultures. *Developmental Psychology,* 1975, *11,* 50–53. (b)

Meacham, J. A. Continuing the dialogue: Dialectics and remembering. *Human Development,* 1976, *19,* 304–309.

Meacham, J. A. A transactional model of remembering. In N. Datan & H. W. Reese (Eds.), *Life-span developmental psychology: Dialectical perspectives on experimental research.* New York: Academic Press, 1977. Pp. 261–284. (a)

Meacham, J. A. Soviet investigations of memory development. In R. V. Kail, Jr., & J. W. Hagen (Eds.), *Perspectives on the development of memory and cognition.* Hillsdale, New Jersey: Erlbaum, 1977. (b)

Meacham, J. A., & Riegel, K. F. Dialectical perspectives on Piaget's theory. In G. Steiner (Ed.), *Piaget's developmental and cognitive psychology within an extended context, Vol. 7 (The psychology of the 20th century).* Zürich: Kindler, 1978.

Mead, G. H. *Mind, self, and society* (C. W. Morris, Ed.). Chicago: Chicago Univ. Press, 1934.

Mead, M. *Coming of age in Samoa.* New York: Morrow, 1928.

Merleau-Ponty, M. *The phenomenology of perception.* London: Routledge & Kegan Paul, 1962.

Miller, S. A. *Contradiction, surprise, and cognitive change: The effects of disconfirmation of belief on conservers and nonconservers.* Unpublished report. Department of Psychology, University of Michigan, 1972.

Miller, W., & Ervin, S. The development of grammar in child language. In U. Bellugi and R. Brown (Eds.), *The acquisition of language. Monographs of the Society for Research in Child Development,* 1964, *29* (no. 92), 43–78.

Minkowski, E. *Lived time.* Chicago: Northwestern Univ. Press, 1970.

Mishler, E. G. Studies in dialogue and discourse: An exponential law of successive questioning. *Language in Society,* 1975, *4,* 31–51. (a)

Mishler, E. G. Studies in dialogues and discourse: II. Types of discourse initiated by and sustained through questioning. *Journal of Psycholinguistic Research,* 1975, *4,* 99–121. (b)

Mitroff, I. I., & Betz, F. Dialectic decision theory: A metatheory of decision making. *Management Science,* 1972, *19,* 11–24.

Moerk, E. Principles of interaction in language learning. *Merrill-Palmer Quarterly,* 1972, *18,* 229–257.

Moerk, E. Changes in verbal child–mother interactions with increasing language skills of the child. *Journal of Psycholinguistic Research,* 1974, *3,* 101–116.

Moss, H. A. Sex, age, and state as determinants of mother–infant interaction. *Merrill-Palmer Quarterly.* 1967, *13,* 19–36.

Murphey, G., & Murphey, L. B. *Asian psychology.* New York: Basic Books, 1968.

Nelson, K. Structures and strategies in learning to talk. *Monograph of the Society for Research in Child Development,* 1973, *38,* No. 149.

Nesselroade, J. R., & Reese, H. W. (Eds.). *Life-span developmental psychology: Methodological issues.* New York: Academic Press, 1973.

Neugarten, B. L., & Datan, N. Sociological perspectives of the life cycle. In P. B. Baltes & K. W. Schaie (Eds.), *Life-span developmental psychology: Personality and socialization.* New York: Academic Press, 1973. Pp. 53–69.

Olson, F. A. Language and thought: Aspects of a cognitive theory of semantics. *Psychological Review,* 1970, *77,* 257–273.

Osborn, H. F. *The origin and evolution of life.* New York: Scribner, 1917.

Overton, W. General systems, structure, and development. In K. F. Riegel & G. C. Rosenwald (Eds.), *Structure and transformation: Developmental aspects.* New York: Wiley, 1975.

Papalia, D. E. The status of several conservation abilities across the life-span. *Human Development,* 1972, *15,* 229–243.

Payne, T. R. *S. L. Rubinstein and the philosophical foundations of Soviet psychology.* New York: Humanities Press, 1968.

References

Phillips, J. R. Syntax and vocabulary of mother's speech to young children: Age and sex comparisons. *Child Development*, 1973, *44*, 182-185.

Piaget, J. *Le langage et la pensee chez l'enfant.* Neuchatel: Delachaux & Niestle, 1923. [*The language and thought of the child.* New York: Harcourt, 1926.]

Piaget, J. *La naissance de l'intelligence chez l'enfant.* Neuchatel: Delachaux & Niestle, 1936. [*The origins of intelligence in children.* New York: International University Press, 1952.]

Piaget, J. *La psychologie de l'intelligence.* Paris: Armand Colin, 1947. [*The psychology of intelligence.* London: Routledge & Kegan Paul, 1950.]

Piaget, J. *Psychologie der Intelligenz.* Zurich: Rascher, 1958.

Piaget, J. *Les mechanisms perceptifs.* Paris: Presses Universitaires de France, 1961. [*The mechanisms of perception.* New York: Basic Books, 1968.]

Piaget, J. *Play, dreams, and imitation in childhood.* New York: Norton, 1962.

Piaget, J. *The origins of intelligence in children.* New York: Norton, 1963.

Piaget, J. *The child's conception of number.* New York: Norton, 1965.

Piaget, J. *Le structuralisme.* Paris: Presses Universitaires de France, 1968 [*Structuralism.* New York: Basic Books, 1970.]

Piaget, J. *Genetic epistemology.* New York: Columbia Univ. Press, 1970.

Piaget, J. *The child's conception of movement and speed.* New York: Ballantine, 1970.

Piaget, J. Intellectual evolution from adolescence to adulthood. *Human Development*, 1972, *15*, 1-12.

Piaget, J. & Inhelder, B. *The child's conception of space.* New York: Norton, 1967. (London: Routledge & Kegan Paul, 1956.)

Planck, M. *Wege zur physikalischen Erkenntnis.* (2 Aufl.). Leipzig: Hirzel, 1934.

Quarterman, C. J., & Riegel, K. F. Age differences in the identification of concepts of the natural language. *Journal of Experimental Child Psychology*, 1968, *6*, 501-509.

Quillian, M. R. Word concepts: A theory and simulation of some basic semantic capabilities. *Behavioral Science*, 1967, *12*, 410-430.

Rashevsky, N. *Looking at history through mathematics.* Cambridge, Massachusetts: MIT Press, 1968.

Reese, H. W. Models of memory development. *Human Development*, 1976, *19*, 291-303.

Reese, H. W. Discrimination learning and transfer: Dialectical perspectives. In N. Datan & H. W. Reese (Eds.), *Life-span developmental psychology: Dialectical perspectives on experimental research.* New York: Academic Press, 1977. Pp. 205-252.

Reichenbach, M. *The philosophy of time and space.* New York: Dover, 1958.

Reichenbach, M., & Mathern, A. The place of time and aging in the natural sciences and scientific philosophy. In J. E. Birren (Ed.), *Handbook of aging and the individual.* Chicago: Univ. of Chicago Press, 1959. Pp. 43-80.

Rheingold, H. L. The effect of environmental stimulation upon social and exploratory behavior in the human infant. In B. M. Foss (Ed.), *Determinants of infant behavior.* (Vol. 1). New York: Wiley, 1961. Pp. 143-177.

Riegel, K. F. *Untersuchung über intellektuelle Fähigkeiten älterer Menschen.* Doctoral dissertation, University of Hamburg, 1957.

Riegel, K. F. Die Bedeutung der Statistik für das psychologische Experiment. *Psychologische Beiträge*, 1958, *3*, 595-618.

Riegel, K. F. Untersuchungen sprachlicher Leistungen und ihrer Veränderungen. *Zeitschrift für allgemeine und angewandte Psychologie*, 1968, *15*, 649-692.

Riegel, K. F. History as a nomothetic science: Some generalizations from theories and research in developmental psychology. *Journal of Social Issues*, 1969, *25*, 99-127.

Riegel, K. F. The language acquisition process: A reinterpretation of selected research findings. In L. R. Goulet & P. B. Baltes (Eds.), *Life-span developmental psychology: Research and Theory.* New York: Academic Press, 1970. Pp. 357–399.

Riegel, K. F. On the history of psychological gerontology. In C. Eisdorfer & M. P. Lawton (Eds.), *Psychology of adult development and aging.* Washington, D.C.: American Psychological Association, 1972. (a)

Riegel, K. F. Time and change in the development of the individual and society. In H. W. Reese (Ed.), *Advances in child development and behavior,* (Vol. 7). New York: Academic Press, 1972. Pp. 81–113. (b)

Riegel, K. F. The influence of economic and political ideologies upon the development of developmental psychology. *Psychological Bulletin,* 1972, *78,* 129–141. (c)

Riegel, K. F. Cardinal Chomsky's Platonic revival movement or linguistics out of HIS mind: A rejoinder to Professor Weimar's paper. *American Psychologist,* 1973, *28,* 1013–1016. (a)

Riegel, K. F. Developmental psychology and society: Some historical and ethical considerations. In J. R. Nesselroade & H. W. Reese (Eds.), *Life-span developmental psychology: Methodological issues.* New York: Academic Press, 1973. (b)

Riegel, K. F. (Ed.). *Intelligence: Alternative views of a paradigm.* Basel: Karger, 1973. (c)

Riegel, K. F. The recall of historical events. *Behavioral Science,* 1973, *18,* 354–363. (d)

Riegel, K. F. Contrastive and recursive relations. *Research Memoradum RM-74-23.* Princeton, New Jersey: Educational Testing Service, 1974.

Riegel, K. F. Adult life crises: Toward a dialectic theory of development. In N. Datan & L. H. Ginsberg (Eds.), *Life-span developmental psychology: Normative life crises.* New York: Academic Press, 1975. Pp. 97–124. (a)

Riegel, K. F. (Ed.) *The development of dialectical operations.* Basel: Karger, 1975. (b)

Riegel, K. F. Subject-object alienation in psychological experimentation and testing. *Human Development,* 1975, *18,* 181–193. (c)

Riegel, K. F. From traits and equilibrium toward developmental dialectics. In W. J. Arnold & J. K. Cole (Eds.), *1974–1975 Nebraska Symposium on Motivation.* Lincoln: Univ. of Nebraska Press, 1976. Pp. 349–407. (a)

Riegel, K. F. *The psychology of development and history.* New York: Plenum, 1976. (b)

Riegel, K. F. The dialectics of time. In N. Datan & H. W. Reese (Eds.), *Life-span developmental psychology: Dialectical perspectives on experimental research.* New York: Academic Press, 1977.

Riegel, K. F., & Meacham, J. A. (Eds.). *The developing individual in a changing world* (2 Vols.). The Hague: Mouton, 1976.

Riegel, K. F., & Meacham, J. A. Dialectics, transaction, and Piaget's theory. In L. Pervin & M. Lewis (Eds.), *Perspectives in interactional psychology.* New York: Plenum, 1978.

Riegel, K. F., & Riegel, R. M. An investigation into denotative aspects of word meaning. *Language and Speech,* 1963, *6,* 5–21.

Riegel, K. F., & Riegel, R. M. Development, drop and death. *Developmental Psychology,* 1972, *6,* 303–319.

Riegel, K. F., & Rosenwald, G. C. (Eds.) *Structure and transformation: Developmental and historical aspects.* New York: Wiley, 1975.

Rosenthal, R. *Experimenter effects in behavioral research.* New York: Appleton-Century-Crofts, 1966.

Rommetveit, R. *Words, meanings, and messages.* New York: Academic Press, 1968.

Rubinstein, S. L. *Grundlagen der allgemeinen Psychologie.* Berlin: Volk und Wissen, 1958.

Rubinstein, S. L. *Prinzipien und Wege der Entwicklung der Psychologie.* Berlin: Akademie Verlag, 1963.

References

Rychlak, J. F. *Introduction to personality and psychotherapy*. New York: Houghton & Mifflin, 1973.

Rychlak, J. F. *Dialectic: Humanistic rationale for behavior and development* Basel: Karger, 1976. (a)

Rychlak, J. F. Psychological science as a humanist views it. In W. S. Arnold & J. K. Cole (Eds.), *1974–1975 Nebraska symposium on motivation*. Lincoln: Univ. of Nebraska Press, 1976. (b)

Sameroff, A. Transactional models in early social relations. *Human Development*, 1975, *18*, 65–79.

Sanders, S., Laurendeau, M., & Bergeron, J. Aging and the concept of space: The conservation of surface. *Journal of Gerontology*, 1966, *21*, 281–285.

Saussure, F. de *Cours de linguistique generale*. Paris: Payot, 1916. [*Course in general linguistics*. New York: McGraw-Hill, 1959.]

Schaie, K. W. A general model for the study of developmental problems. *Psychological Bulletin*, 1965, *64*, 92–107.

Schaltenbrand, G. Consciousness and time. *Annals of the New York Academy of Sciences*, 1967, *138*, 632–645.

Schmid, H. *Anthropologische Konstanten und literarische Struktur*. Unpublished manuscript, University of Bochum, Germany, 1973.

Scholes, P. A. *The Oxford compendium to music*. (10th edition). London: Oxford Univ. Press, 1970.

Shatz, M., & Gelman, R. The development of communication skills: Modifications in the speech of young children as a function of listener. *Monographs of the Society for Child Development*, 1973, *38*, No. 152.

Shugar, G. W. A method of descriptive analysis of child activity in the period of language acquisition. In K. Ohnesorge (Ed.), *Colloquium Paedololinguisticum: Proceedings of the First International Symposium of Paedolinguistics*. The Hague: Mouton, 1972. Pp. 242–253.

Slobin, D. I. Imitation and grammatical development in children. In N. S. Endler, L. R. Butler, & H. Osser (Eds.), *Contemporary issues in developmental psychology*. New York: Holt, 1968.

Slobin, D. *The ontogenesis of grammar*. New York: Academic Press, 1971.

Snow, C. E. Mother's speech to children learning language. *Child Development*, 1972, *43*, 549–565.

Sokal, R. R., & Sneath, P. H. A. *Principles of numerical taxonomy*. San Francisco: Freeman, 1963.

Soll, I. *An introduction to Hegel's metaphysics*. Chicago: Univ. of Chicago Press, 1969.

Spengler, O. *Der Untergang des Abendlandes*. München, Beck, 1918–1922 [*The decline of the West*. New York: Knopf, 1946.]

Spitz, R. Life and the dialogue. In M. Gaskill (Ed.), *Counterpoint*. New York: International Univ. Press, 1963. (a)

Spitz, R. The evolution of the dialogue. In M. Schur (Eds.), *Drives, affects, and behavior*. New York: International Univ. Press, 1963. (b)

Spitz, R. The derailment of dialogue: Stimulus overload, action cycles, and the completion gradient. *Journal of the American Psychoanalytical Association*, 1964, *12*, 752–775.

Spranger, E. *Psychologie des Jugendalters*. Leipzig: Quelle & Meyer, 1924.

Stern, C., & Stern, W. *Die Kindersprache*. Leipzig: Barth, 1907.

Stevens, S. S. Mathematics, measurement, and psychophysics. In S. S. Stevens (Ed.), *Handbook of experimental psychology*. New York: Wiley, 1951. Pp. 1–49.

Sutton-Smith, B. Developmental structures in fantasy narratives. *Human Development*, 1976, *19*, 1–13.

Thomae, H. Development and value orientation: The contribution of Edward Spranger to a differential developmental psychology. In K. F. Riegel & J. A. Meacham (Eds.), *The developing individual in a changing world.* The Hague: Mouton, 1976.

Titunik, I. R. The formal method and the sociological method (M. M. Baxtin, P. N. Medvedev, V. N. Voloshinov) in Russian theory and study of literature. In V. N. Voloshinov (Ed.), *Marxism and the philosophy of language.* New York: Seminar Press, 1973. Pp. 175-202.

Trabasso, T. *Reasoning and the processing of negative information.* Paper presented at the 78th Annual Convention of the American Psychological Association, Washington, D. C., September 1970.

Trier, J. *Der Deutsche Wortschatz im Sinnbezirk des Verstandes.* Heidelberg: Winter, 1931.

Tulving, E. & Donaldson, W. (Eds.) *Organization of memory.* New York: Academic Press, 1972.

van den Daele, L. Qualitative models in developmental analysis. *Developmental Psychology,* 1969, *1,* 303-310.

van den Daele, L. Ego development in dialectic perspective. *Human development,* 1975, *18,* 129-142.

Velikovsky, I. *Worlds in collision.* New York: Macmillan, 1950.

Velikovsky, I. *Earth in upheaval.* New York: Doubleday, 1955.

Voloshinov, V. N. *Marxism and the philosophy of language.* New York: Seminar Press, 1973.

Vygotsky, L. S. *Thought and language.* Cambridge, Massachusetts: MIT Press, 1962.

Wason, P. C. The processing of positive and negative information. *Quarterly Journal of Experimental Psychology,* 1959, *11,* 92-107.

Watzlawick, P., Beavin, J. H., & Jackson, D. D. *Pragmatics of human communication.* New York: Norton, 1967.

Weeks, T. Speech registers in young children. *Child Development,* 1971, *42,* 1119-1131.

Weir, R. H. *Language in the crib.* The Hague: Mouton, 1962.

Werner, H. *Einführung in die Entwicklungspsychologie.* Leipzig: Barth, 1926. [*Comparative psychology of mental development.* New York: Follett, 1948.]

Wozniak, R. H. A dialectic paradigm for psychological research: Implications drawn from the history of psychology in the Soviet Union. *Human Development,* 1975, *18,* 18-34. (a)

Wozniak, R. H. Dialecticism and structuralism: The philosophical foundations of Soviet psychology and Piagetian cognitive developmental theory. In K. F. Riegel & G. C. Rosenwald (Eds.), *Structure and transformation: Developmental and historical aspects.* New York: Wiley, 1975. Pp. 24-45. (b)

Wundt, M. *Hegel's Logik und die moderne Physik.* Köln: Westdeutscher Verlag, 1949.

Wundt, W. Uber Ausfrageexperimente und über die Methoden zur Psychologie des Denkens. *Psychologische Studien,* 1907, *3,* 301-360.

Wundt, W. *Volkerpsychologie, Bd. 1 & 2, Die Sprache.* Leipzig: Engelmann, 1911-1912.

Wyatt, F. A psychologist looks at history. *Journal of Social Issues,* 1962, *16,* 182-190.

Wyatt, F. The reconstruction of the individual and collective past. In R. W. White (Ed.), *The study of lives.* New York: Appleton-Century-Crofts, 1963. Pp. 304-320.

Zaporozhets, A. V., & Elkonin, D. B. *The psychology of preschool children.* Cambridge, Massachusetts: MIT Press, 1971.

Zivian, M. T., & Riegel, K. F. Word identification as a function of semantic clues and association frequency. *Journal of Experimental Psychology,* 1969, *79,* 336-341.

Author Index

A

Ainsworth, M. D., 99
Ajuriaguerra, J. de, 4–8
Alden, J. R., 123
Anderson, E. S., 89n
Archimedes, 178
Aristotle, 145
Austin, G. A., 80

B

Balance, W., 147
Baldwin, A. L., 100
Balfour, G., 45
Baltes, P. B., 3, 15, 126, 172
Bavink, B., 37
Beavin, J. H., 85
Bell, S. M., 99
Bellugi-Klima, U., 98, 102
Bergeron, J., 48
Berko Gleason, J., 89n
Bertalanffy, L. von, 22
Betz, F., 15
Bickford, B., 45
Birren, J. E., 164
Blonsky, P. P., 28

Bloom, L., 76
Blount, B. G., 89n
Blumenthal, A., 11, 147
Bonvillian, J. D., 89n
Boring, E. G., 145, 151
Bourne, L. E., Jr., 80
Braine, M. D. S., 98
Brentano, F., 86
Brinkmann, W., 147
Brown, R., 79, 98, 102, 103
Bruner, J. S., 79, 80, 89n
Buck-Morss, S., 15
Buehler, C., 133, 135
Buehler, K., 61
Burgess, E., 15

C

Caesar, J., 123, 124
Carlyle, T., 168, 169
Carnap, R., 76
Cartwright, D., 72
Cassirer, E., 159
Cazden, C. B., 102
Chandler, M. J., 15
Charles XII, 66

Chomsky, N., 48, 68, 69, 85, 102
Clark, H. H., 45, 77
Clive, J., 168
Cipolla, C. M., 62
Cohen, D., 162n
Coombs, C. H., 80
Copernicus, N., 26
Cuvier, G., 153

D
Darwin, C., 18
Datan, N., 15, 126, 131, 142, 157n, 179
Dedekind, R., 75
De Paulo, B. M., 89n
Descartes, R., 86
Donaldson, M., 45
Donaldson, W., 3
Donders, J. C., 86
Du Bois-Reymond, E., 145
Duncan, S., 89n

E
Ebbinghaus, H., 117
Einstein, A., 178
Elkonin, D. B., 43
Engels, F., 29, 54, 69
Erikson, E., 112, 133–135
Ervin-Tripp, S., 89n, 98, 102, 103

F
Fanshel, D., 85
Farwell, C. B., 89n
Fechner, G. T., 86
Ferguson, C. A., 89n
Fieguth, R., 7, 91, 101
Fillmore, C. J., 76
Fischer, R., 177
Flavell, J. H., 19, 48
Fraser, C., 89n, 98
Fraser, J. T., 177
Freedle, R., 7, 15, 89n, 99, 166
Frege, B., 75
Fresnel, A. J., 35
Freud, S., 15, 51
Fröbel, F., 15
Furth, H. G., 19, 50, 51

G
Gadamer, H. G., 178n
Gaettens, R., 62

Galileo, 178
Galton, F., 19, 149
Gelman, R., 89n
Giorgi, A., 20
Görtz, G. H. von, 66
Goethe, J. W. von, 88
Goffman, W., 120
Goodnow, S. S., 80
Gould, R., 133
Goulet, L. R., 126
Greenfield, P. M., 98
Griffiths, J. A., 45
Günther, G., 178

H
Halliday, M. A. K., 89, 102
Harary, F., 72
Hardesty, F. P., 19
Harris, A. E., 7, 15, 89n, 98
Hass, W. A., 85
Havighurst, R., 15
Hefner, R., 10
Hegel, F., 14, 32, 36–38, 50, 54
Heisenberg, W., 36, 87
Helmholtz, H. L. F. von, 86
Heraclitus, 89
Higgins, E. T., 45, 77
Hobbes, T., 18
Hölder, O., 81
Holzman, M., 89n
Hooper, F. H., 48
Hume, D., 86
Hunt, J. McV., 126
Husserl, E., 170
Huttenlocher, J., 45, 77
Huygens, C., 35

I
Inhelder, B., 42, 75, 160

J
Jackson, D. D., 85
Jaeger, W., 145
Jaffe, J., 100
Jammer, M., 159
Jenkins, J. J., 72
Jesperson, O., 68
Johnson, C. E., 89n
Jordan, P., 35, 37

K

Kant, I., 50, 86, 124
Kaufman, W. A., 38
Kaye, K., 100
Keynes, J. M., 24
Kochen, M., 120
Kominski, C. A., 48
Kosok, M., 179
Krüger, F., 15
Kuhlen, R. G., 133, 135
Kuhn, T., 11, 26, 139, 151
Kvale, S., 15, 170, 174

L

Labov, W. L., 61, 85, 91, 102, 169
Laurendau, M., 48
Lawler, J., 7, 15, 51
Lehman, H. C., 133, 145
Leibniz, G. W., 19, 86, 100
Lenin, V., 29, 32, 38, 54, 69
Leontiev, A. N., 29
Levinson, D., 133
Levi-Strauss, C., 51, 68
Lewin, K., 88
Lewis, M., 7, 15, 89n, 99, 166
Lieberman, P., 99
Linde, C., 169
Locke, J., 18, 86
Looft, W., 45
Louis XV, 66
Luria, A. R., 29
Lynd, S., 125

M

McCarthy, D., 143
McLaughlin, G. H., 25, 26, 41, 45, 51, 105
McNeill, D., 78, 102, 167
Magenis, A., 123
Magnus, R., 145
Malinowski, B., 62
Mann, T., 149
Mannheim, K., 15
Mao Tse-tung, 7, 101
Marx, K., 14, 23, 29, 54, 69
Matejka, L., 85
Mathern, A., 162
Meacham, J. A., 15, 33, 68, 91
Mead, M., 137
Merleau-Ponty, M., 178n
Mill, J. S., 86

Miller, S. A., 43
Miller, W., 98
Minkowski, E., 157
Mishler, E. G., 89n
Mitroff, I. I., 15
Moerk, E., 89n
Montessori, M., 19
Moss, H. A., 7, 100
Mueller, J., 145
Murphy, G., 17
Murphy, L. B., 17

N

Nelson, H., 98
Nelson, K., 89n
Nesselroade, J. R., 15, 126
Neugarten, B., 15, 131, 142
Newton, I., 26, 35
Norman, R. Z., 72

O

Oleshansky, B., 10
Olson, D., 79
Osborn, H. F., 153
Overton, W. F., 22

P

Palermo, D. S., 72
Papalia, D. E., 48
Pavlov, I., 28, 29, 31, 33, 69, 71
Payne, T. R., 16, 28, 31, 54, 69
Peary, J. C., 100
Pestalozzi, J. H., 19, 153
Phillips, J. R., 89n
Piaget, J., 4–7, 14, 15, 19, 20, 25, 26, 33, 38,
    40–57, 59, 68, 75, 88, 94, 105, 130, 143–
    153, 158, 160, 164, 166
Planck, M., 35
Plato, 15, 85
Ptolemy, 26

Q

Quarterman, C. J., 131
Quillian, M. R., 58

R

Rashevsky, N., 120
Rebecca, M., 10
Reese, H. W., 15, 126, 157n, 170, 179
Reichenbach, M., 162

Rheingold, H. A., 7, 100
Riegel, R. M., 48, 58, 75
Roberts, N., 89n
Rogers, C., 94
Rommitveit, R., 79
Rosenthal, R., 88
Rousseau, J.-J., 19, 20, 153
Rubinstein, S. L., 16, 28, 29, 31, 54, 69
Rychlak, J. F., 15, 179
Ryder, N. B., 15

S
St. Veronica, 124
Saltzman, E., 98
Sameroff, A., 7, 15, 100
Sanders, S., 48
Sapir, E., 68
Saussure, F. de, 61, 85, 158
Schaie, K. W., 3, 15, 126, 172
Schaltenbrand, G., 165, 178n
Schelling, F. W. J. von, 145
Schmid, H., 7, 91, 101
Shantz, C. A., 45
Sheehy, G., 133
Shatz, M., 89n
Scholes, P. A., 175
Shugar, G. W., 94
Sigel, I. E., 45
Skinner, B. F., 71
Slobin, D. I., 78, 102
Sneath, P. H. A., 72
Snow, C. E., 89n
Socrates, 15
Sokal, R. R., 72
Soll, I., 38
Spengler, O., 26
Spitz, R., 85
Spranger, E., 19, 153
Stern, C., 79

Stern, D. N., 100
Stern, W., 51, 79
Stevens, S. S., 80
Sutton-Smith, B., 98

T
Thomae, H., 19
Titchener, E. B., 29, 147
Titunik, I. R., 85
Trabasso, T., 79
Trier, J., 58
Tulving, E., 3

V
Vaillant, G., 133
van den Daele, L. D., 15, 50, 120, 152
Velikovsky, I., 153
Voloshinov, V. N., 85
Vygotsky, L. S., 29, 69, 85, 143

W
Waletsky, J., 91, 169
Washington, G., 120
Wason, P. C., 80
Watzlawick, P., 85
Weeks, T., 89n
Weir, R. H., 79
Werner, H., 15, 51, 57
Wohlwill, J. F., 48
Wozniak, R. H., 15
Wundt, M., 38
Wundt, W., 3, 15, 20, 29, 38, 86, 87, 142, 145–147, 168, 169, 178
Wyatt, F., 112

Z
Zaporozhets, A. V., 43
Zivian, M. T., 72

Subject Index

A

Abilities, 2–4
Absolute time, 160, 175
Accommodation, 96–164
Adulthood, 48–50, 129–156
Aging, 12–14, 47–50
Alienation, 42–45, 50, 51
Arts, 151
Assimilation, 96, 164

B

Barter systems, 60–62
Behaviorism, 29

C

Career development, 138–142
Change, concept of, 158–162
Changes, *see also* Progressions
   cohort, 172–174
   cultural-sociological, 172–174
   dialectical, 8–16
   individual-psychological, 168–171
   inner-biological, 162–168
Classes, 40–42
   criteria for, 74

Closed systems, 22–27
Cognitive development, 4, 25–27, 35–55, 68
Cognitive dissonance, 4
Cohort changes, 172–174
Coinage systems, 62–65
Comparatives, 45–47
Conditions, 32, *see also* Progressions
Consciousness, 28, 29
Constitutive relationism, 31, 32
Contradiction, 35–38, 44–44, 130
Crises, 9–12
   adult life, 129–156
   extrascientific bases, 152–154
Cultural-sociological changes, 172–174

D

Debenture systems, 65–68
Development, 12–14, *see also* Cognitive development
   of careers, 138–142
Dialectical changes, 8–16
Dialectical idealism, 32, 54
Dialectical logic, 177
Dialectical operations, 35–55
Dialectical paradigm, 20–22

Subject Index

Dialectical thinking, 38, 47
Dialectical time, 161, 175
Dialectic psychology, 20, 28
Dialectics
  historical, 29, 32
  material, 32
  primitive and scientific, 7, 15, 51, 98
Dialogical units, 94, 166
Dialogues, 5
  developmental, 97–105
  incomplete, 95–97
  mother–child, 7, 98–105, 166
  properties of, 92–95
  situational, 89–97
  temporal organization of, 85–110
Dimensions, 8–14, 161, *see also* Progressions

E
Education, 19, 28
Equilibrium, 4, 5, 14, 109, 129
Event sequences, 160–168
  biological, 162–165
  psychological, 165–168
  types of, 161, 162
Exchanges, 61, 63, 167
Experimental psychology, 2, 20, 88

F
Faculty psychology, 2
Family, 10–12, 135, 137, 149
Formalism, 14

H
Historical dialectics, 29, 32
Historical interpretations, 123–125
Historical materialism, 69
History, 17–34, 111–127

I
Idealism, 16
  dialectical, 32, 54
Identity, 36–40
Individual differences, 20, 49
Individual-psychological changes, 168–171
Inner-biological changes, 162–168
Intelligence, 4
Interactions, 20, 54
  dialogic, 5–8
  double, 29–32, 68

intersection of, 16
language, 65–68
subject and object, 36, 86–89
systems of, 68
Interpretations, historical, 123–125
Introspection, 29, 87
Inversion, 79

L
Language, 57–83
  acquisition, 102–105
  interaction, 65–68
  proto-, 60–62
  relational basis of, 45–48, 70–82
  token, 62–65
Laws, 17
Linguistic systems, 60–70
Logic
  dialectical, 177
  formal, 177
  operations, 40–42

M
Marxism, 16, 23
Material dialectics, 32
Materialism, 16
Meaning, 3
Mechanism, 14, 16, 22, 27, 32
Mechanistic paradigm, 17–19
Memory, 111–117
  temporality of, 170
Memory span, 25–27
Mentalism, 14, 16, 22, 27, 33, 68, 86
Mentalistic paradigm, 19, 20
Mind, 29
Monetary systems, 60–70
Monologues, 90–92
Mother–child dialogues, 7, 98–105, 166
Music, 174

N
Narratives, 90–92, 168–170
Nations, 150
Negation, 79

O
Objectification, 86, 88, 125, 167
Open systems, 22–27

Operations
    dialectical, 35–55
    linguistic, 45–48
    logical, 40–42
    transformational, 67

P

Paradigms, 17, 142
    dialectical, 20–22
    mechanistic, 17–19
    mentalistic, 19, 20
Positivism, 37
Progressions, 8–16, 132, 162–174
Psychology
    dialectic, 20, 28
    experimental, 2, 20, 88
    faculty, 2
    Soviet, 27–32

Q

Questions, 88

R

Recollections, 111–127
    historical, 120–123
Reflexes, 28, 33
Relational time, 160, 215
Relationism, constitutive, 31
Relations, 39, 45–48, 57–83
    compounding of, 77
    explicit, 76
    extralingual, 127
    implicit, 76
    intersection of, 72
    intralingual, 74
    relations of, 16, 78
    subject–object, 86–89

S

Science, 151
    history of, 17–34
    revolutions in, 26
Scientists, careers of, 10, 138–147
Semantics, 59
Sequences, *see* Progressions
Sociology, 23
Soviet psychology, 27–32
Stages, 19, 25–27, 50–53
Structuralism, 7, 68
    Piagetian, 144
Subject–object relations, 36, 86–89
Symbolic interactionism, 33
Syntax, 59
Systems
    of interactions, 29–32, 68
    open and closed, 22

T

Testing, 4, 28
Thought, mature, 38, 47, 48
Time
    absolute, 160, 175
    dialectical, 161, 175
    dialectics of, 157–180
    in dialogues, 85–110
    in music, 174
    properties of, 158–161
    relational, 160, 175
Transactions, 68
Transformational grammar, 68
Transformations
    linguistic, 81
    Piagetian, 144

W

Women, 10, 12